CONTENTS

Title Page
Copyright
Dedication
Acknowledgments
Preface
About This Book
Introduction ... 1
Chapter 1: Introduction to Christian Education ... 2
Chapter 2 The Practice of Christian Education ... 25
Chapter 3: The Contexts of Christian Education ... 86
Chapter 4: The Goal of Christian Education ... 141
Chapter 5: From Covenant to Kingdom ... 172
Chapter 6: Doctrine ... 239
Chapter 7: Prayer ... 253
Chapter 8: Fasting ... 263
Chapter 9: Women of Faith ... 273
Epilogue ... 316
References ... 319
Final Blessing ... 321
About The Author ... 323

AN IN-DEPTH INTRODUCTION TO CHRISTIAN EDUCATION

Building Lives through Christ-Centered Learning

Dr. RUSHAYNE STEWART

Copyright © 2025 DR. RUSHAYNE STEWART

All rights reserved

This book is based on the author's original research, interpretation, and lived experiences. While biblical texts and scholarly sources are cited, the analysis, conclusions, and recommendations presented herein reflect the author's perspective. This work is not intended to provide legal, psychological, or any professional advice, but rather to provide insight into spiritual teaching from the author's perspective. Readers are encouraged to consult appropriate professionals for such guidance. Unless otherwise indicated, Scripture quotations are taken from the King James Version of the Bible.

Printed in the United States of America.

Dedication

This book is dedicated to every teacher, pastor, counselor, parent, and student who believes that education is a divine calling, where truth transforms hearts and knowledge shapes destinies.

May you continue to teach, lead, and learn in the spirit of Christ, the Master Teacher.

To every parent who whispers prayers over a child, to every teacher who patiently sows seeds of truth, to every pastor who feeds the flock with the Word, and to every learner who hungers for wisdom. This work is dedicated to you.
May your labor in the Lord never be in vain, and may the generations that follow rise up to know, love,
and serve Christ through the gift of faithful education.

ACKNOWLEDGMENTS

I give all glory to God, who is the source of wisdom and the author of all truth. His grace made every word of this work possible.

My gratitude extends to my mentors, colleagues, and students who have walked with me through years of teaching and learning. To my family and friends, thank you for your patience, encouragement, and unwavering belief in my calling.

A special thanks to all who labor in Christian education. Your dedication to teaching truth, shaping character, and nurturing faith continues to light the path for generations to come.

PREFACE

"The fear of the Lord is the beginning of wisdom, and knowledge of the Holy One is understanding." Proverbs 9:10

This book was born out of both study and lived experience. Over the years, I have seen how education, when rooted in Christ, can heal, guide, and transform lives. I have also witnessed how, when divorced from God's truth, it can leave hearts empty and souls searching. My desire in writing is not only to share biblical foundations and practical insights, but also to encourage others who are called to teach, to disciple, and to serve. Whether you are a parent, pastor, student, or educator, my prayer is that these pages will strengthen your faith, sharpen your vision, and renew your commitment to Christ-centered education. May what you read here inspire you to see teaching as ministry, learning as discipleship, and education as a lifelong journey with Christ at the center.

"Impress them on your children. Talk about them when you sit at home and when you walk along the road." Deuteronomy 6:7

From the earliest pages of Scripture, God placed the responsibility of teaching upon His people. Parents were commanded to diligently teach their children the ways of the Lord. Prophets and priests were charged with reminding Israel of God's covenant promises. Jesus Himself taught in parables, illustrating eternal truths with simple stories. The Great Commission calls the church to "make disciples...teaching them to observe all things." At every stage of redemptive history, education has been central to God's plan of shaping His people.

"Do not conform to the pattern of this world, but be transformed by the renewing of your mind." Romans 12:2

Yet today, Christian education often finds itself in tension with a world that measures success by knowledge without wisdom, progress without morality, and freedom without responsibility. The call to write this book grew out of that tension. I became increasingly aware that many believers, though passionate in faith, lacked a clear framework for understanding how education can be faithfully Christian. I longed to contribute to that conversation, drawing from both my academic research and my personal journey.

"The unfolding of your words gives light; it gives understanding to the simple." Psalm 119:130

In my years of ministry and study, I have observed the transformative power of Christ-centered teaching. I have seen students whose lives were redirected when they encountered Scripture in a classroom setting. I have met teachers whose faith grew deeper as they integrated biblical truth into their instruction. I have listened to parents testify how intentional discipleship in the home prepared their children to stand firm in a shifting culture. These stories convinced me that education, when guided by the Spirit, is one of the most powerful tools God has given the church.

"My people are destroyed for lack of knowledge." Hosea 4:6

At the same time, I have encountered the challenges and shortcomings of Christian education. Too often, it is reduced to a label without substance, Christian in name, but secular in philosophy. Sometimes it becomes legalistic, focusing on rules rather than transformation. Other times, it is disconnected from the realities of students' lives, leaving learners ill-equipped to face the pressures of society. These shortcomings compelled me to dig deeper: What does it truly mean for education to be Christian? What principles set it apart from other systems? How can it remain faithful in the midst of cultural change?

"Teach me your decrees, O Lord; to them I will hold fast." Psalm 119:33

The chapters that follow are my attempt to answer these questions. They are not exhaustive, nor do they claim to offer a perfect model. Rather, they represent an effort to explore the biblical, historical, and practical foundations of Christian education. I hope that educators, pastors, students, and families will find encouragement here, as well as practical guidance for the journey of teaching and learning.

"Commit your works to the Lord, and your thoughts will be established." Proverbs 16:3

Writing this book has been both an academic exercise and a spiritual pilgrimage. It demanded study, reflection, and prayer. It required revisiting my own experiences, moments of success and failure, of joy and disappointment. At times, I wrestled with questions about what it means to live faithfully as both a scholar and a believer. Yet through it all, I sensed God's guiding hand, reminding me that education is not merely about information but about transformation.

"Remember your leaders, who spoke the word of God to you. Consider the outcome of their way of life and imitate their faith." Hebrews 13:7

I am deeply indebted to the many voices who shaped my understanding of this subject. Scholars who have written extensively on theology and pedagogy laid much of the groundwork for my own reflections. Pastors and mentors who modeled faithful teaching inspired me to pursue this path. Students who asked hard questions pushed me to think more deeply. Family and friends who encouraged me along the way gave me the strength to continue writing when the task felt overwhelming. To each of them, I owe a debt of gratitude.

"Always be prepared to give an answer to everyone who asks you to give the reason for the hope that you have." 1 Peter 3:15

This book is also an expression of hope. I believe we stand at a critical moment in history, where the world is hungering for truth yet often rejecting the One who is Truth. Christian education is not a luxury; it is a necessity. If the next generation is to be prepared to live faithfully in a world of confusion, they must be grounded in the Word of God, formed by the Spirit, and guided by teachers who understand that their role is nothing less than discipleship.

"So whether you eat or drink or whatever you do, do it all

for the glory of God." 1 Corinthians 10:31

At its core, Christian education is about shaping whole persons for the glory of God. It speaks to the intellect, the emotions, the will, and the spirit. It invites learners to see the world through the lens of Scripture and to live with integrity, compassion, and courage. It is not simply about producing graduates but about forming disciples who will bear fruit in their families, communities, and churches. That vision is what keeps me passionate about this subject.

"Encourage one another and build each other up." 1 Thessalonians 5:11

I recognize that readers will come to this book with different backgrounds and expectations. Some may be seasoned educators, looking for fresh insight. Others may be parents trying to navigate the challenges of raising children in the faith. Still others may be pastors or church leaders seeking to equip their congregations. My prayer is that no matter your role, you will find here a reminder that you are not alone in this work. The God who calls you to teach and to disciple is the same God who promises to be with you always.

"Therefore, go and make disciples of all nations... teaching them to obey everything I have commanded you." Matthew 28:19-20

It is my conviction that every believer has a part to play in Christian education. Some teach in classrooms, others in pulpits, others around dinner tables. Some disciples through formal instruction, others through everyday conversations. Wherever teaching happens, there lies an opportunity to shape lives for eternity. This book is written with all of you in mind.

"All Scripture is God-breathed and is useful for teaching, rebuking, correcting, and training in righteousness." 2 Timothy 3:16

As you read, you will notice that I draw upon both Scripture and scholarship, weaving together biblical truth with practical reflection. I believe this integration is essential. Christian education must be rooted in the Word, yet it must also speak to the real issues facing learners today. My approach is therefore both theological and practical, academic and personal.

"Examine yourselves to see whether you are in the faith; test yourselves." 2 Corinthians 13:5

I encourage you, as you engage with these chapters, not only to analyze the arguments but also to reflect on your own calling. Ask yourself: How is God inviting me to teach and to learn? In what ways can I make Christ more central in my educational practice? How can I encourage others on this journey? If these pages move you toward deeper reflection and faithful action, then they will have accomplished their purpose.

"Now to the King eternal, immortal, invisible, the only God, be honor and glory forever and ever." 1 Timothy 1:17

Finally, I offer this book as an act of worship. Education is not an end in itself, but a means of glorifying God. My hope is that every paragraph, every example, and every reflection will point you back to Him, the true Teacher, the source of wisdom, and the goal of all learning. To Him be the glory, both now and forevermore.

ABOUT THIS BOOK

An In-Depth Introduction to Christian Education: Building Lives through Christ-Centered Learning explores how education becomes a sacred act when Christ is at the center. Drawing on biblical truth, research, and real-life ministry experience, this book equips readers to teach, to make disciple, and lead with wisdom and compassion.

You will discover the purpose of Christian education, the importance of prayer and fasting in leadership, the harmony of grace and mercy, and the faith-filled stories of men and women who shaped generations through obedience to God.

This book is both a guide and an invitation, to see education not merely as instruction, but as participation in God's redemptive work.

INTRODUCTION

Education is never neutral. Every system, whether it acknowledges it or not, communicates a vision of truth, morality, and purpose. For the Christian, education cannot be separated from discipleship, for at the heart of learning is the call to follow Christ. From the earliest pages of Scripture, God's people were instructed to teach His Word diligently, to recount His mighty works, and to prepare each generation to walk in covenant faithfulness.

This book grows out of that conviction: that Christian education is not merely an academic exercise, but a sacred responsibility. It is about shaping lives, not only minds; forming character, not merely conveying knowledge; and preparing disciples to live faithfully in a world that often rejects God's truth.

Here you will find a journey through the foundations, practices, and goals of Christian education. We will look at what makes education distinctively Christian, why it matters for the church and the world, and how it transforms both learners and teachers alike. I hope that as you read, you will be reminded that teaching is not just about information but about transformation, and that Christ Himself remains the foundation, the content, and the goal of all true education.

CHAPTER 1: INTRODUCTION TO CHRISTIAN EDUCATION

Biblical Foundations

The story of God's people has always been a story of learning. From the earliest days, the Lord entrusted His covenant community with the responsibility of instruction. *"These words, which I command thee this day, shall be in thine heart: and thou shalt teach them diligently unto thy children"* (Deuteronomy 6:6-7). Education was never an optional addition to Israel's life; it was the very means of ensuring that future generations would walk in covenant faithfulness. Psalm 78:4-7 emphasizes the same charge: parents were to recount God's mighty deeds so that their children would hope in Him and not forget His works.

Joshua was instructed to meditate on the Book of the Law Day and night so that he would be careful to obey it (Joshua 1:8). Ezra is described as a man who "set his heart to study the Law of the Lord, and to do it, and to teach His statutes and rules in Israel" (Ezra 7:10). Prophets such as Isaiah and Jeremiah also functioned as educators, calling the people back to God's truth when they strayed. In every generation, the faithful passed on the knowledge of God through teaching.

In the New Testament, this educational mandate continues with even greater clarity. Jesus is constantly presented as a teacher. His parables, sermons, and personal mentoring shaped His disciples not only in doctrine but in daily living. He concluded His ministry with the Great Commission: *"Go therefore and make disciples of all nations, baptizing them... and teaching them to observe all that I have commanded you"* (Matthew 28:19-20). Teaching is not an afterthought to discipleship; it is its heartbeat.

The apostolic church carried on this mission. Acts 2:42 records that the early believers "devoted themselves to the apostles' teaching and to fellowship, to the breaking of bread and to prayer." Paul discipled Timothy, urging him to continue in the Scriptures he had learned from childhood (2 Timothy 3:15). Titus was instructed to appoint elders who could "give instruction in sound doctrine" (Titus 1:9). The New Testament witness is clear: the life of the church depends on faithful Christian education.

The Worldview Contrast

Every educational system conveys a worldview. Even when not explicitly stated, assumptions about truth, morality, human dignity, and destiny are embedded in teaching. Secular education often views humanity as autonomous, truth as relative, and success as measured by personal achievement or economic progress. By leaving God out of its framework, it implicitly trains students to interpret the world without reference to Him.

Christian education begins with the conviction that *"the fear of the Lord is the beginning of wisdom"* (Proverbs

9:10). It recognizes God as Creator (Genesis 1:1), acknowledges humanity's fall into sin (Romans 3:23), proclaims redemption through Christ (John 3:16), and points to the hope of new creation (Revelation 21:1-5). In this framework, every discipline, history, science, mathematics, language, and the arts is studied through the lens of God's truth.

Consider practical contrasts: Secular education may teach evolution as a purely natural process, while Christian education acknowledges God as Designer and Sustainer of life. Secular systems may treat morality as socially constructed, but Christian education grounds it in God's unchanging law and the example of Christ. Secular philosophy often elevates human reason as supreme, but Christian education humbly submits reason to divine revelation.

The distinction, then, is not in sprinkling prayers or Bible verses into a curriculum. The difference is foundational: secular education trains people to live *without* God; Christian education trains people to live *for* God.

Christ as the Foundation

At the very center, Christian education is not just a set of doctrines or even a book, but a spoke of the foundation, Jesus Christ. The Gospels repeatedly refer to Him as "Teacher" (John 13:13). He taught with authority, unlike the scribes (Matthew 7:28-29), with compassion for the multitudes (Mark 6:34), and with methods suited to His hearers, parables for the crowds, probing questions for His disciples, and clear rebuke for the self-righteous.

For Christian education, Christ is both the content and the model. He is the subject of our teaching, for all Scripture testifies of Him (John 5:39). He is also the pattern of how we teach, for He combined truth with love, authority with humility, and knowledge with example. Paul expressed this Christ-centered aim when he wrote, *"Him we proclaim, warning everyone and teaching everyone with all wisdom, that we may present everyone mature in Christ"* (Colossians 1:28).

Church history affirms this centrality. Augustine argued that all truth is God's truth, and therefore all learning ultimately points to Christ. Martin Luther insisted that Scripture must govern education, exalting Christ as the source of wisdom. John Calvin emphasized that true knowledge begins with knowing God and ourselves rightly in His light. The Reformation itself can be seen as a renewal of Christian education, grounding faith and learning in the person of Christ.

To separate education from Christ is to strip it of its essence. Christian education exists not merely to inform the mind but to bring learners into communion with the Living Word.

Transformation as the Aim

The purpose of Christian education is not intellectual achievement alone but transformation. Paul exhorts believers in Romans 12:2: *"Be not conformed to this world, but be ye transformed by the renewing of your mind."* This renewing of the mind is the ongoing work of Christian teaching, shaping believers to live differently in thought, desire, and conduct.

Transformation extends beyond doctrine. A student

may memorize Scripture or recite a catechism yet remain unchanged if truth does not penetrate the heart. Understanding Christian education results in character formation, humility, integrity, love, and obedience. As Paul said in 2 Corinthians 3:18, *"We all are being transformed into his image with ever-increasing glory, which comes from the Lord, who is the Spirit."*

This aim distinguishes Christian education from secular schooling. Where the latter is equipped for careers, the former equips for discipleship. Where the world measures success by achievement, Christian education measures it by Christlikeness. The goal is not scholars alone, but saints, not intellectuals alone, but disciples.

The Communal Nature of Christian Education

Christian education is never an isolated endeavor. While personal study and devotion are vital, formation occurs most powerfully in community. God has established the family, the church, and the fellowship of believers as the primary arenas of education.

The family is the child's first school. Parents are charged to nurture children in the training and admonition of the Lord (Ephesians 6:4). Faith is often caught before it is taught, as children witness prayer, worship, discipline, and love in the home.

The church then builds on this foundation. Through preaching, teaching, fellowship, worship, and discipline, believers are continually formed. In the early church, catechesis (systematic instruction in the faith) was central to preparing believers for baptism and discipleship. Today, Sunday schools, Bible studies, youth groups, and discipleship programs carry on this tradition.

Schools and seminaries also play a role, particularly in providing structured education that integrates biblical truth with academic learning. Yet even these institutions serve best when connected to the broader life of the home and church.

Christian education is thus communal by design. Proverbs 27:17 reminds us, *"Iron sharpeneth iron; so, a man sharpeneth the countenance of his friend."* Believers are shaped together, holding one another accountable, encouraging one another in love, and growing together into maturity in Christ.

What is Christian Education?

Defining "Christian"

The word *Christian* first appears in Acts 11:26: *"And the disciples were called Christians first in Antioch."* The term identified believers as those who belonged to Christ, not simply as admirers, but as His disciples. To be a Christian is to confess Him as Savior, submit to Him as Lord, and walk in obedience as His follower.

A Christian is one who has been made new by the Spirit (John 3:3-5), who is united with Christ in His death and resurrection (Galatians 2:20), and who belongs to a chosen people, called out of darkness into light (1 Peter 2:9). This identity is not cultural, traditional, or inherited by birth. One does not become a Christian by association, by attending church, or by embracing moral values apart from Christ. True Christianity is a transformation brought about through the gospel.

Therefore, when we describe something as *Christian*, including education, we mean that it is anchored in Christ, flowing from Him, and directed toward His glory. It is defined not by religious appearance but by allegiance to the living Christ.

Defining "Education"

Education, in its broadest sense, is the intentional process of shaping knowledge, skills, values, and habits. The Latin word *educare* means "to bring up" or "to draw out." Every society has developed systems of education because human beings are formed, not only born.

In ancient Israel, education was covenantal and holistic. Children were taught the stories of God's mighty acts, the Law, and the Psalms so that they might grow into faithful covenant-keepers (Deuteronomy 6:6-7; Psalm 78:4-7). In Greco-Roman culture, education centered on rhetoric, philosophy, and civic responsibility. In the early church, catechesis (systematic instruction in the faith) was developed to prepare believers for baptism and discipleship. Each of these illustrates that education is never neutral; it always reflects assumptions about what is true, what is good, and what it means to live well.

From a biblical perspective, education cannot be reduced to information transfer. It is about shaping the whole person in wisdom and obedience to God. Moses commanded Israel to *teach diligently* (Deut. 6:7), and Paul instructed fathers to bring up their children in the *"nurture and admonition of the Lord"* (Ephesians 6:4). Education is both intellectual and moral; it is the drawing out of knowledge and the cultivation of godly character.

Bringing the Two Together

When the two words are joined, *Christian education* emerges as something entirely unique. It is not secular instruction with religious elements sprinkled in, nor is it merely a program of Bible knowledge. Rather, it is the Spirit-led process of forming disciples of Christ by means of truth, in the context of faith, for the purpose of godliness.

Several distinctives define this reality:

Christ-Centered: Jesus is the content, the model, and the goal. Christian education is about knowing Him (Philippians 3:10), becoming like Him (Romans 8:29), and serving Him (Colossians 3:17).

Scripture-Rooted: God's Word is the foundation. *"All Scripture is God-breathed and profitable for teaching"* (2 Timothy 3:16).

Spirit-Empowered: The Holy Spirit illumines the mind, convicts the heart, and transforms the will (John 14:26).

Holistic: It shapes intellect, affections, and behavior together.

Missional: It equips disciples not only for personal growth but for service in God's kingdom (Matthew 28:19-20).

Practical contrasts help illustrate this uniqueness. In history classes, secular education may present events as random sequences or human achievements alone; Christian education presents them as unfolding under God's providence. In science, secular education may insist on materialism; Christian education affirms God as Creator and Sustainer. In ethics, secular models may treat morality as relative; Christian education grounds it in God's eternal character.

Voices from History

Throughout history, Christian thinkers have emphasized this distinct vision.

Origen (3rd century) believed education should bring the soul into harmony with divine wisdom.

Augustine (4th century) taught that all truth is God's truth and that learning should lead the soul toward the enjoyment of God.

Thomas Aquinas (13th century) emphasized that reason and revelation work together under God's authority.

Martin Luther (16th century) declared that children must be instructed in both the liberal arts and the Scriptures, so that they might glorify God in every sphere of life.

John Calvin (16th century) argued that education was essential for the health of both church and society, since true knowledge of God leads to reverence and obedience.

John Wesley (18th century) insisted that education must form both head and heart, producing holiness and service.

Ellen G. White (19th century) described Christian education as preparation "for the joy of service in this world and for the higher joy of wider service in the world to come."

Randolph Crump Miller (20th century) emphasized that Christian education is not merely about teaching religion, but about forming disciples in faith and practice.

Each voice echoes the same truth: Christian education is transformative, holistic, and always anchored in

Christ.

Contexts of Christian Education

Christian education unfolds in three main contexts, each with a distinct but complementary role:

> **The Home:** Parents are the first teachers. Children learn faith by observing prayer, discipline, worship, and love in daily family life. Proverbs 22:6 calls parents to "train up a child in the way he should go." The home is where Christian education begins.
>
> **The Church:** The Body of Christ nurtures discipleship through preaching, teaching, worship, sacraments, and fellowship. The early church modeled this in Acts 2:42, where they devoted themselves to teaching and prayer. Today, churches carry this on through Sunday schools, catechism, small groups, and discipleship ministries.
>
> **The School or Seminary:** Christian institutions provide formal instruction, integrating biblical truth with academic disciplines. Here, students are equipped not only for ministry but for faithful service in every vocation from business to science to the arts.

These three strands work together like a braided cord. The home lays the foundation, the church strengthens and sustains, and the school provides structure and depth. Together, they shape disciples for life and eternity.

Purpose of Christian Education

Godliness of Character and Action

The primary aim of Christian education is godliness. It seeks not only to inform but to transform, shaping men and women whose lives reflect the holiness of God. Scripture consistently ties learning to character: *"The fear of the Lord is the beginning of wisdom, and the knowledge of the Holy One is understanding"* (Proverbs 9:10). Wisdom in the biblical sense is not merely intellectual but moral; it produces a life marked by obedience and reverence for God.

Deuteronomy 6 shows this clearly. After commanding Israel to love God with all their heart, soul, and strength, Moses instructs them to teach God's commands diligently to their children. The purpose was not only that the next generation would know the Law but that they would live it, walking in covenant faithfulness. In the same way, Christian education today aims at forming people who live differently because they know Christ.

This goal extends beyond the classroom. In the home, godliness is shaped as children see faith modeled by parents. In the church, believers learn integrity by observing leaders who serve humbly. In the workplace, Christians demonstrate honesty, diligence, and compassion as fruits of their formation. True Christian education cannot be measured by grades or diplomas but by the character of those it shapes.

Spiritual Rebirth as the Foundation

Christian education begins with spiritual rebirth. Jesus made this non-negotiable when He told Nicodemus, *"Except a man be born again, he cannot see the kingdom of God"* (John 3:3). Education apart from regeneration may produce moral citizens or skilled workers, but it cannot produce disciples of Christ.

Yet instruction still has value before conversion. It plants seeds that the Spirit may later bring to life. Timothy is a prime example: from childhood, he was taught the Scriptures by his mother and grandmother (2 Timothy 1:5; 3:15). That early training prepared him to receive Christ when God's Spirit drew him. Likewise, countless children raised in Christian homes or taught in Sunday schools later come to faith because they were surrounded by truth from an early age.

Christian education, therefore, serves as both preparation and fulfillment. It prepares learners for salvation by grounding them in God's Word, and it nurtures those already saved into deeper faith. Unlike secular systems, which may sharpen the mind but leave the soul untouched, Christian education addresses the deepest need of humanity: reconciliation with God.

Growth Toward Maturity in Christ

Conversion is only the beginning. The purpose of Christian education is to guide believers toward maturity. Paul expressed this in Ephesians 4:13, describing the goal as *"the measure of the stature of the fullness of Christ."* Similarly, Hebrews 5:12-14 contrasts "milk" for the immature with "solid food" for those who have been trained to discern good from evil. Growth in faith involves moving from basic truths to deeper wisdom and practice.

Christian education nurtures this process by providing instruction, accountability, and opportunities for spiritual discipline. In the home, children progress from simple prayers to personal study and active service. In the church, believers grow from being hearers of the Word to doers of the Word, serving others in ministry. In Christian schools and seminaries, students learn to think critically about faith and culture, integrating biblical truth with every area of knowledge.

This growth is never automatic. It requires intentional teaching, mentoring, and discipleship. Just as a gardener tends a plant with care, so Christian education cultivates believers step by step, guiding them toward maturity in Christ.

Equipping Believers for Service

Christian education also prepares believers for service. Paul reminds us in Ephesians 4:11-12 that God gave teachers and leaders *"to equip the saints for the work of ministry, for building up the body of Christ."* Education is never an end in itself; it exists to prepare disciples for mission.

The Bible provides vivid examples of this equipping. Moses prepared Joshua to lead Israel into the Promised Land. Elijah mentored Elisha for prophetic ministry. Jesus trained His disciples, not only by teaching them but by sending them to preach and heal. Paul invested in Timothy, Titus, and others, preparing them to carry on the gospel after him.

Today, Christian education serves the same purpose. Some are equipped for pastoral ministry, others for teaching, and still others for service in business, medicine, or the arts. Whatever the vocation, the purpose is the same: to glorify God and extend His kingdom. Christian schools, churches, and seminaries must therefore help students identify their gifts, discern their calling, and develop the skills needed to serve effectively.

Knowledge without service produces arrogance, but knowledge applied in service builds up the body of Christ. Christian education fulfills its purpose when it produces not spectators but servants.

An Eternal Perspective

The final purpose of Christian education reaches beyond this present life. Its horizon is eternity. John writes, *"Beloved, now we are the sons of God, and it doth not yet appear what we shall be: but we know that, when he shall appear, we shall be like him"* (1 John 3:2). The ultimate end of Christian education is not earthly success but eternal transformation.

The New Testament often describes life as a pilgrimage. Paul speaks of running the race to obtain an incorruptible crown (1 Corinthians 9:25). James promises the crown of life to those who persevere (James 1:12). Christian education prepares believers for this journey by fixing their eyes on Christ, the "author and finisher of our faith" (Hebrews 12:2).

The early church understood education in this eternal light. Augustine's *City of God* contrasted the earthly city, focused on temporal power, with the heavenly city, focused on eternal fellowship with God. For Augustine, education was not just preparation for life on earth but training for citizenship in heaven.

In the same way, Christian education today must continually remind learners that they are citizens of another kingdom (Philippians 3:20). It teaches them to hold earthly achievements lightly and to set their affections on things above (Colossians 3:2). Every lesson, every act of teaching, and every moment of discipleship carries this eternal significance.

Explication of Key Terms

Why Clarity Matters

Understanding Christian education requires clarity about the words we use. Language shapes thought and thought shapes practice. If we are careless with our definitions, we risk being careless with our teaching. This is not a matter of semantics but of faithfulness. Throughout history, when God's people failed to guard their language, confusion crept into their worship and their doctrine. Clear words lead to clear convictions; vague words lead to vague discipleship.

Christian education in particular depends on precision. If we misdefine its key concepts, we distort its practice. For instance, if we think of "church" only as a building, we reduce Christian education to a program that happens within four walls. If we define "education" as merely passing along information, we strip it of its moral and spiritual weight. If we approach "methodology" as entertainment, we risk raising consumers instead of disciples.

Three terms are especially foundational: *the Christian Church, education,* and *methodology.* Each carries deep meaning in Scripture and in Christian history. Without a shared understanding of these terms, the purpose and practice of Christian education can easily become vague, shallow, or even contrary to God's design.

The Christian Church

The church is central to Christian education because it is the covenant community in which believers are nurtured, and disciples are formed. Biblically, the church is never defined as a building or a one-hour service. The Greek word *ekklesia* means "assembly" or "called-out ones." It refers to people redeemed by Christ and gathered for worship, fellowship, and mission.

The New Testament describes the church with rich metaphors:

> **The Body of Christ** (1 Corinthians 12:27), every member plays a role in building up the whole. This image carries educational weight: just as the body grows through nourishment and exercise, so believers mature as they learn and practice their faith within the community.
>
> **The Bride of Christ** (Ephesians 5:25-27), beloved, cleansed, and prepared for Christ. The imagery of preparation points to education: the church is continually being taught and sanctified to be presented purely before her Lord.
>
> **The Temple of the Holy Spirit** (1 Corinthians 3:16), God dwells in His people. This makes every act of instruction sacred, for education in the church is not human alone but Spirit-filled.
>
> **The Flock of God** (John 10:16; 1 Peter 5:2), guided and protected by shepherds. This metaphor highlights the pastoral role of teaching, guarding the flock from error, and leading them into truth.

The early church embodied this understanding. Acts 2:42 records that believers devoted themselves "to the apostles' teaching and to fellowship, to the breaking of bread and to prayer." Teaching was woven into every aspect of church life. Catechesis, systematic instruction in doctrine, prepared new believers for baptism. Psalms and hymns were sung to engrain truth in the heart (Colossians 3:16). Even church discipline was educational, designed to restore the wayward and teach holiness (1 Corinthians 5:5).

Historically, the church remained the primary center of learning for centuries. Monasteries preserved literacy and Scripture during times of cultural collapse. The Reformers emphasized catechisms, sermons, and schools as instruments of discipleship. Even today, where churches embrace their role as teaching communities, believers are strengthened in faith and witness.

To misunderstand the church as merely an institution or social club is to gut Christian education of its life. To see the church as the living Body of Christ is to recognize it as God's chosen classroom for discipleship.

Education

The second foundational term is *education.* Modern usage often reduces it to the transmission of facts, the acquisition of skills, or preparation for employment. While these are not unimportant, they fall far short of the biblical vision.

In Scripture, education is covenantal. It is the passing on of faith and wisdom from one generation to the next. Deuteronomy 6:6-7 commands Israel to keep God's words on their hearts and teach them diligently to their children at home, on the road, at bedtime, and at daybreak. Education here is continual, relational, and life-encompassing. It is less about formal lessons and more about embedding truth in the rhythms of daily life.

Proverbs reinforce this: *"Train up a child in the way he should go, and when he is old, he will not depart from it"* (Proverbs 22:6). Education is training, not just telling. It involves discipline, correction, example, and encouragement. Paul carries this forward in the New Testament, urging fathers to raise children "in the nurture and admonition of the Lord" (Ephesians 6:4).

The Bible also shows that education is moral and spiritual. Knowledge divorced from wisdom can lead to pride and destruction. Israel's downfall often came when they knew God's law but did not live it. By contrast, Psalm 119 celebrates learning God's Word as the path to holiness and joy.

The history of the church reflects this covenantal view. The early church developed catechisms to ground new believers in truth. Augustine saw education as training the soul to love rightly. Aquinas integrated faith and reason, insisting that all truth finds unity in God. The Reformers emphasized that Scripture must be central in all teaching, and they established schools to ensure that every child could read God's Word.

Thus, education in the Christian sense cannot be neutral. Every lesson conveys a vision of truth and purpose. Christian education seeks to form disciples who know God's Word, love Him with their whole being, and walk in obedience. It is not content with knowledge alone but presses toward wisdom and faithfulness.

Methodology

The third key term is *methodology*, the way teaching is carried out. Methods are not secondary or insignificant; they shape how truth is received. Wrong methods can distort the message, while faithful methods reinforce it.

God Himself modeled diverse teaching methods. He gave Israel visible signs: the rainbow (Genesis 9) as a covenant reminder, the Passover (Exodus 12) as a memorial meal, the tabernacle (Exodus 25-31) as a living symbol of His holiness and presence. These were not merely rituals, but lessons engraved into the lives of the people.

Jesus, the Master Teacher, employed methods that engaged both mind and heart. He told parables that invited reflection, asked probing questions to reveal motives, performed miracles as living demonstrations of truth, and used repetition to reinforce lessons. Most of all, He taught by example, embodying the message He proclaimed. When He washed His disciples' feet (John 13:14-15), He gave them a lesson they could never forget.

The early church also embraced formative methods. They used creeds to summarize belief, hymns to teach theology, and communal worship to reinforce truth. Catechesis provided structured instruction in doctrine, while mentoring and apprenticeship allowed believers to learn by imitation.

In every age, however, methodology carries dangers. In modern times, there is a temptation to substitute entertainment for discipleship, or to rely on shallow novelty rather than faithful teaching. A method may hold attention but fail to transform lives. Christian methodology must always be tested by Scripture: Does it communicate truth faithfully? Does it lead to obedience? Does it glorify Christ rather than distract from Him?

At its best, Christian methodology is participatory and relational. Proverbs 2:4-6 urges learners to seek wisdom as a hidden treasure, suggesting an active pursuit. Paul often engaged in dialogue with his churches, not only lecturing but reasoning and exhorting (Acts 17:2; 20:7). Effective Christian teaching invites learners to wrestle with truth, apply it in life, and live it out in service.

Thus, methodology is not about style or trend but about faithfulness. The method must serve the message, never overshadow it.

Conclusion - Foundations of Christian Education

Christian education is not a passing trend or a human invention. It is God's design for forming a people who know Him, love Him, and live faithfully in His world. In this chapter, we have seen that its roots lie deep in Scripture and in the life of the church. It is shaped by a worldview that recognizes Christ as the center of all truth and life. It is defined by careful attention to words, for clarity in our language leads to clarity in our practice. And it is directed toward a clear purpose: the transformation of character, the equipping of disciples, and the preparation of God's people for eternity.

These foundations remind us that Christian education is not merely a classroom activity or a program of study. It is a way of life, carried out in families, in congregations, and in every sphere where believers live and serve. It calls us to a high vision: that every believer might grow in wisdom and holiness, that every generation might be taught the fear of the Lord, and that every method of teaching might point to Christ alone.

With these foundations established, we are ready to move from principle to practice. The following chapters will explore how Christian education is lived out day by day in teaching, in discipleship, in the home, in the church, and in the wider world. Only when the foundations are laid firmly can the building rise strong. And only when Christ Himself remains the cornerstone can Christian education fulfill its God-given purpose.

CHAPTER 2 THE PRACTICE OF CHRISTIAN EDUCATION

The Importance of Christian Education

Christian education is not an optional ministry or a side activity of the church; it is central to the mission of God's people. From the beginning, God has commanded His people to be a teaching community. Israel was told to rehearse God's mighty acts and laws to their children so that they would not forget (Deuteronomy 6:6-7; Psalm 78:4-7). The early church was described as being devoted to "the apostles' teaching and to fellowship" (Acts 2:42). In both the Old and New Testaments, education was never an extra; it was at the very heart of God's covenant purposes.

The importance of Christian education becomes even clearer when we remember that every society educates. The question is never whether people will be taught, but what they will be taught, and by whom. Every culture passes down its values, beliefs, and assumptions. Secular systems emphasize knowledge and skills but often leave truth, virtue, and faith untended. Left on its own, the world will always train people to live without God.

For this reason, Christian education matters profoundly. It is the means by which the people of God preserve His truth, transmit faith to the next generation, shape character in accordance with Scripture, and equip believers for service in the world. Without strong Christian education, churches risk raising members who attend services but are not rooted in Christ. With it, churches raise disciples who are firmly grounded, prepared to live faithfully in a culture that is often hostile to the gospel.

The stakes could not be higher. A weak or neglected approach to Christian education results in shallow discipleship, compromise with worldly thinking, and eventually, the loss of biblical truth. But a strong, intentional commitment to Christian education results in believers who are mature, steadfast, and fruitful. It produces homes where parents teach and model faith, churches where the Word is central, and communities where truth is preserved against error.

For these reasons, Christian education must never be treated as optional or secondary. It is the lifeline of the church, the safeguard of truth, and the God-ordained path for making disciples in every generation.

Preserving the Truth of the Gospel

One of the greatest reasons Christian education is indispensable is that it preserves the truth of the gospel from one generation to the next. Without teaching, truth is quickly lost. Scripture gives us a sobering picture of what happens when this responsibility is neglected. After Joshua and his generation passed away, Judges 2:10 records: *"There arose another generation after them, which knew not the Lord, nor yet the works which he had done for Israel."* The result was spiritual decline, idolatry, and chaos. The failure of instruction produced a failure of faith.

The same danger threatens the church today. Truth does not remain alive in the hearts of God's people automatically; it must be taught diligently. If Christian Education is weak, shallow, or neglected, the church risks raising a generation that knows church activities but does not know the living God. Paul's warning to Timothy rings with urgency: *"The time will come when they will not endure sound doctrine... and they shall turn away their ears from the truth"* (2 Timothy 4:3-4). Christian education stands as a guardrail, preserving the faith "once delivered unto the saints" (Jude 3).

History provides clear evidence of this principle. When the early church faced heresies such as Gnosticism or Arianism, it was education through catechism, creeds, and systematic teaching that preserved orthodoxy. The Apostles' Creed and the Nicene Creed were not written to decorate worship services; they were educational tools, safeguarding the truth for believers and passing it to the next generation. In the medieval church, monasteries preserved biblical manuscripts and taught theology when much of society was illiterate. During the Reformation, Luther's *Small Catechism* and Calvin's *Genevan Catechism* were written for households and churches to ensure that every child and adult could articulate the essentials of the faith.

This preserving function of Christian education is no less important today. In a culture flooded with competing voices, relativism that denies truth, materialism that denies God, and individualism that denies accountability, Christian education is the anchor. It roots believers in the unchanging Word of

God. Paul urged Timothy: *"Hold fast the form of sound words... that good thing which was committed unto thee keep by the Holy Ghost"* (2 Timothy 1:13-14). The language of "holding fast" and "keeping" underscores the protective role of teaching. Education is not simply about imparting knowledge; it is about guarding the deposit of faith.

Practical examples illustrate this necessity. A child who learns the stories of Scripture from an early age carries a framework for understanding the world. A congregation that hears sound preaching week after week is fortified against deception. A seminary that faithfully trains ministers ensures that pulpits will not be filled with empty words but with the living truth of God. Wherever Christian education is strong, the gospel is preserved. Wherever it is neglected, the faith begins to fade.

For this reason, the importance of Christian Education cannot be overstated. It is the God-ordained means of protecting truth in a world bent on distortion. Just as Israel was commanded never to forget the Lord's mighty works, the church is called to "teach faithful men, who shall be able to teach others also" (2 Timothy 2:2). Preservation requires education, and education requires diligence. Without it, the church risks repeating the tragedy of Judges, a generation rising that knows not the Lord.

Passing the Faith to the Next Generation

Christian education is also essential because it ensures that the faith is passed on faithfully to the next generation. The Bible is clear: faith does not pass automatically from parent to child. Every new generation must be taught, reminded, and formed in the truth. That is why God gave such strong commands to His people about instructing their children. *"And these words, which I command thee this day, shall be in thine heart: and thou shalt teach them diligently unto thy children"* (Deuteronomy 6:6-7). This teaching was not to be confined to the temple or synagogue but was to saturate daily life, spoken at home, on the road, at bedtime, and in the morning.

The psalmist echoes this responsibility: *"We will not hide them from their children, shewing to the generation to come the praises of the Lord, and his strength, and his wonderful works that he hath done... that they might set their hope in God, and not forget the works of God, but keep his commandments"* (Psalm 78:4, 7). Christian education is thus not a luxury; it is obedience to God's design for the continuity of faith. Without it, children grow up with little foundation and are easily swept away by the currents of culture.

Examples in Scripture highlight both failure and success in this task. Eli, the priest, neglected to discipline and instruct his sons, and they grew corrupt, bringing shame and judgment (1 Samuel 2:12-17, 29). By contrast, Timothy was nurtured in the Scriptures from childhood by his grandmother Lois and mother Eunice (2 Timothy 1:5; 3:15). That early teaching gave him a firm foundation to serve faithfully alongside Paul. The difference lay in whether the next generation was diligently taught or left to drift.

The history of the church also underscores this principle. The early church catechized children and new believers alike, grounding them in basic truths of the faith. The Reformers pressed for Christian schools not as optional additions but as necessary for the survival of the faith in each community. John Calvin insisted that every child should be taught not only to read but to know the Scriptures, so that Geneva would remain a city founded on God's Word. John Wesley, centuries later, emphasized catechism and Bible instruction within the Methodist movement to ensure that Methodism would not become a form without power. Each generation of Christians recognized that education was the link between faith remembered and faith forgotten.

In practice, passing the faith requires intentionality in every context. In the home, parents must teach and model devotion, making prayer and Scripture part of family life. In the church, pastors and teachers must expound the Word clearly, while congregations reinforce truth through worship, fellowship, and service. In schools, Christian teachers must integrate faith with learning so that subjects like history and science are not presented apart from God but as part of His story.

Without this intentional passing on of the faith, a church may appear strong for one generation but will wither in the next. With it, the church grows stronger, producing believers who set their hope in God and remain steadfast in Him. This is why Christian education is of such great importance: it is God's appointed means of ensuring that the torch of faith is never extinguished but passed on, burning brightly, from one generation to another.

Shaping Character and Conduct

Christian education is not only about transmitting knowledge; it is about forming lives. Scripture consistently links teaching to the transformation of character. *"The fear of the Lord is the beginning of wisdom: and the knowledge of the holy is understanding"* (Proverbs 9:10). True wisdom is not measured in facts accumulated but in the reverence of God and the shaping of one's conduct according to His truth.

Proverbs 22:6 reminds us: *"Train up a child in the way he should go: and when he is old, he will not depart from it."* The word "train" implies guidance, correction, and discipline. It is the slow and steady work of shaping the heart as well as the mind. This is where Christian education differs radically from secular systems. While secular education may prepare students to achieve, compete, or succeed materially, it often neglects the moral and spiritual dimensions of life. Christian education insists that character is inseparable from knowledge.

The Bible gives vivid examples of the consequences when character is neglected. Eli's sons, though raised in the temple, were described as "sons of Belial; they knew not the Lord" (1 Samuel 2:12). They had access to the rituals of religion but were never trained in godliness, and their corruption led to judgment on their family. By contrast, Daniel and his companions, though trained in the wisdom of Babylon, remained steadfast in integrity because they were grounded in the fear of the Lord (Daniel 1:8-20). Their character, formed through faithful teaching, enabled them to stand firm in a hostile culture.

The early church also understood this dimension of education. Instruction for baptismal candidates was not limited to doctrinal memorization; it included moral teaching, shaping believers to renounce sin and embrace holiness. Augustine emphasized that education should train the soul to love rightly, to order desires toward God rather than toward self. The Reformers likewise connected education to moral formation. Luther's catechisms taught not only the Apostles' Creed and the Lord's Prayer but also the Ten Commandments, grounding students in the life of obedience.

Practical Christian education today must hold this same emphasis. In the home, parents shape character by modeling honesty, forgiveness, humility, and perseverance before their children. In the church, pastors and teachers guide conduct through instruction, accountability, and discipleship. In schools, Christian educators must resist the temptation to reduce education to grades and performance. They must remind students that diligence, respect, and love of neighbor are as essential as academic achievement.

Character formation is not optional. Without it, education produces clever sinners rather than faithful saints. Knowledge divorced from godliness leads to arrogance and ruin, but knowledge united with virtue leads to wisdom and service. Christian education's importance, therefore, is not only in what it teaches but in the kind of people it forms, men and women whose conduct reflects Christ in every sphere of life.

Equipping for Service in the World

The importance of Christian education is also seen in its role of equipping believers for service in the world. Education is never meant to terminate in the classroom. Its purpose is to prepare disciples who live out their faith in every sphere of life. Paul describes this equipping function in Ephesians 4:11-12: *"And he gave some, apostles; and some, prophets; and some, evangelists; and some, pastors and teachers; for the perfecting of the saints, for the work of the ministry, for the edifying of the body of Christ."* Teaching within the church is meant to strengthen believers so they may build up others.

Christian education equips believers to serve in diverse contexts. In the home, it trains parents to nurture children in godliness. In the church, it prepares members to lead, teach, and minister with wisdom. In society, it sends Christians into business, medicine, government, and the arts with a biblical worldview that shapes their work. Every calling becomes an opportunity to glorify God when Christians are properly trained to see vocation as service.

The New Testament gives many examples of this pattern. Jesus spent three years instructing His disciples, not so they could remain students forever but so they could be sent out to preach, heal, and establish the church (Matthew 28:19-20; Acts 1:8). Paul mentored Timothy and Titus so that they could lead and teach others (2 Timothy 2:2). Aquila and Priscilla, though tentmakers by trade, instructed Apollos more accurately in the way of God (Acts 18:26). Each of these examples shows education flowing into service.

History also affirms this principle. The catechisms of the Reformation did not stop with belief; they called believers to live out their faith in work, worship, and citizenship. The Puritans in New England founded schools like Harvard and Yale, not merely to educate ministers but to prepare a society shaped by biblical truth. John Wesley's emphasis on Methodist teaching was linked directly to service; teaching was to produce holiness, and holiness was to express itself in works of mercy and evangelism.

Today, the need is just as urgent. The world does not need Christians who can merely recite doctrine but believers who embody Christ in their daily vocations. Christian doctors must practice with compassion, Christian business leaders with integrity, Christian teachers with patience and truth. Christian education provides the biblical foundation and spiritual training for such service. Without it, believers may drift into careers shaped by secular values. With it, they see their work as kingdom service.

In this way, Christian education prevents discipleship from becoming self-focused. It reminds believers that knowledge is not an end but a means to equip them for ministry and mission. As James reminds us, *"Be ye doers of the word, and not hearers only"* (James 1:22). Christian education forms hearers who become doers, disciples who become servants, and learners who become leaders in the cause of Christ.

The Content of Christian Education

Every system of education has content. Whether acknowledged or not, every school, every teacher, and every curriculum communicates more than facts; it communicates values, assumptions, and a vision of life. This is why the content of Christian education matters so deeply. It is not enough for Christian education to exist in name; its strength lies in what it teaches. If the content is vague, shallow, or compromised, the results will be weak and worldly disciples. But when the content is faithful to God's Word, believers are grounded in truth, shaped in character, and equipped to live for Christ.

The Bible continually stresses the importance of sound content. Paul warned Timothy that *"the time will come when they will not endure sound doctrine"* (2 Timothy 4:3). Instead of neglecting doctrine, Timothy was urged to *"hold fast the form of sound words"* (2 Timothy 1:13) and to *"commit these things to faithful men, who shall be able to teach others also"* (2 Timothy 2:2). These instructions remind us that the content of Christian teaching is not a matter of preference but a sacred trust. The gospel must be handed down intact from generation to generation through faithful teaching.

The history of the church also underscores this truth. The early church defended itself against heresy by clarifying its teaching in the form of creeds. The Apostles' Creed and the Nicene Creed were not empty statements but carefully crafted summaries of biblical truth, designed to protect and pass on the essentials of the faith. During the Reformation, Luther wrote his *Small Catechism* so that every father could teach his household the basics of faith. **Calvin's Genevan Catechism** served a similar purpose. John Wesley's catechisms for Methodist societies carried on the same tradition. At every stage of church history, when the content of Christian education was solid and biblical, the church grew strong; when content was neglected or distorted, the church declined.

This reality is no different today. A family that does not fill its children with God's Word will find that the world is quick to fill them with its philosophies. A church that entertains but does not teach sound doctrine may draw crowds, but will fail to form disciples. A school that pursues excellence in academics while neglecting the fear of the Lord produces capable minds but unanchored hearts. Content is never neutral. What is taught, and what is omitted, shapes a generation.

The Word of God as the Foundation

At the foundation of all Christian education stands the Word of God. Scripture is not one subject among many; it is the fountain from which all true knowledge flows. Paul reminds us that *"All scripture is given by inspiration of God, and is profitable for doctrine, for reproof, for correction, for instruction in righteousness"* (2 Timothy 3:16). This verse outlines the very heart of Christian educational content. The Bible provides the truths we believe (doctrine), exposes the errors we must reject (reproof), shows us the path of correction when we stray, and trains us in righteousness for daily living.

This means that the Bible must not be treated as a supplemental text but as the central textbook of life. In the Old Testament, God commanded His people to keep His words ever before them: *"These words, which I command thee this day, shall be in thine heart: and thou shalt teach them diligently unto thy children"* (Deuteronomy 6:6-7). The Word was to be spoken in the home, on the road, at night, and in the morning. The psalmist likewise declared, *"Thy word have I hid in mine heart, that I might not sin against thee"* (Psalm 119:11). Scripture was not a mere subject; it was the guide for all of life.

The New Testament shows the same pattern. Jesus Himself continually taught from the Scriptures, opening the Law, the Prophets, and the Psalms to His disciples (Luke 24:27, 44-45). The early church devoted itself to "the apostles' teaching" (Acts 2:42), which was rooted in the Old Testament and illuminated by the words of Christ. Paul told the Colossians, *"Let the word of Christ dwell in you richly in all wisdom"* (Colossians 3:16). Christian education, therefore, can only be faithful when it begins and ends with God's Word.

Historically, this conviction gave rise to practices such as catechism, Bible memorization, and expository preaching. Families gathered daily to read and rehearse Scripture. Schools established by Christians made the Bible central to their curriculum. Wherever God's Word was at the core, Christian education flourished.

In practical terms, this means that in the Christian home, Scripture should be read, memorized, and applied in family life. In the church, preaching and teaching must remain anchored in the Bible, not in human wisdom or popular opinion. In Christian schools and institutions, every subject, mathematics, history, science, and literature must be taught in light of God's Word, revealing His order, sovereignty, and truth. Scripture is not just one part of the content of Christian education; it is the foundation upon which everything else rests.

Moral and Ethical Content

Christian education is not complete if it teaches Scripture and doctrine but fails to shape conduct. The Bible makes clear that true learning must be expressed in holy living. James 1:22 warns: *"But be ye doers of the word, and not hearers only, deceiving your own selves."* Education that stops at the mind without reaching the heart and will is incomplete. For this reason, moral and ethical instruction is a vital part of Christian education's content.

God's Word consistently ties teaching to obedience. In Deuteronomy 6, Israel was commanded not only to know God's laws but to "walk in all His ways." The Ten Commandments (Exodus 20) were not abstract truths but concrete directives for daily living, honoring parents, keeping the Sabbath, speaking truth, respecting property, and rejecting covetousness. The wisdom literature expands this, offering moral instruction for integrity, honesty, diligence, humility, and self-control. Proverbs is filled with reminders that wisdom shows itself in right conduct: *"He that walketh uprightly walketh surely: but he that perverteth his ways shall be known"* (Proverbs 10:9).

Jesus likewise tied His teaching to behavior. In the

Sermon on the Mount (Matthew 5-7), He called His followers not only to believe but to live differently from the world: to love enemies, to give in secret, to pray sincerely, and to forgive freely. He concluded with the parable of the wise and foolish builders, making clear that the difference between the two was not in hearing His words but in doing them. Paul followed the same pattern in his letters. After teaching doctrine, he always moved to practical exhortations: put off lying, anger, and immorality; put on kindness, humility, and love (Ephesians 4:22-32; Colossians 3:5-17). Doctrine provides the foundation, but morality and ethics are the building blocks.

The church throughout history has reinforced this connection. Early catechisms not only summarized beliefs but also included instruction in the Ten Commandments and the Lord's Prayer as guides for holy living. Augustine insisted that education should train the soul to love rightly, to love God above all and neighbor as oneself. Thomas Aquinas emphasized the formation of virtues such as prudence, justice, temperance, and courage, alongside theological virtues of faith, hope, and love. The Reformers, too, insisted that Christian education was incomplete without shaping conduct. Luther's *Small Catechism* placed equal weight on creed, commandments, and prayer. John Wesley later declared, "There is no holiness but social holiness," highlighting that ethics must be lived in community.

In practice, moral and ethical content must be woven into every level of Christian education. In the home, children should learn not only Bible verses but habits of respect, honesty, and service. In the church, teaching should address real-life issues such as marriage, money, speech, and integrity in work. In Christian schools, subjects like literature and history must be taught with moral reflection, asking what actions honor or dishonor God. Ethics should not be treated as an optional course for advanced students but as a thread running through all education.

The danger of neglecting this content is clear. Knowledge without virtue leads to pride and destruction. Paul warned that "knowledge puffeth up, but charity edifieth" (1 Corinthians 8:1). A church may produce well-informed members who can recite doctrine but live hypocritically. A school may graduate students with excellent grades but little moral compass. Without moral and ethical teaching, Christian education produces clever sinners rather than faithful disciples.

When moral and ethical content is present, however, education produces lives of integrity and holiness. Believers who are trained to "walk worthy of the Lord" (Colossians 1:10) become witnesses of God's truth in their families, workplaces, and communities. They embody the character of Christ in their daily conduct, showing the world that Christian education is not theoretical but transformational.

Worldview Content

A crucial element of Christian education is the shaping of a worldview. A worldview is the lens through which people interpret reality, how they answer questions about origins, purpose, morality, and destiny. Every system of education communicates a worldview, whether explicitly or subtly. Secular education often assumes that the universe is the product of chance, that morality is relative, and that truth is subjective. This worldview shapes students to see themselves as autonomous individuals accountable only to themselves.

Christian education presents a radically different vision. It begins with the confession that *"In the beginning God created the heaven and the earth"* (Genesis 1:1). Life is not an accident but a gift, and creation is purposeful, ordered, and good. Humanity is made in the image of God (Genesis 1:27), fallen into sin (Romans 3:23), redeemed in Christ (John 3:16), and destined for eternity (Revelation 21:1-5). These truths form the framework for how Christians understand every aspect of life.

Paul explains this in Colossians 2:8: *"Beware lest any man spoil you through philosophy and vain deceit, after the tradition of men, after the rudiments of the world, and not after Christ."* Christian education resists empty worldviews by rooting learners in Christ, "in whom are hid all the treasures of wisdom and knowledge" (Colossians 2:3). Because all truth belongs to God, every subject must be studied in relation to Him.

This means that history is not random events but the unfolding of God's providence. Science is not chaotic forces, but the discovery of the order God has woven into creation. Literature is not merely human imagination but the expression of humanity's struggle with sin and longing for redemption. Mathematics reflects God's consistency and design. Even the arts, when approached with discernment, reflect creativity given by the Creator. In this way, Christian education integrates all knowledge into a coherent worldview centered on Christ.

The church has long understood the importance of worldview. Augustine argued that all truth is God's truth and that Christians should not reject learning but reclaim it under Christ's lordship. Aquinas built on this by showing how reason and faith, though distinct, are united in the pursuit of truth. The Reformers insisted that education should not divide the sacred from the secular but should teach every subject with reference to God's Word. Abraham Kuyper, a later Reformed thinker, famously declared, "There is not a square inch in the whole domain of our human existence over which Christ, who is Sovereign overall, does not cry: Mine!"

Practically, worldview content means that Christian education must avoid compartmentalization. Faith cannot be confined to Sunday worship or Bible classes. It must shape how believers think about economics, politics, science, art, and culture. A Christian student studying biology must see God's hand in creation. A Christian studying history must recognize God's providence guiding nations. A Christian artist must understand creativity as a gift for glorifying God rather than self. When education integrates worldview in this way, learners see all of life under the reign of Christ.

The absence of worldview content leaves believers vulnerable. Without it, they may confess Christian doctrine on Sundays but live according to secular assumptions the rest of the week. They may know

Bible verses but interpret life through the lens of materialism, relativism, or nationalism. This divided mind leads to instability and compromise. But when worldview is central, Christian education produces disciples whose minds are renewed, who "bring into captivity every thought to the obedience of Christ" (2 Corinthians 10:5).

Worldview content gives Christian education its coherence. It prevents fragmentation by showing that faith touches every part of life. It trains believers not only to think biblically but to live faithfully in the midst of a fallen world. It prepares them to engage culture with wisdom, to discern truth from error, and to glorify Christ in every calling.

Practical Application of Content

The final element of Christian educational content is practical application. Knowledge, doctrine, morality, and worldview are essential, but if they remain abstract, they fall short of their purpose. Christian education must move truth from the page into life, shaping not only what learners know and believe but also how they live, serve, and witness. Jesus made this clear in the Great Commission: *"Teaching them to observe all things whatsoever I have commanded you"* (Matthew 28:20). The goal of teaching is obedience, not information.

Scripture continually emphasizes this connection. Deuteronomy 30:14 declares, *"The word is very nigh unto thee, in thy mouth, and in thy heart, that thou mayest do it."* Psalm 119 links delight in God's Word with walking in His ways. James 1:22 warns that hearing without doing leads to self-deception. Paul reminds the Philippians, *"The things which ye have both learned, and received, and heard, and seen in me, do: and the God of peace shall be with you"* (Philippians 4:9). In every case, teaching finds its fulfillment in practice.

The early church modeled this integration of truth and life. Believers "continued steadfastly in the apostles' doctrine and fellowship, and in breaking of bread, and in prayers" (Acts 2:42). Instruction was not divorced from worship, community, or service; it was woven into daily practice. Early catechisms trained not only the mind but also habits of prayer, worship, fasting, and generosity. Augustine's *Confessions* reveal that his own learning became meaningful only when it led to obedience and transformation.

The Reformers also insisted on application. Luther's *Small Catechism* did not stop with explanation but included daily prayers and guidance for Christian living. The Puritans taught that education must cultivate habits of holiness in family life, work, and public witness. John Wesley designed Methodist societies not merely for study but for accountability and practical service, combining doctrine with disciplined practice. In every age, faithful Christian education has linked content to obedience.

Practically, this means that Christian education today must train believers to live what they learn. In the home, children should not only memorize Scripture but be guided in applying it through kindness to siblings, obedience to parents, and respect for others. In the church, teaching should connect doctrine with discipleship, showing how truths about God shape decisions in marriage, money, and mission. In schools, students must be challenged to see how their knowledge can be used to serve God and neighbor, whether through vocation, creativity, or civic responsibility.

The absence of application produces shallow discipleship. Learners may become well-informed but unchanged, able to discuss doctrine but unwilling to forgive, to recite Scripture but slow to serve. This was the failure of the Pharisees, who knew the law but neglected mercy and love (Matthew 23:23). When application is neglected, education becomes sterile and powerless. But when application is emphasized, believers live out their faith with integrity, and the world sees the gospel embodied in daily conduct.

Practical application also makes Christian education missional. It prepares believers not merely to survive in the world but to engage it with wisdom and courage. Jesus told His disciples, *"Ye are the light of the world. A city that is set on a hill cannot be hid"* (Matthew 5:14). Christian education equips believers to let their light shine in families, workplaces, communities, and nations. It ensures that truth is not confined to classrooms but carried into every sphere of life.

In this way, the application brings all the elements of Christian education together. Scripture provides the foundation, doctrine clarifies belief, morality shapes conduct, worldview guides understanding, and application sends believers out to live faithfully. Content that is not applied remains incomplete. But content that is lived out fulfills its purpose, forming disciples who know the truth, love God, serve others, and glorify Christ in all things.

The Teachers of Christian Education

Christian education depends on teachers. God's truth is living and powerful, but He has chosen to communicate it through human instruments, men and women who faithfully teach others. Paul asks in Romans 10:14, *"How shall they hear without a preacher?"* and by extension, how shall disciples be formed without teachers? Teachers are not optional in Christian education; they are central to its practice. Without them, the content of Christian education would remain abstract, never translated into the minds and hearts of learners. With them, God's truth is explained, modeled, and applied to daily life.

The importance of teachers can be seen throughout the biblical story. From the beginning, God raised up men and women to guide His people through instruction. Abraham was called to command his children after him in the way of the Lord (Genesis 18:19). Moses was commanded to "teach [the people] statutes and ordinances" so they might do them in the land God gave them (Deuteronomy 4:1-2). The prophets, though often remembered for their warnings, were also teachers who reminded Israel of the covenant and called them to return to obedience. Their ministry shows that God does not leave His people without instruction; He raises teachers to keep them aligned with His Word.

This pattern culminates in Jesus Christ, the supreme Teacher. More than a preacher of truth, He embodied the truth He proclaimed (John 14:6). The crowds marveled because He taught "as one having authority, and not as the scribes" (Matthew 7:29). He spoke in parables that opened the kingdom of God to ordinary people, and He invested deeply in His disciples, teaching them both publicly and privately. His command at the end of His earthly ministry makes clear how central teaching is to the mission of the church: *"Go ye therefore, and teach all nations... teaching them to observe all things whatsoever I have commanded you"* (Matthew 28:19-20). For Jesus, discipleship is inseparable from teaching.

The apostles carried this mission forward. Acts 2:42 describes the early church as devoted to "the apostles' teaching." Paul instructed Timothy not only to guard the truth but also to pass it on: *"The things that thou hast heard of me among many witnesses, the same commit thou to faithful men, who shall be able to teach others also"* (2 Timothy 2:2). This verse shows four generations of teachers, Paul to Timothy, Timothy to faithful men, and faithful men to others. Christian education advances only when teachers embrace their calling to preserve and transmit the truth. James 3:1 adds a sober reminder: *"My brethren, be not many masters [teachers], knowing that we shall receive the greater condemnation."* The role of a teacher is weighty, requiring both seriousness and integrity, for the spiritual lives of learners are profoundly shaped by their instruction.

Because of this, teachers hold a sacred trust. They are not inventors of truth but stewards of it. Their task is not to impress, entertain, or manipulate but to faithfully explain God's Word and live it out before those they instruct. When teachers are faithful, Christian education flourishes, churches remain strong, and generations are equipped to walk in the ways of the Lord. When teachers fail through neglect, error, or hypocrisy, the entire work of education collapses. For this reason, teachers stand at the very center of Christian education's practice.

Biblical Foundations for Teachers

The Bible is full of teachers appointed by God, showing that instruction has always been at the heart of His plan for His people. From the Old Testament through the New Testament, teaching is central to covenant life, discipleship, and the growth of the church.

In the Old Testament, Moses stands as the model of a teacher. He not only received the law of God but was charged to teach it to Israel. After leading the people out of Egypt, his role was not simply political or military; it was instructional. Deuteronomy 4:1 records his words: *"Now therefore hearken, O Israel, unto the statutes and unto the judgments, which I teach you, for to do them, that ye may live, and go in and possess the land which the Lord God of your fathers giveth you."* For Israel, learning was tied to obedience, and obedience was tied to life in the land. Moses also commanded the Levites to read the law aloud publicly every seven years so that all would hear and learn (Deuteronomy 31:10-13). This practice shows that teachers were essential for reminding God's people of His covenant and ensuring that His Word was never forgotten.

Ezra is another striking example. After the exile, when Israel returned to rebuild its life and worship, Ezra is described as a man who had *"set his heart to study the Law of the Lord, and to do it, and to teach His statutes and rules in Israel"* (Ezra 7:10). Here the threefold pattern of the teacher's role is made clear: study God's Word, live it out, and then teach it to others. Teachers are not only conveyors of information but examples of obedience whose instruction flows from their own submission to God.

The prophets also carried out a teaching role. They were not merely predictors of future events but instructors who called the people back to the covenant. Through their preaching, explanation, and illustration, they reminded Israel of God's law and urged repentance. Their teaching was often confrontational, challenging the people to reject idols and return to the Lord. In this way, they demonstrate that teachers must sometimes disturb false comfort in order to bring learners back to the truth.

In the New Testament, Jesus is presented as the supreme Teacher. The Gospels frequently refer to Him by this title (John 13:13). His teaching was unique in its authority: *"And it came to pass, when Jesus had ended these sayings, the people were astonished at his doctrine: for he taught them as one having authority, and not as the scribes"* (Matthew 7:28-29). He taught through parables that conveyed deep truths in simple images. He preached the Sermon on the Mount, laying out the principles of life in the kingdom of God. He invested personally in His disciples, explaining truths to them privately and patiently shaping their understanding. His ministry culminated in the Great Commission, which placed teaching at the very heart of the church's mission: *"Go ye therefore, and teach all nations... teaching them to observe all things whatsoever I have commanded you"* (Matthew 28:19-20).

The apostles carried this teaching ministry forward. Acts 2:42 describes the early believers as devoted to "the apostles' teaching." Paul instructed Timothy to "preach the word, reprove, rebuke, exhort with all longsuffering and doctrine" (2 Timothy 4:2). He also commanded him to entrust the truth to faithful men who would be able to teach others also (2 Timothy 2:2), showing the generational chain of teaching that sustains the church. James warns of the seriousness of this calling: *"My brethren, be not many masters [teachers], knowing that we shall receive the greater condemnation"* (James 3:1). Teaching carries both privilege and accountability.

From beginning to end, Scripture portrays teachers as God's appointed instruments for passing on His truth. They preserve the law, proclaim the gospel, and form disciples. Their ministry is indispensable to the life of God's people. Without teachers, truth fades, worship declines, and discipleship falters. With faithful teachers, the Word of God is preserved, lived, and multiplied across generations.

Qualifications of Teachers

Because teachers have such influence, Scripture places serious emphasis on their qualifications. Christian education is not merely about transferring knowledge but about forming disciples in the truth of God. For this reason, the teacher must be both competent in knowledge and exemplary in character. A teacher who knows the Word but fails to live it distorts the message. A teacher who is godly but ignorant of truth cannot give sound instruction. Both knowledge and holiness are required.

Paul gives clear qualifications when describing overseers and elders in 1 Timothy 3 and Titus 1. These passages highlight that teachers must be above reproach, faithful in family life, sober-minded, self-controlled, hospitable, and able to teach. The phrase "able to teach" shows the need for skill in communicating truth, but the surrounding qualities emphasize the integrity of life. Christian teachers must embody the message they proclaim. Knowledge without holiness is dangerous, for it leads to hypocrisy and undermines trust. Conversely, zeal without knowledge misleads learners and spreads confusion.

Faithfulness to Scripture is another vital qualification. Teachers are not free to invent their own ideas or follow the trends of culture. They are stewards of God's Word, entrusted with a deposit that must be guarded and proclaimed. Paul charged Timothy: *"Preach the word; be instant in season, out of season; reprove, rebuke, exhort with all longsuffering and doctrine"* (2 Timothy 4:2). Teachers must be diligent students of Scripture, rightly handling the word of truth (2 Timothy 2:15). Their authority does not come from personal charisma or human wisdom but from the faithful exposition of God's Word.

Humility is also an essential qualification. James 3:1 warns: *"Be not many masters [teachers], knowing that we shall receive the greater condemnation."* Teaching carries weighty accountability, for those who lead others astray will answer to God for their negligence. This should drive every teacher to depend on the Spirit, to teach with prayer, and to acknowledge that wisdom comes from God. Paul asks, *"What hast thou that thou didst not receive?"* (1 Corinthians 4:7). A true Christian teacher recognizes that all knowledge and ability are gifts entrusted by God for the benefit of His people.

The history of the church confirms this biblical standard. The early Fathers, such as Augustine, warned that a teacher's life must match his teaching, lest his example discredit his words. Thomas Aquinas argued that teachers must possess both knowledge and virtue, for without virtue, knowledge becomes destructive. The Reformers insisted that pastors and teachers be examined not only for theological accuracy but also for upright conduct. John Wesley was careful in appointing Methodist class leaders, requiring that they demonstrate both understanding of the gospel and lives marked by holiness.

For today's Christian educators, whether pastors, parents, schoolteachers, Sunday or Sabbath school teachers, or college professors, these qualifications remain the same. They must know the Scriptures well, teach them faithfully, and live them consistently. They must resist the temptation to chase popularity or innovation at the expense of truth. They must cultivate humility, recognizing that their influence over students can either build faith or tear it down. Above all, they must depend on the Spirit of God, who alone enables them to instruct with power and integrity.

When teachers embody these qualifications, Christian education becomes effective. Learners not only hear the truth but see it lived out before them. Instruction is reinforced by example, and the Word of God is honored. But when teachers neglect these qualifications, the damage is great. For this reason, the church must take seriously the selection, preparation, and accountability of its teachers, ensuring that those who instruct others do so with knowledge, holiness, and humility.

The Teacher's Responsibility

If qualifications describe who teachers must be, responsibilities describe what teachers must do. The responsibility of teachers in Christian education is threefold: to teach truth, to model holiness, and to shepherd learners. These are not optional tasks but essential callings that together define faithful Christian teaching.

1. Teachers must teach the truth faithfully.
The teacher's first responsibility is to handle the Word of God with care and to communicate it clearly. Paul charges Titus that a teacher "must hold firm to the trustworthy word as taught, so that he may be able to give instruction in sound doctrine and also to rebuke those who contradict it" (Titus 1:9). This requires diligence in study, courage in proclaiming truth, and clarity in instruction. Teachers are not entertainers or motivators but stewards of God's Word. Their aim is not to please human ears but to feed hungry souls with the bread of life. Paul's words to Timothy are instructive: *"Preach the word; be instant in season, out of season"* (2 Timothy 4:2). Teachers must remain faithful whether or not their message is popular.

2. Teachers must model holiness.
Instruction is never only verbal. Learners inevitably

observe the life of their teachers, and example often speaks more powerfully than words. Paul urged the Corinthians, *"Be ye followers of me, even as I also am of Christ"* (1 Corinthians 11:1). The Thessalonians could imitate Paul because they had seen his labor, love, and endurance among them (1 Thessalonians 1:5-7). A teacher who proclaims Christ but lives in hypocrisy undermines the very message he teaches. By contrast, a teacher whose life displays integrity reinforces the truth and demonstrates what it means to follow Christ. This is why Scripture consistently ties teaching to character. Holiness gives credibility to instruction, while sin discredits it.

3. Teachers must shepherd learners.
Education is more than the transfer of knowledge; it is the shaping of lives. Teachers are called not only to instruct but to nurture, encourage, correct, and guide. Paul described his ministry in Thessalonica as being "gentle among you, even as a nurse cherishes her children" (1 Thessalonians 2:7). At the same time, he exhorted, comforted, and charged them to walk worthy of God (1 Thessalonians 2:11-12). This pastoral dimension of teaching requires patience and care, for learners often struggle, doubt, or resist. A faithful teacher walks with them, pointing them back to Christ and urging them toward maturity.

The history of the church confirms these responsibilities. Augustine, in his *On Christian Teaching*, emphasized that teachers must not only explain Scripture but also stir love for God in their hearers. Thomas Aquinas argued that the goal of teaching is the formation of virtue, which requires both instruction and guidance. The Reformers insisted that pastors were shepherds as well as teachers, responsible for the care of souls. John Wesley required Methodist leaders to give both doctrinal instruction and personal oversight, combining teaching with pastoral care.

In practical terms today, this means that Christian teachers, whether parents at home, pastors or teachers in the church, or educators in schools, must embrace all three dimensions. They must labor in study to teach God's Word faithfully. They must pursue holiness in their own lives so that their example reinforces their teaching. And they must shepherd their learners, investing personally in their growth and walking with them toward maturity. When teachers embrace these responsibilities, Christian education fulfills its purpose of forming disciples who know the truth, love God, and live for His glory.

Historical Witness

The church has always recognized the vital role of teachers in Christian education. From the earliest centuries, Christian leaders understood that the strength of the church depended not only on evangelism and worship but also on faithful instruction. Each generation of believers needed teachers who could preserve truth, refute error, and form disciples in the likeness of Christ.

In the early church, figures such as Origen and Augustine wrote works of instruction that shaped

Christian thought for centuries. Origen developed systematic approaches to Scripture, training disciples to read the Word with depth and discernment. Augustine, in his *On Christian Teaching*, stressed that teachers must not only explain Scripture but also help learners grow in love for God and neighbor. For him, education was not merely intellectual but spiritual, intended to lead the soul to holiness.

During the medieval period, teaching remained central to the church's mission. Monastic schools preserved learning and trained generations of clergy. Thomas Aquinas, one of the great teachers of the Middle Ages, emphasized that education must form both intellect and virtue. He insisted that truth and goodness are inseparable, and that the goal of teaching is wisdom, knowledge ordered toward God. These medieval teachers demonstrated that Christian education is at its best when it unites doctrine, morality, and devotion.

The Reformation renewed this emphasis on teachers. Martin Luther not only preached the gospel but also wrote catechisms for households, equipping fathers to be the first teachers of their children. His *Small Catechism* asked simple but profound questions, giving families a practical tool for passing on the faith. John Calvin established schools in Geneva, training ministers and laypeople alike. His vision was that every believer, not just clergy, should be taught the truths of Scripture. By institutionalizing education, Calvin ensured that the Reformation would not be a passing movement, but a lasting transformation rooted in teaching.

The Wesleyan revival carried this tradition into the

modern era. John Wesley organized Methodist societies and classes where lay leaders instructed believers in doctrine and holy living. These small groups were not only for fellowship but for education and accountability. Wesley knew that revival would wither without structure, so he appointed teachers to ensure that believers grew in knowledge and holiness.

In every age, the strength of the church has been closely tied to the quality of its teachers. Where teachers were faithful, the church flourished; where teaching was neglected or corrupted, the church declined. This historical witness affirms what Scripture already makes clear: teachers are indispensable instruments in God's plan for preserving truth and forming disciples. The church today stands in continuity with this great tradition, called to raise up teachers who, like those before them, will faithfully pass on the truth of Christ to the next generation.

Practical Implications Today

The role of teachers in Christian education remains as vital today as in any period of history. Though times and cultures change, the need for faithful instructors of God's truth never diminishes. In fact, the modern world, with its flood of information, competing worldviews, and moral confusion, makes the task of teachers more urgent than ever.

The first implication is that parents must embrace their role as the primary teachers of their children. Scripture is clear that fathers and mothers are responsible for training their children in the nurture and admonition of the Lord (Ephesians 6:4). This responsibility cannot be outsourced to schools or even to the church alone. From the earliest commands in Deuteronomy 6, parents were instructed to speak of God's Word "when thou sittest in thine house, and when thou walkest by the way, and when thou liest down, and when thou risest up." Family life itself is meant to be a classroom of faith, where children see God's truth taught and lived.

Second, pastors and elders carry the weighty responsibility of teaching the church. Acts 20:28 calls them to "feed the church of God, which he hath purchased with his own blood." The strength of a congregation depends not on programs or popularity but on the faithful preaching and teaching of Scripture. Pastors must resist the temptation to cater to cultural trends or tickle ears, and instead remain steadfast in expository teaching. Elders and leaders, too, must guide through instruction, ensuring that sound doctrine permeates the life of the church.

Third, Christian schoolteachers and educators hold a unique position of influence. They are entrusted with shaping both the minds and the hearts of students. Their role is not simply to add Bible verses to a secular curriculum but to integrate biblical truth into every subject. Mathematics reveals God's order, science displays His handiwork, literature reflects humanity's moral struggle, and history unfolds His providence. Faithful teachers help students see that Christ is Lord over all knowledge. In doing so, they prepare students not only for careers but for lives of faithful discipleship.

The modern cultural climate makes these responsibilities even more pressing. Teachers today face a society that denies absolute truth, exalts personal autonomy, and often ridicules faith. They must have the courage to stand firm, patience to persevere in difficulty, and deep trust in the sufficiency of God's Word. They are called to be countercultural witnesses, shaping learners who can resist deception and live faithfully in a hostile environment.

Practically, this means the church must invest in teachers. Parents must be trained and encouraged in their role at home. Pastors and church leaders must be equipped through sound theological training. Schools must support Christian educators with resources, prayer, and accountability. The church cannot treat teaching as an afterthought but must see it as a frontline ministry essential to its survival and growth.

When teachers embrace their calling with integrity and devotion, Christian education thrives. Learners are rooted in truth, disciples are formed in Christ's likeness, and the next generation is equipped to live faithfully. But when teaching is neglected, compromised, or corrupted, the consequences are devastating. In every age, the flourishing of the church depends on its teachers. Today is no different. The practical implication is clear: Christian education requires faithful teachers in the home, the church, and the school, who will pass on the truth of Christ with courage, clarity, and love.

The Learners of Christian Education

If teachers are indispensable to Christian education, so too are learners. Teaching has no effect if there are no hearts ready to receive, and the ministry of instruction is wasted if hearers are indifferent or rebellious. Christian education is not only about faithful teachers delivering truth but also about faithful learners receiving it with humility and obedience. Just as the farmer must sow good seed, the soil must be ready to receive it. In the same way, the Word of God bears fruit only when learners approach it with the right attitude.

The Bible consistently presents God's people as learners. In the Old Testament, Israel was commanded to hear and obey. *"Hear, O Israel: The Lord our God is one Lord"* (Deuteronomy 6:4). The command begins with hearing, with listening attentively, and receiving instruction. Throughout Israel's history, the nation was called not only to receive God's law but to meditate on it day and night, to teach it to their children, and to obey it in practice. The prophets often rebuked Israel for having ears but not listening, for rejecting the teaching of the Lord. Their failure as learners led to disobedience and judgment.

In the New Testament, Christ Himself identifies His followers as learners. The word "disciple" literally means "learner." Jesus invited people not merely to admire Him but to follow Him as students follow a master. He said, *"Take my yoke upon you, and learn of me; for I am meek and lowly in heart: and ye shall find rest unto your souls"* (Matthew 11:29). His disciples spent years listening to His words, watching His example, and being corrected when they misunderstood. The church was born from this group of learners who were willing to be taught and then sent out to teach others.

The early church continued in this pattern. Acts 2:42 describes the first believers as those who *"continued steadfastly in the apostles' doctrine."* They did not treat learning as optional but as essential to discipleship. Paul urged the Thessalonians to "receive the word of God... not as the word of men, but as it is in truth, the word of God" (1 Thessalonians 2:13). The Colossians were told, *"Let the word of Christ dwell in you richly"* (Colossians 3:16). These passages show that faithful learners are marked by devotion to teaching, receptivity to truth, and eagerness to grow.

Christian education, therefore, is not a one-sided task. It requires both teachers and learners, those who faithfully proclaim the Word and those who faithfully receive it. The posture of learners determines whether teaching produces fruit. A humble, teachable heart is like good soil where seed can flourish (Mark 4:20). A proud or distracted heart, by contrast, is like rocky or thorny ground, where the Word is quickly lost. The success of Christian education depends not only on faithful teaching but on learners who are willing to hear, believe, and obey.

In our time, the need for faithful learners is just as urgent. We live in an age of constant noise, endless distractions, and widespread skepticism of authority. Many hear but few truly listen. For this reason, Christian education must not only focus on the qualifications of teachers but also cultivate the qualities of learners' humility, hunger for truth, perseverance in study, and obedience. Only when teachers and learners work together, under the guidance of the Spirit and in submission to Scripture, does Christian education fulfill its God-given purpose.

Biblical Foundations for Learners

The foundation of Christian learning is firmly rooted in Scripture. From the earliest days of God's covenant with His people, He emphasized not only the giving of His Word but the receiving of it. Israel's identity as the people of God depended on their willingness to listen, believe, and obey. *"Hear, O Israel: The Lord our God is one Lord: and thou shalt love the Lord thy God with all thine heart, and with all thy soul, and with all thy might"* (Deuteronomy 6:4-5). The Shema begins not with doing but with hearing. The very posture of the covenant people was that of learners before their God.

God commanded Israel to pass His Word diligently to their children: *"And these words, which I command thee this day, shall be in thine heart: and thou shalt teach them diligently unto thy children"* (Deuteronomy 6:6-7). This shows a twofold pattern, parents as teachers and children as learners. The health of Israel's covenant life depended on both roles being fulfilled. When children listened, received, and obeyed, God's blessings followed. When they hardened their hearts, ignored instruction, and went after idols, judgment fell. The prophets repeatedly indicted Israel for being "a rebellious people, lying children, children that will not hear the law of the Lord" (Isaiah 30:9). The tragedy of Israel's history shows the danger of failing to learn.

The wisdom literature likewise emphasizes the learner's role. Proverbs opens with a call to the young to hear and receive instruction: *"The fear of the Lord is the beginning of knowledge: but fools despise wisdom and instruction"* (Proverbs 1:7). The entire book is framed as a father teaching a son, with constant exhortations: "Hear, my son, your father's instruction, and forsake not your mother's teaching" (Proverbs 1:8). The wise learner is humble, attentive, and responsive; the fool is proud, careless, and resistant. Christian education stands on this biblical pattern: learners must not only be exposed to truth but also embrace it with reverence and obedience.

In the New Testament, the pattern continues. The word "disciple" itself means "learner." To be a disciple of Jesus is to be a student under His authority. Jesus invited His followers with the words, *"Take my yoke upon you, and learn of me"* (Matthew 11:29). His disciples spent years listening to His teaching, asking questions, and receiving correction. When they misunderstood, Jesus patiently instructed them again. Their identity as learners prepared them to become teachers who would one day disciple others.

The early church preserved this emphasis. Acts 2:42 describes believers as those who "continued steadfastly in the apostles' doctrine." They did not treat learning as an optional extra but as central to their new life in Christ. Paul praised the Thessalonians because they received his words "not as the word of men, but as it is in truth, the word of God" (1 Thessalonians 2:13). The Colossians were exhorted to "let the word of Christ dwell in you richly" (Colossians 3:16). Again and again, the responsibility of the learner is emphasized: to receive truth with humility, to retain it faithfully, and to live it out consistently.

This biblical foundation underscores that Christian education is a two-way covenant: God provides teachers and truth, but learners must respond with open hearts. Without attentive, obedient learners, the ministry of teaching is hindered. But when learners hear, receive, and obey, the Word of God takes root and bears fruit, producing lives of wisdom, holiness, and service.

The Attitude of Learners

If the Bible makes clear that God's people are called to be learners, then the heart posture of the learner becomes critical. The effectiveness of Christian education is not determined by the brilliance of the teacher alone but also by the responsiveness of the learner. A seed may be pure and the Sower faithful, yet if the soil is hardened or choked with thorns, it cannot bear fruit. Jesus' parable of the Sower (Mark 4:1-20) illustrates this truth vividly: some hear the Word but let Satan snatch it away; others receive it with joy but have no root; still others are choked by cares and riches. Only the good soil, the humble, receptive heart, bears fruit.

The first essential attitude of a learner, then, is humility. Proverbs 1:7 declares, *"The fear of the Lord is the beginning of knowledge: but fools despise wisdom and instruction."* To fear the Lord is to acknowledge dependence on Him and openness to His truth. A proud learner, convinced of self-sufficiency, rejects correction and despises instruction. By contrast, a humble learner recognizes the need for guidance and gladly receives wisdom. This humility is seen in young Samuel, who, as a boy, responded to God's call with, *"Speak, Lord; for thy servant heareth"* (1 Samuel 3:9). His attitude of listening and obedience prepared him for a life of faithful service.

The second essential attitude is obedience. Learning in Scripture is never abstract or purely intellectual. God's Word is given to be obeyed. In Deuteronomy 5:1, Moses says, *"Hear, O Israel, the statutes and judgments which I speak in your ears this day, that ye may learn them, and keep, and do them."* True learning results in action. James echoes this truth in the New Testament: *"Be ye doers of the word, and not hearers only, deceiving your own selves"* (James 1:22). The attitude of the learner must therefore be readiness to apply instruction. A person who delights in Bible study but resists change in life is not truly a learner.

A third necessary attitude is hunger for truth. The psalmist declares, *"As the hart panteth after the water brooks, so panteth my soul after thee, O God"* (Psalm 42:1). The Bereans in Acts 17:11 are commended because "they received the word with all readiness of mind, and searched the scriptures daily, whether those things were so." They were eager learners, testing teaching against Scripture and delighted to grow in knowledge. A faithful learner approaches instruction not with apathy or boredom but with expectation, believing that God speaks through His Word and His teachers.

The early church fathers also emphasized learner attitudes. Augustine wrote that the best students are those who "love to learn what God teaches," reminding us that education must stir affection as well as intellect. Thomas à Kempis, in *The Imitation of Christ*, exhorted believers to be "humble and peaceable learners" who desire transformation more than curiosity. Throughout history, the greatest learners of the faith were those whose hearts were teachable and eager for holiness.

For today's Christian learner, these attitudes are just as necessary. In an age of distraction, pride, and shallow curiosity, humility, obedience, and hunger for truth are countercultural. Students must resist the temptation to treat learning casually or skeptically. Instead, they must come with reverence for God's Word, readiness to obey, and a genuine desire to grow. Parents, pastors, and teachers can help cultivate these attitudes, but ultimately the learner must choose them.

When these attitudes are present, Christian education becomes transformative. The Word of God takes root, instruction shapes character, and disciples grow into maturity. But when learners are proud, resistant, or indifferent, even the best teaching fails to bear fruit. The posture of the learner is therefore not secondary but central to the success of Christian education.

The Responsibility of Learners

While teachers bear the responsibility of faithfully transmitting truth, learners carry an equal responsibility to receive and apply it. Christian education is not a passive activity where knowledge is poured into empty vessels; it is a covenant of accountability. Teachers will give an account for what they have taught (James 3:1), but learners will also give an account for what they have heard. Jesus Himself warned, *"Take heed therefore how ye hear"* (Luke 8:18). The way truth is received determines whether it bears fruit or is wasted.

The first responsibility of learners is to listen attentively. In both the Old and New Testaments, hearing is emphasized as the foundation of obedience. *"Hear, O Israel"* begins the Shema (Deuteronomy 6:4), showing that listening is the starting point of covenant life. Jesus often concluded His parables with the phrase, *"He that hath ears to hear, let him hear"* (Matthew 13:9). True learning requires focus, attention, and a willingness to receive instruction. A distracted or careless listener cannot be transformed by truth.

The second responsibility is to apply the Word. Knowledge alone is insufficient; it must be translated into practice. Moses told Israel, *"These words, which I command thee this day, shall be in thine heart; and thou shalt teach them diligently unto thy children"* (Deuteronomy 6:6-7). God's Word was not to remain external but to penetrate the heart and shape daily living. Jesus reinforced this in Matthew 7:24-27, contrasting the wise man who built his house on the rock by hearing and doing His words with the foolish man who heard but did not act. Learners who fail to apply teaching deceive themselves, as James warns: *"Be ye doers of the word, and not hearers only, deceiving your own selves"* (James 1:22).

A third responsibility of learners is to grow continually. Learning is not a one-time event but a lifelong pursuit. The writer of Hebrews rebuked believers who, by that time, should have been teachers but still needed "milk" instead of "strong meat" (Hebrews 5:12-14). This shows that learners are responsible for progressing their understanding and maturity. Paul urged the Colossians to let the word of Christ dwell in them richly (Colossians 3:16) and prayed for the Philippians to "abound yet more and more in knowledge and in all judgment" (Philippians 1:9). Growth is not automatic; it requires diligence, perseverance, and willingness to be stretched.

Church history also affirms this responsibility. The early catechumens preparing for baptism devoted themselves to years of instruction and practice before entering the church fully. They embraced the responsibility of learning as preparation for discipleship. The Reformers expected laypeople to study Scripture, memorize catechisms, and participate actively in their learning. Wesley's Methodist societies required members not only to listen but to demonstrate growth in holiness and service. Learners who resisted growth were lovingly corrected and guided back to faithfulness.

For today's believers, the responsibilities of learners are even more pressing. In an age of distraction, Christians must discipline themselves to listen carefully to God's Word rather than allowing their attention to be consumed by noise. In a culture that values information without transformation, they must be diligent to apply what they learn in obedience to Christ. And in a time of spiritual complacency, they must embrace continual growth, pressing toward maturity rather than remaining in spiritual infancy.

Ultimately, learners will be judged not by how much they have heard but by how faithfully they have responded. Jesus declared, *"To whom much is given, of him shall be much required"* (Luke 12:48). Every lesson, sermon, or Scripture reading carries responsibility. Learners who hear and obey grow in wisdom and holiness. Those who hear and neglect harden their hearts and increase their guilt. Christian education, therefore, is not a privilege without obligation but a sacred trust for which every learner must one day give account.

Challenges for Learners Today

While Scripture sets forth the calling and responsibilities of learners, the reality is that learning is often difficult, especially in the modern age. Every generation faces obstacles, but our time presents unique challenges that can hinder disciples from receiving truth. Christian education must therefore recognize these barriers and help learners overcome them through the grace of God and the power of the Spirit.

One major challenge is distraction. We live in an age of constant noise, where screens, media, and endless streams of information compete for attention. Learners are often conditioned to skim, scroll, and move quickly from one thought to the next, rather than meditate deeply on God's Word. Yet Scripture calls believers to stillness and focus: *"Be still, and know that I am God"* (Psalm 46:10). The psalmist delighted in God's law and meditated on it day and night (Psalm 1:2). Such meditation requires discipline and silence, practices increasingly rare in our culture. Without overcoming distraction, learners will struggle to hear and retain the truth.

Another challenge is secularism and competing worldviews. Modern education often presents life as if God were irrelevant or nonexistent. From science to philosophy, learners are subtly taught to interpret the world without reference to the Creator. This undermines faith and creates divided minds. Paul warns against this danger: *"Beware lest any man spoil you through philosophy and vain deceit, after the tradition of men, after the rudiments of the world, and not after Christ"* (Colossians 2:8). Christian learners today must guard their hearts and minds, filtering every idea through the truth of God's Word. Without vigilance, secularism seeps into their thinking and erodes their faith.

A third challenge is spiritual apathy. Many learners approach Christian education with indifference, treating it as optional or secondary. They may attend classes or services but remain disengaged, showing little hunger for truth. Jesus warned of this in the parable of the soils, describing those who receive the Word with joy but quickly fall away, or those whose growth is choked by "the cares of this world, and the deceitfulness of riches" (Matthew 13:22). Apathy robs the Word of its power in a learner's life, not because the Word is weak but because the heart is closed. Teachers may sow faithfully, but if learners do not value the truth, it bears little fruit.

A fourth challenge is resistance to authority. Our culture prizes autonomy and often views submission to instruction with suspicion. Yet learning requires humility and a willingness to be corrected. Proverbs warns, *"Whoso loveth instruction loveth knowledge: but he that hateth reproof is brutish"* (Proverbs 12:1). Hebrews 13:17 exhorts believers to obey their leaders and submit to them, "for they watch for your souls." Modern learners, shaped by a culture of self-expression, may resist the accountability that true learning demands. Overcoming this challenge requires a renewed trust in God's appointed teachers and a recognition that submission to godly authority is part of discipleship.

Finally, learners today face the challenge of being busy. Life is filled with obligations, work, school, family, and countless activities. Spiritual learning is easily pushed aside. Yet Jesus rebuked Martha, who was "cumbered about much serving," and commended Mary, who chose "that good part" by sitting at His feet (Luke 10:38-42). Learners must intentionally prioritize time for study, prayer, and instruction. Without this priority, the urgent often crowds out the essential.

Despite these challenges, Scripture assures us that learners can overcome by God's grace. The Spirit empowers believers to focus, resist deception, hunger for truth, and persevere in growth. Teachers must help learners recognize these obstacles and equip them with practical strategies to resist distraction, stand firm against false ideas, cultivate zeal, submit humbly, and guard time for God's Word. By doing so, learners can flourish even in a hostile world, becoming faithful disciples who bear fruit for the kingdom.

Transition to Methodology

The role of learners in Christian education cannot be overstated. Teachers may sow faithfully, but unless learners receive with humility, obedience, and perseverance, the Word bears little fruit. Scripture, history, and experience all affirm that discipleship depends on both faithful instruction and faithful reception. Christian education is, therefore, a sacred partnership between those who teach and those who learn, both under the guidance of the Holy Spirit.

Yet even when both teachers and learners are committed, a further question arises: *how* does the process of education best take place? How should truth be communicated so that it is not only heard but understood, remembered, and lived out? This brings us to the next essential element of Christian education and its methodology. Just as seed must be sown wisely and soil cultivated carefully, so the methods of teaching and learning shape the effectiveness of education. Having considered the teachers and the learners, we now turn to the ways in which Christian instruction is carried out.

The Methodology of Christian Education

If Christian education is to be effective, it must not only have faithful teachers, willing learners, and sound content, but also wise methodology. Methodology refers to the ways and means by which truth is communicated and received. It is the practical expression of the teaching process, the strategies, tools, and patterns that enable God's Word to be understood, retained, and lived. Without sound methodology, even the best content can fail to take root, for learners may not grasp it or may forget it quickly.

The Bible itself recognizes the importance of method. God did not give His Word randomly but communicated it through diverse means: commandments written on tablets, stories told through generations, songs embedded in worship, visions and parables that stirred imagination, and, ultimately, the living Word in Jesus Christ. Each method had a purpose, suited to the audience and the moment. The psalmist declared, *"I will open my mouth in a parable: I will utter dark sayings of old... that the generation to come might know them"* (Psalm 78:2, 6). Jesus followed this same pattern, teaching crowds in parables and then explaining the meaning privately to His disciples (Mark 4:34). His use of questions, illustrations, and object lessons shows that method matters.

Throughout church history, the methodology of Christian education has been carefully considered. The early church used catechesis, a question-and-answer method, to prepare converts for baptism. Medieval schools used lectures, disputations, and memorization to form both intellect and character. The Reformers revived catechisms, hymns, and preaching as central methods of instruction. Wesley and the Methodists emphasized small groups, accountability, and experiential learning. In each era, the method was shaped by the conviction that truth must not only be declared but also grasped and lived.

In our time, the challenge is to identify methods that remain faithful to Scripture, effective for learners, and adaptable to diverse contexts. Methodology must never replace content or undermine truth, but it must serve as the vessel by which truth is carried. Christian education, therefore, requires prayerful wisdom in choosing and practicing methods that honor God, serve learners, and lead to transformation.

Biblical Methods of Teaching

The Bible itself demonstrates that methodology matters. God did not reveal His truth in one rigid form, but used a variety of methods suited to different times, audiences, and purposes. These biblical models provide patterns for Christian education today, showing that how we teach is as important as what we teach.

One of the most common biblical methods is storytelling. Much of the Old Testament is narrative, recounting God's dealings with His people through events and characters. Stories of creation, the Exodus, the judges, and the kings were not only historical records but teaching tools that revealed God's character and covenant faithfulness. Psalm 78 emphasizes this: *"We will not hide them from their children, showing to the generation to come the praises of the Lord, and his strength, and his wonderful works that he hath done"* (v. 4). Story embeds truth in memory, making it easier to recall and apply. For this reason, God commanded Israel to rehearse His mighty acts continually before their children (Deuteronomy 6:20-25).

Another biblical method is the use of symbols and rituals. God gave Israel festivals, sacrifices, and ceremonies that served as ongoing lessons. The Passover meal, for instance, was a vivid reenactment of God's deliverance, teaching each generation to remember His salvation (Exodus 12:26-27). These practices engaged not only the mind but also the senses, reinforcing truth through repeated action. In the New Testament, baptism and the Lord's Supper continue this pattern, serving as visible words that communicate spiritual realities.

Jesus, the Master Teacher, employed a wide range of methods. He taught with parables, simple stories that contained profound truths. Parables like the Sower, the prodigal son, and the good Samaritan invited listeners to reflect deeply, drawing them into the lesson rather than delivering abstract principles. Jesus also used questions to provoke thought and self-examination: "Whom do men say that I am?" (Matthew 16:13). He employed object lessons, such as pointing to a child to teach humility (Matthew 18:2-4), or washing His disciples' feet to model servanthood (John 13:12-15). His methods were varied, creative, and always purposeful, engaging both heart and mind.

The apostles continued these methods. They used preaching as a central tool, proclaiming the gospel with boldness and clarity (Acts 2:14-36). They also engaged in dialogue and reasoning, as Paul did in the synagogue and marketplace (Acts 17:2, 17). Letters to the churches served as written instruction, often combining doctrine, exhortation, and practical application. Early Christian communities also employed memorization and recitation of Scripture and creeds, ensuring that truth was deeply ingrained.

These biblical examples reveal several key principles. First, effective teaching is varied. Different methods reach different learners and reinforce truth in different ways. Second, effective teaching is engaging. Stories, questions, and symbols draw learners into active participation rather than passive listening. Third, effective teaching is practical. Jesus and the apostles always connected truth to life, showing learners how to live out what they had been taught.

For Christian education today, these methods remain instructive. Storytelling can be used to communicate biblical truths in memorable ways. Rituals such as family devotions, weekly worship, and the sacraments reinforce God's Word in rhythm and practice. Teachers can employ questions, illustrations, and object lessons to stimulate thought and foster understanding. Preaching, discussion, and memorization remain vital tools. What matters most is that the methods align with Scripture, serve the content faithfully, and aim at transformation.

In sum, the Bible itself demonstrates that God values

methodology. His truth was communicated through stories, symbols, questions, and actions that engaged the whole person. Jesus modeled creativity and intentionality in His teaching. The apostles continued this pattern, ensuring that truth was not only declared but understood. Christian educators today must follow these biblical examples, using methods that honor God, engage learners, and lead to obedience.

Historical Methods of Christian Education

As the church grew and spread across cultures and centuries, it developed methods of teaching that reflected biblical patterns while responding to new challenges. These historical approaches illustrate both the creativity and the consistency of Christian education, reminding us that methodology is not a modern concern but a timeless necessity.

In the early church, catechesis became the primary method for forming believers. New converts, called catechumens, underwent a period of systematic instruction before baptism. This teaching was often conducted through a question-and-answer format, ensuring that learners could both understand and confess the essentials of the faith. Catechesis emphasized memorization of Scripture, the Apostles' Creed, the Lord's Prayer, and the Ten Commandments. Far from being superficial, this method trained the mind and heart, embedding truth deeply into the life of the church.

As the church entered the medieval period, monastic schools became centers of education. Monks devoted themselves to copying Scripture, preserving learning, and instructing novices. The method of Lectio Divina, reading, meditation, prayer, and contemplation, shaped not only the intellect but also the spiritual life of learners. Education was not separated from devotion but integrated with worship and discipline. Later, cathedral schools and universities expanded this model, using lectures, disputations, and commentaries to train clergy and scholars. These methods emphasized rigorous study and debate, ensuring careful handling of Scripture and theology.

During the Reformation, the focus shifted back to the whole people of God. Reformers like Martin Luther and John Calvin emphasized the importance of catechisms and preaching as primary methods of instruction. Luther's *Small Catechism* was designed for use in the home, with fathers as the first teachers of their children. Calvin established schools in Geneva to train both ministers and laypeople, integrating biblical truth with broader subjects such as languages and history. The method of systematic, repeated instruction ensured that entire communities were shaped by the Word. Hymn singing also became a powerful teaching tool, embedding doctrine in the hearts of believers through worship.

The post-Reformation era saw the rise of new methods, particularly in the movements of John Wesley and the Methodists. Wesley organized believers into societies, classes, and bands, where instruction was combined with accountability and fellowship. These small groups allowed for interactive teaching, personal application, and mutual encouragement. Methodology here emphasized not only knowledge but also spiritual growth and practical holiness. Wesley's method demonstrated that effective Christian education involves both structured teaching and relational discipleship.

In the modern era, Christian education has employed a variety of methods, from Sunday schools to mission schools, from preaching in revival meetings to Bible institutes and seminaries. Sunday schools in particular, beginning in the 18th century, revolutionized Christian education by making systematic instruction available to children and the poor. These schools used repetition, memorization, and graded lessons to ensure that learners of all ages could grasp biblical truth.

Across all these periods, a common thread emerges: Christian education has always sought methods that are faithful to Scripture, appropriate to context, and effective for learners. Whether through catechisms, lectures, hymns, small groups, or schools, the goal has remained the same: to transmit God's truth clearly and form disciples in obedience. Historical methods remind us that methodology is not static but adaptable, yet it must always serve the unchanging content of God's Word.

For today's educators, the witness of history offers both encouragement and guidance. It shows that faithful teaching has always required intentional methods. It also warns that when methods lose connection to Scripture and discipleship, education becomes hollow. The church must therefore learn from the past, adopting methods that honor God, engage learners, and equip disciples for faithfulness in their time.

Practical Methods for Today

While the methods of Christian education have taken different forms across centuries, the central challenge remains the same: how to communicate God's truth in ways that are faithful, clear, and transformative. Today's world offers both new opportunities and new obstacles for teaching, making it necessary to draw from biblical principles and historical wisdom while also adapting to contemporary realities.

One practical method is interactive teaching. Scripture shows that Jesus often engaged His disciples through questions and dialogue (Matthew 16:13-15). Today, small groups, Bible studies, and classroom discussions allow learners to wrestle with truth, ask questions, and apply lessons to real life. Interactive methods prevent passive listening and encourage deeper understanding. Learners are not empty vessels but active participants, and good methodology creates space for engagement.

Another method is the intentional use of story and illustration. Just as Jesus taught in parables, teachers today can use stories, testimonies, and case studies to connect doctrine with lived experience. Stories capture the imagination and make abstract truths concrete. A child may forget a definition of grace but remember a story that reveals its beauty. Modern Christian educators can employ biblical narratives, missionary accounts, or personal testimonies as powerful tools for shaping faith.

Memorization and repetition remain essential, even in an age of instant access to information. The psalmist declared, *"Thy word have I hid in mine heart, that I might not sin against thee"* (Psalm 119:11). Memorization plants truth deep in the soul, equipping believers to recall God's Word in times of trial. Though undervalued in today's culture, practices such as learning Scripture, hymns, and creeds ensure that faith is anchored in truth rather than fleeting opinion.

The use of technology presents both opportunities and challenges. Digital tools allow for wide access to sermons, Bible studies, and teaching resources. Online platforms can extend education to those who cannot attend in person. However, reliance on technology must not replace personal discipleship. Education in the church is not merely the transfer of information but the formation of character, which requires relationship. Teachers must use technology wisely, as a supplement, not a substitute, for embodied teaching.

Another crucial method is experiential learning. Wesley's small groups modeled this by combining teaching with accountability and service. Today, learners grow not only by hearing but by doing. Service projects, mission trips, mentoring relationships, and community involvement help learners embody the truths they are taught. When students serve the poor, share their faith, or participate in worship leadership, they move from theory to practice, allowing learning to shape their lives.

Finally, family-based education must not be neglected. Scripture calls parents to be the primary instructors of their children (Deuteronomy 6:7). Churches and schools should equip parents to fulfill this calling, encouraging family devotions, prayer, and Scripture reading in the home. When teaching is reinforced daily in family life, learners are more likely to retain and live out what they have been taught.

These practical methods highlight a key principle: no single method is sufficient. Just as the Bible used varied approaches, story, law, symbol, parable, and command, so Christian educators today must employ a variety of tools. What matters is not novelty or tradition for its own sake but faithfulness to Scripture and effectiveness in forming disciples. Teachers must ask not simply, "What will keep learners entertained?" but "What will help learners hear, understand, and obey the Word of God?"

When practical methods are chosen wisely, Christian education becomes holistic, engaging both mind and heart, and preparing learners for faithfulness in a complex world. The challenge is great, but the opportunity is greater, for God continues to use faithful teachers, willing learners, and wise methods to accomplish His purposes.

Conclusion: The Practice of Christian Education

The practice of Christian education rests on a delicate but powerful harmony. It requires faithful teachers who are equipped and called, learners who receive truth with humility and obedience, content that is firmly rooted in God's Word, and methods that communicate truth with clarity and effectiveness. None of these elements can stand alone; each depends on the others. Teachers without learners labor in vain, learners without teachers stumble into confusion, content without method is easily forgotten, and method without content becomes empty form. But when all are brought together under the authority of Scripture and the guidance of the Spirit, Christian education fulfills its God-ordained purpose.

At the heart of this practice is the conviction that God Himself is both the source and the goal of education. He calls teachers, shapes learners, gives content, and blesses methods. His Word is the foundation on which all instruction rests, and His Spirit is the power that brings knowledge to life and transforms hearts. Paul reminded the Corinthians, *"I planted, Apollos watered; but God gave the increase"* (1 Corinthians 3:6). Teachers plant, methods water, learners receive, but only God brings growth. This keeps Christian education from pride on the one hand and despair on the other, for its ultimate success does not rest in human skill alone but in divine grace.

The church throughout history has borne witness to this truth. From the catechumens of the early church to the reformers with their catechisms, from the monasteries that preserved Scripture to the Sunday schools that trained generations of children, faithful Christian education has always combined these essential elements. Where teachers were diligent, learners receptive, content biblical, and methods wise, the church was strengthened and the faith passed on. Where any of these were neglected, the church faltered. History teaches us what Scripture already declares: Christian education thrives when truth is faithfully taught, faithfully received, and faithfully lived.

Today, the practice of Christian education faces new challenges, distractions, secularism, apathy, resistance to authority, and the misuse of technology. Yet the same God who sustained His people through past trials equips His church now. The task remains the same: to teach all nations, making disciples who observe all that Christ commanded (Matthew 28:19-20). The methods may adapt to context, but the mission never changes.

In the end, the practice of Christian education is not about techniques or institutions alone but about forming disciples of Jesus Christ. It is about shaping minds, hearts, and lives in conformity to His truth. When teachers embrace their calling with holiness, learners humble themselves to receive, content is drawn from the riches of God's Word, and methods are employed with wisdom, then Christian education accomplishes its goal: lives transformed for the glory of God.

CHAPTER 3: THE CONTEXTS OF CHRISTIAN EDUCATION

Christian Education in the Home

The home is the first and most foundational context of Christian education. Long before there were churches, schools, or seminaries, God entrusted parents with the sacred duty of training their children in His ways. The family is the primary classroom, and parents are the first teachers. What is learned in the home shapes not only individual lives but also the future of the church and society.

Scripture consistently emphasizes this truth. In Deuteronomy 6:6-7, God commands: *"And these words, which I command thee this day, shall be in thine heart: and thou shalt teach them diligently unto thy children, and shalt talk of them when thou sittest in thine house, and when thou walkest by the way, and when thou liest down, and when thou risest up."* Christian education is not confined to formal instruction but woven into the rhythms of daily life. The home is meant to be a place where God's Word is spoken, remembered, and lived.

The psalmist echoes this calling: *"We will not hide them from their children, shewing to the generation to come the praises of the Lord, and his strength, and his wonderful works that he hath done"* (Psalm 78:4). God intends His truth to pass from generation to generation, and the home is His appointed channel. In the New Testament,

Paul exhorts fathers, *"Provoke not your children to wrath: but bring them up in the nurture and admonition of the Lord"* (Ephesians 6:4). The responsibility rests not only with the church but squarely on the shoulders of parents.

Throughout history, the strongest seasons of the church have been those in which families embraced their role in education. Early Christians instructed their children in the Scriptures and prayers of the church. The Reformers, particularly Luther and Calvin, emphasized the role of the home in catechesis, with fathers leading daily devotions and mothers nurturing children in godliness. John Wesley designed his small groups to strengthen family discipleship as well as church fellowship. In every age, where homes have been faithful, the church has flourished.

In our time, however, the home is under tremendous pressure. Families are fragmented by busyness, technology, and competing influences. Many parents feel unequipped to teach their children or assume that the church alone bears this responsibility. Yet Christian education cannot be outsourced. The church and school may assist, but they cannot replace the home. God has appointed parents as the primary teachers for their children, and when they fulfill this calling, they lay a foundation for lifelong faith.

The home, then, is not a secondary or optional context of Christian education but the very heart of it. Here, values are formed, habits are shaped, and the gospel is first seen and heard. If Christian education is neglected in the home, no amount of church or school instruction can fully compensate. But if it is faithfully practiced, the home becomes a wellspring of faith that strengthens both church and society.

Parents as Primary Teachers

In God's design, parents are the first and most influential teachers in the lives of their children. Long before a child enters a classroom or joins a church program, they are shaped by the rhythms, words, and examples of the home. Christian education begins not in the pulpit or the school desk, but at the family table, during bedtime prayers, and through daily conversations. Parents bear a God-given responsibility to form their children in the knowledge of God and the ways of Christ.

Fathers, in particular, are addressed in Ephesians 6:4: *"Fathers, provoke not your children to wrath: but bring them up in the nurture and admonition of the Lord."* The phrase "nurture and admonition" points to both loving care and intentional instruction. Mothers also play a vital role, as seen in Timothy's upbringing. Paul reminds Timothy of "the unfeigned faith that is in thee, which dwelt first in thy grandmother Lois, and thy mother Eunice" (2 Timothy 1:5). From them he learned the Holy Scriptures, which made him wise unto salvation (2 Timothy 3:15). Parents and grandparents together share in the sacred duty of teaching faith by word and example.

The influence of parents is unique because it is both constant and personal. Teachers in schools or churches may have limited contact hours, but parents shape a child's worldview every day. Their words, actions, priorities, and habits are lessons in themselves.

Children learn what is truly important not only by what parents say but by what they do, whether family worship is prioritized, whether Scripture is read, whether prayer is practiced, and whether Christ is honored in the rhythms of life.

Throughout church history, leaders have recognized the central role of parents. Martin Luther wrote his catechisms not for the clergy but for fathers to use in instructing their households. He declared that "the home is the first school, and the father is the first teacher." John Calvin likewise urged parents to take responsibility for teaching their children, insisting that the covenant promises of God include the duty to pass on faith within the family. John Wesley was profoundly shaped by his mother, Susanna Wesley, who devoted time each week to teaching each of her children individually, instilling Scripture and piety in their hearts. These examples remind us that when parents embrace their role as teachers, the home becomes a fertile ground for faith.

In our time, many parents feel unqualified to teach. They may lack formal theological training or feel overwhelmed by their own spiritual struggles. Yet Christian education in the home does not require expertise so much as faithfulness. Parents are not called to answer every question or deliver polished lectures, but to faithfully share God's Word, model Christian living, and create an environment where Christ is honored. Even simple practices, by reading a Bible story, praying before meals, and discussing God's goodness in everyday events, can have a lasting impact.

Parents must therefore embrace their role with

seriousness and joy. Neglect in this area cannot be fully compensated for by the church or school. When parents abdicate their teaching role, children often drift, shaped more by culture than by Christ. But when parents take up their calling, even imperfectly, God uses their faithfulness to sow seeds of truth that can bear fruit for a lifetime. In God's plan, parents are not just caregivers or providers but primary teachers of Christian education, entrusted with the souls of the next generation.

Daily Practices of Home Education

If parents are the primary teachers in God's design, then the daily life of the home becomes the classroom where Christian education takes place. This does not mean that every moment must be a formal lesson, but rather that the rhythms of family life should be infused with Scripture, prayer, and godly conversation. Christian education in the home is less about rigid programs and more about a consistent atmosphere where Christ is honored and His Word is central.

Deuteronomy 6 gives a model for this; the command is practical, showing that education happens in ordinary moments at meals, walks, bedtime, and morning routines. These daily practices form children more powerfully than occasional lectures or special events.

One daily practice is family worship. From the earliest days of the church, believers gathered in households for prayer, Scripture reading, and singing. Parents can lead their families in short times of devotion, reading a passage of Scripture, explaining its meaning, praying together, and singing hymns or psalms. Such times need not be long or complex but should be consistent. Regular family worship establishes in children's minds that God's Word is the foundation of life.

Another essential practice is prayer woven into daily routines. Children learn the value of prayer not only by being told to pray but by hearing their parents pray. Morning prayers, blessings before meals, and prayers at bedtime create a rhythm of dependence on God. Parents who pray with and for their children teach by example that every part of life is lived in God's presence.

Scripture memorization is another powerful daily tool. The psalmist declared, *"Thy word have I hid in mine heart, that I might not sin against thee"* (Psalm 119:11). When parents encourage their children to memorize verses, catechisms, or hymns, they equip them with truth that can guide and sustain them in temptation and trial. Repetition at meals or during car rides can make memorization natural and enjoyable.

Conversations about God in everyday life are equally important. Parents are called to speak of God's works and commands not only in formal settings but during ordinary activities. A sunset may lead to a conversation about God's creation; a conflict between siblings may become a lesson in forgiveness; an answered prayer provides an opportunity to give thanks. These conversations show children that faith is not confined to Sunday but integrated into every aspect of life.

History gives us many examples of such daily practices. The Puritans emphasized family worship, seeing the home as a "little church." John Wesley's mother, Susanna Wesley, devoted specific time each week to instruct each of her children individually in Scripture and prayer. Families in the Reformation era gathered around catechisms, repeating questions and answers until children could recite them with confidence. These practices, though simple, shaped generations of believers who lived with deep knowledge of Scripture and devotion to God.

In our time, daily practices of home education face obstacles, busy schedules, digital distractions, and the breakdown of family rhythms. Yet even small, intentional habits can make a lasting difference. A short devotion at breakfast, a prayer before school, a hymn sung at night, these may seem ordinary, but God uses them to plant seeds of truth. Parents must remember that consistency matters more than perfection. The goal is not to create flawless routines but to cultivate an atmosphere where Christ is acknowledged, honored, and loved.

Ultimately, daily practices of home education are about shaping hearts. Knowledge is important, but children must also see faith lived out in their parents' example. When Scripture, prayer, and godly conversation permeate the home, children grow up understanding that following Christ is not a compartment of life but its center. These daily practices transform the home into a living classroom of discipleship.

Historical Witness of Family Discipleship

Throughout the history of the church, the home has been recognized as the first and most important context of Christian education. Generations of believers have understood that parents bear responsibility for shaping their children's faith, and when families embraced this calling, the church was strengthened. Historical witness confirms what Scripture commands: the family is the seedbed of discipleship.

In the early church, families passed down the faith through daily instruction and example. The *Didache* (a first-century Christian manual) exhorted believers to train their children in the "way of life" and to keep them from the "way of death." Household baptism signified not only the inclusion of children in the covenant community but also the expectation that parents would nurture them in the teachings of Christ. Early Christian families gathered for prayer, the reading of Scripture, and the breaking of bread, making the home a miniature church.

During the Patristic period, church fathers such as Augustine emphasized the role of parents in catechesis. Augustine recalled how his mother, Monica, instilled in him a deep reverence for God through her prayers and example, even when he strayed. He observed that children who received training in the home carried those impressions throughout life, for better or worse. Fathers were repeatedly reminded of their duty to be spiritual leaders in the household, guiding both wives and children in their faith.

In the medieval era, family life was deeply shaped by the rhythms of the church. Parents taught children to recite the Lord's Prayer, the Apostles' Creed, and the Ten Commandments. Monastic communities influenced lay families, encouraging regular prayer and Scripture reading in the home. Though literacy was limited, oral instruction and repetition ensured that children learned the essentials of the faith from their parents.

The family altar, whether simple or elaborate, was a visible reminder that God's Word had a place at the center of the household.

The Reformation brought renewed attention to the family as the first school of faith. Martin Luther insisted that fathers were responsible for teaching the catechism to their children, calling the household "the real school." His *Small Catechism* was written not for scholars but for families, providing a simple framework for instruction in the home. John Calvin, likewise, urged parents to lead their children in daily prayer and catechism, insisting that covenant promises obligated families to nurture their children in the Lord. The Reformers saw the home as the foundation of the church, and they designed their teaching tools accordingly.

In the Puritan tradition, family discipleship reached a high point. Puritan homes were known as "little churches," where fathers acted as pastors and mothers nurtured in faith. Daily family worship was expected, including Scripture reading, prayer, and singing. Richard Baxter and other Puritan leaders wrote manuals instructing parents on how to lead their households spiritually. For Puritans, the home was not merely a private sphere but a place of intentional Christian education that shaped entire communities.

In the modern era, examples like Susanna Wesley stand as shining witnesses to the power of family discipleship. As the mother of John and Charles Wesley, she devoted one evening each week to instruct each of her many children individually, teaching Scripture, prayer, and godly living. Her faithfulness bore fruit in the revival movements that transformed England and beyond. In the 18th and 19th centuries, Sunday schools arose to supplement but not replace family instruction. Leaders like Robert Raikes emphasized that parents still bore the primary responsibility, while Sunday schools offered additional support.

This long history demonstrates that when Christian families prioritize discipleship, the church flourishes. Where homes were faithful, generations were anchored in the truth. Where homes neglected their responsibility, the church struggled, regardless of the strength of its institutions. The witness of history affirms that family discipleship is not optional but essential. Parents who teach, model, and pray with their children stand in a great tradition that has sustained the faith through centuries.

Challenges and Opportunities Today

While Scripture and history affirm the central role of the home in Christian education, families today face unique challenges that make this responsibility both difficult and essential. Modern culture presents obstacles that threaten to crowd out spiritual instruction, yet these same challenges also create opportunities for the gospel to shine more clearly in the home.

One major challenge is the busyness of modern life. Parents often juggle demanding work schedules, children's extracurricular activities, and endless household responsibilities. In such a climate, intentional discipleship can easily be neglected. Family worship, prayer, and conversation about God are often replaced by hurried meals and fragmented routines. Yet even here lies an opportunity: when families intentionally set aside time for Scripture and prayer, they bear countercultural witness that Christ, not busyness, rules their home.

Another challenge is the influence of technology and media. Screens dominate much of family life, shaping values and desires often in opposition to the gospel. Children are discipled daily by television, social media, and online platforms. Parents may feel powerless against these influences. Yet the opportunity lies in reclaiming technology for God's purposes, using it to access Scripture, Christian music, and teaching resources, while modeling discernment and restraint. Parents who guide their children in wise media use teach them how to live faithfully in a digital age.

A third challenge is secularism and competing worldviews. Schools, peers, and society often promote values contrary to biblical truth. Children may be taught to question the authority of Scripture, embrace relativism, or prioritize self-fulfillment over obedience to God. This makes the home even more critical as a place of grounding in truth. Parents who consistently teach God's Word, discuss cultural issues from a biblical perspective, and model faithfulness provide their children with a firm foundation. In a world of shifting values, the home becomes an anchor of stability.

A further challenge is parental insecurity. Many parents feel inadequate to teach, assuming that pastors, teachers, or church programs are more qualified. They fear they lack the knowledge or ability to answer their children's questions. Yet this too provides an opportunity: parents can model humility by learning alongside their children. By opening Scripture together, asking questions, and seeking answers in God's Word, families grow in faith together. The example of parents who are willing learners encourages children to value learning as a lifelong pursuit.

Finally, families face the challenge of fragmentation. Divorce, absent parents, and broken homes make consistent discipleship difficult. But even here, God's grace provides opportunity. Grandparents, extended family members, and church communities can step in to support children spiritually. The home may be fractured, but God is faithful to provide teachers and examples where parents are absent. Single parents, though bearing heavy burdens, can powerfully shape their children's faith through consistent love, prayer, and instruction.

Amid these challenges, the opportunities for Christian education in the home are profound. Families that prioritize Christ stand out in a culture of distraction. Children raised in homes where the Bible is read, prayer is practiced, and Christ is honored often carry those lessons into adulthood. Parents who disciple their children, however imperfectly, participate in God's promise that His Word will not return void (Isaiah 55:11).

The home remains the primary context of Christian education. Its challenges are real, but so are its opportunities. In every era, faithful families have passed on the faith in the midst of cultural pressures. Today is no different. When parents embrace their calling with prayer and perseverance, God uses the home as a powerful witness of His truth, equipping the next generation to live for His glory.

Transition to the Church

The home is God's first and foundational classroom, where parents and families are entrusted with the sacred duty of teaching the next generation His truth. Yet God has not left families to labor alone. From the beginning, He also established the gathered community of believers as a place of teaching, worship, and discipleship. The church complements the work of the home, reinforcing and expanding what is taught there, and providing the broader fellowship of God's people.

If the home is the seedbed where faith is planted, the church is the garden where it is cultivated and strengthened. Together, they form a partnership in Christian education, each supporting and reinforcing the other. Having considered the home as the first context of discipleship, we now turn to the church, the household of God, to see how Christian education takes shape in the life of the gathered body of Christ.

Christian Education in the Church

The church is God's household, the gathered community of believers where instruction, worship, fellowship, and service come together under Christ's lordship. While the home is the first and most personal context of Christian education, the church is the public and corporate one. Together they form a partnership: parents plant seeds of faith in the home, while the church nourishes and strengthens those seeds through preaching, teaching, and shared discipleship. Neither can replace the other; both are essential.

From the earliest days of God's people, the gathered assembly was a place of learning. In Israel, the law was read publicly so that "men, women, and children, and the foreigners residing in your towns may listen and learn to fear the Lord your God" (Deuteronomy 31:12). The synagogue became the center of instruction, where Scripture was read, explained, and discussed. Jesus Himself participated in this pattern, standing in the synagogue to read from Isaiah and proclaim its fulfillment in Him (Luke 4:16-21). The people of God have always been a people of the Word, gathered not only to worship but also to learn.

The New Testament church continued this pattern. Acts 2:42 describes the first believers as devoted to "the apostles' teaching and the fellowship, to the breaking of bread and the prayers." Instruction was central to their shared life. Apostles, prophets, pastors, and teachers were appointed to equip the saints for the work of ministry (Ephesians 4:11-12). Paul commanded

Timothy to devote himself to "the public reading of Scripture, to exhortation, to teaching" (1 Timothy 4:13). The local church became the primary setting where believers were built up in the knowledge of Christ and equipped to live faithfully in the world.

Throughout history, the church has recognized its role as an educational community. The early church used sermons, catechesis, and liturgy to form believers. Hymns and creeds were teaching tools, embedding doctrine in worship. In the Middle Ages, cathedrals and parish churches became centers of both worship and instruction, teaching even the illiterate through stained glass, artwork, and ritual. The Reformers placed preaching at the center of worship and insisted that every believer be instructed in Scripture. Sunday schools in the 18th and 19th centuries expanded this mission, making biblical education accessible to children and the poor. In every era, the church has embraced its calling to be a teaching fellowship.

Today, the church's role in Christian education remains vital. Families may be scattered, schools may be secularized, and culture may resist biblical truth, but the church continues to gather God's people for worship and learning. In preaching, believers hear the Word proclaimed. In Bible studies, they discuss and apply truth. In fellowship, they encourage one another. In service, they learn obedience. The church is not merely a place where individuals come to receive but a community where disciples are formed together.

Christian education in the church, therefore, is not an optional program but a defining characteristic of the body of Christ. A church that neglects teaching ceases to be faithful to its calling. But a church that prioritizes instruction, discipleship, and mutual encouragement fulfills Christ's command to make disciples of all nations. As we explore this context, we will see how the church, through preaching, sacraments, fellowship, and teaching ministries, continues to shape believers into the likeness of Christ.

Preaching and Teaching in the Church

At the heart of Christian education in the church stands the ministry of the Word through preaching and teaching. From the days of Israel's public readings of the Law to the apostolic sermons of the New Testament, the proclamation of God's Word has been central to the gathered people of God. Preaching and teaching are not optional features of church life but essential means by which disciples are formed, faith is strengthened, and the body of Christ is built up.

The Old Testament gives clear precedent. Moses commanded that every seven years the law should be read publicly before all the people so that they might "hear, and that they may learn, and fear the Lord your God, and observe to do all the words of this law" (Deuteronomy 31:12). Ezra modeled this in Nehemiah 8 when he read the law aloud, and the Levites "gave the sense, and caused them to understand the reading" (v. 8). Teaching was not simply reciting Scripture but explaining it, ensuring that the people understood and could obey.

In the New Testament, preaching takes center stage. Jesus Himself went about "teaching in their synagogues, and preaching the gospel of the kingdom" (Matthew 4:23). His Sermon on the Mount (Matthew 5-7) remains the supreme model of kingdom instruction, combining clarity, authority, and practical application. After His resurrection, He commanded His apostles to "teach all nations... teaching them to observe all things whatsoever I have commanded you" (Matthew 28:19-20). The church's mission is inseparable from teaching.

The book of Acts portrays the early church as devoted to the apostles' teaching (Acts 2:42). Peter's sermon at Pentecost (Acts 2:14-36), Stephen's defense before the council (Acts 7), and Paul's addresses in synagogues and marketplaces (Acts 17) show the centrality of proclamation. Paul charged Timothy to "preach the word... reprove, rebuke, exhort with all longsuffering and doctrine" (2 Timothy 4:2). Preaching was to be faithful, urgent, and grounded in Scripture, not in human speculation.

Throughout church history, preaching has remained the primary vehicle of Christian education in the gathered body. The church fathers saw preaching as central to pastoral ministry. Augustine's *On Christian Teaching* gave guidelines for interpreting Scripture and communicating it clearly, insisting that the goal of preaching was not eloquence alone but transformation. In the Middle Ages, sermons and homilies reinforced the faith, often accompanied by visual instruction in art and liturgy for the illiterate. The Reformers, especially Luther and Calvin, restored preaching to the center of worship, declaring that where the Word of God is faithfully preached, there the true church exists.

Teaching in the church has also taken many forms

alongside preaching. Catechisms, Bible classes, and discipleship groups extend the ministry of the Word beyond the pulpit. From the Sunday school movement in the 18th century to modern Bible study fellowships, the church has multiplied opportunities for believers to be instructed systematically in Scripture and doctrine. Whether through sermons, classes, or informal study, the goal is the same: that the Word of Christ may dwell richly among God's people (Colossians 3:16).

Today, the church faces the challenge of competing voices. Many sermons are reduced to motivational talks, and biblical teaching is sometimes neglected in favor of entertainment. Yet the calling remains unchanged: the church is to be a pillar and ground of the truth (1 Timothy 3:15). Faithful preaching and teaching remain the lifeblood of Christian education in the church. They must be grounded in Scripture, centered on Christ, empowered by the Spirit, and directed toward obedience.

When preaching and teaching hold their rightful place, the church is nourished, faith is strengthened, and disciples grow. Believers are equipped to resist error, to live holy lives, and to serve faithfully in the world. The ministry of the Word remains the foundation of Christian education in the church, just as it has been from the beginning.

Worship and Liturgy as Education

Christian education in the church is not limited to formal preaching and teaching. Worship itself is a form of education, shaping believers through repeated words, actions, and symbols. The prayers we pray, the songs we sing, the sacraments we receive, and the liturgies we follow all instruct us in the truths of the faith. Worship is not only an expression of devotion but also a school of discipleship.

In the Old Testament, God gave Israel patterns of worship that carried deep teaching significance. The festivals of Passover, Pentecost, and Tabernacles were not mere ceremonies but lessons in God's salvation and faithfulness. Each year, children would ask, *"What mean ye by this service?"* (Exodus 12:26), and parents would explain God's mighty acts of deliverance. The sacrificial system taught the seriousness of sin and the necessity of atonement, preparing the way for Christ, the true Lamb of God. Worship was pedagogy, embedding truth in the life of the people through ritual, repetition, and symbol.

The New Testament continues this pattern. Jesus instituted the Lord's Supper, commanding His disciples to "do this in remembrance of me" (Luke 22:19). The breaking of bread was not only an act of fellowship but a continual lesson in the gospel, Christ's body given, His blood shed for the forgiveness of sins. Baptism likewise teaches, portraying death to sin and new life in Christ (Romans 6:3-4). These sacraments are visible words, instructing believers each time they are observed.

The early church recognized worship as formative education. Acts 2:42 describes believers as devoted to the apostles' teaching, fellowship, breaking of bread, and prayers. Early liturgies combined Scripture reading, prayer, hymns, and the Eucharist, ensuring that worship reinforced doctrine. The Nicene Creed, for example, was not only a doctrinal statement but a confession repeated in worship, embedding Trinitarian truth in the hearts of believers. Augustine remarked that "singing is praying twice," highlighting the educational power of hymns and psalms. Through worship, the faith was taught, remembered, and passed on.

In the medieval church, liturgy continued to serve as education, even for the illiterate. Stained-glass windows, church art, and ritual actions all communicated biblical stories and theological truths. The cycle of the church year, Advent, Christmas, Lent, Easter, Pentecost, structures time around the story of salvation. Worship was a classroom that engaged the senses and imagination, reinforcing the truths proclaimed in Scripture.

The Reformers emphasized that worship must be grounded in the Word, but they too saw its educational role. Luther insisted that congregational singing was vital for teaching the faith, composing hymns that conveyed doctrine. Calvin structured worship around the reading and preaching of Scripture but also retained the Psalms as the church's songbook, embedding biblical truth in the hearts of the people. For both, worship was not only a reverent offering to God but a school where believers were formed in truth.

Today, worship and liturgy continue to serve as powerful tools of Christian education. Hymns, songs, prayers, Scripture readings, and the sacraments all teach. However, churches face the temptation to reduce worship to entertainment, where music and ritual are chosen for emotional effect rather than formative depth. When this happens, worship loses its educational power. Yet when worship is saturated with Scripture, rooted in historic practices, and centered on Christ, it continues to shape hearts and minds.

The rhythms of worship teach believers how to pray, what to believe, and how to live. Children who grow up hearing the creeds, singing hymns rich in doctrine, and watching the sacraments learn truth not only intellectually but experientially. Adults are continually reminded of the gospel through prayers of confession, assurances of pardon, and songs of praise. Worship becomes the context where education is lived, where truth is rehearsed until it becomes part of the fabric of life.

Christian education in the church, then, is inseparable from worship. Liturgy is not empty repetition but formative instruction. When the church gathers to sing, pray, and receive the Word and sacraments, it is not only worshiping God but also being taught by Him. Worship and education, in God's design, are two sides of the same reality: disciples are made as they adore and as they learn.

Discipleship and Fellowship

While preaching and worship are central to the church's educational ministry, Christian education is not confined to the pulpit and liturgy. The church is also a fellowship of believers, a community where discipleship takes place through relationships, accountability, and mutual encouragement. Education in the church is not only about receiving information but also about being formed together in Christlikeness through shared life.

The New Testament presents the church as a body in which each member contributes to the growth of the whole. Paul writes, *"From whom the whole body fitly joined together and compacted by that which every joint supplieth... maketh increase of the body unto the edifying of itself in love"* (Ephesians 4:16). Discipleship is therefore communal, not individualistic. Believers learn not only from pastors and teachers but also from one another as they share wisdom, bear burdens, and model obedience.

Acts gives us a vivid picture of this fellowship. The early believers "continued steadfastly in the apostles' doctrine and fellowship, and in breaking of bread, and in prayers" (Acts 2:42). Their fellowship included shared meals, mutual care, and generosity, so that "all that believed were together, and had all things common" (v. 44). This community life was itself an education, teaching believers how to live out the gospel in love, service, and unity. Discipleship was not abstract but embodied in relationships.

Jesus Himself modeled discipleship as fellowship. He did not merely lecture His disciples but lived with them, walking, eating, and serving alongside them. He corrected them when they erred, encouraged them when they faltered, and sent them out on missions to practice what they had learned. This relational method shows that true discipleship is holistic, involving both instruction and shared life.

Throughout history, the church has cultivated discipleship and fellowship as essential parts of education. The early monastic communities emphasized shared prayer, work, and study, forming believers in discipline and holiness. In the medieval period, guilds and confraternities provided structures for lay discipleship. The Reformers emphasized small group study of Scripture, while Puritans encouraged "conference", believers gathering to discuss the sermon and apply it together. John Wesley's Methodist movement organized believers into societies, classes, and bands, where they encouraged one another, confessed sins, and held each other accountable. These structures show that fellowship has always been a vital context for education.

Today, discipleship and fellowship remain indispensable. Bible study groups, prayer meetings, mentorship relationships, and service teams all provide opportunities for believers to learn together. Fellowship meals, retreats, and informal gatherings reinforce the bonds of love that make discipleship possible. In these settings, believers see faith modeled in real life, receive encouragement in trials, and find accountability in obedience.

At the same time, fellowship in the church faces challenges. Modern culture prizes individualism, making it easy for Christians to view faith as a private matter. Busyness and digital isolation also undermine meaningful relationships. Yet the church must resist these tendencies, for discipleship cannot flourish in isolation. Believers are called to "consider one another to provoke unto love and to good works: not forsaking the assembling of ourselves together" (Hebrews 10:24-25). Fellowship is not optional; it is essential to Christian growth.

When the church embraces discipleship and fellowship, Christian education becomes holistic. Believers are not only taught but also nurtured, corrected, and encouraged. They learn not only from sermons but from conversations, meals, and shared service. Education moves from the head to the heart and hands, shaping character and conduct. In this way, the church fulfills its calling as a community of disciples who learn Christ together.

The Role of the Church Today

In our time, the church remains one of the most vital contexts of Christian education. Families and schools play important roles, but the church uniquely gathers God's people around Word, worship, and fellowship. Its calling is not simply to provide programs but to form disciples, grounding them in truth and equipping them to live faithfully in the world.

One of the church's primary responsibilities today is to proclaim biblical truth clearly and faithfully. In a culture marked by confusion, relativism, and competing worldviews, the church must stand as "the pillar and ground of the truth" (1 Timothy 3:15). Preaching, teaching, and catechesis must remain centered on Scripture rather than shifting with cultural trends. The temptation is strong to reduce sermons to entertainment or to dilute teaching to avoid offense. Yet the church's task is not to conform to the world but to transform minds by God's Word (Romans 12:2).

The church also bears the responsibility to equip believers for daily life. Christian education is not limited to doctrine but extends to practice. Paul writes that pastors and teachers are given "for the perfecting of the saints, for the work of the ministry, for the edifying of the body of Christ" (Ephesians 4:12). This means churches must train members to live out their faith in homes, workplaces, and communities. Parenting, marriage, work, and service must all be shaped by the teaching of the church. Classes, discipleship groups, and mentoring relationships are practical ways this responsibility is fulfilled.

A third responsibility is to provide intergenerational training. The church gathers all ages, from infants to elders, and each contributes to the educational task. Older believers are called to teach and model faith for younger ones, as Paul exhorted Titus: "That the aged women teach the young women... to be sober, to love their husbands, to love their children" (Titus 2:3-4). Youth learn not only from peers but from the witness of mature saints. The church, unlike any other institution, brings together generations in a shared life of discipleship, making it a unique and powerful context for learning.

The church must also embrace diversity within unity. In a globalized and multicultural world, congregations often include people from varied backgrounds. This creates challenges but also rich educational opportunities. Believers learn from one another as they see the gospel expressed in different cultures and contexts. The church models the truth that Christ has broken down dividing walls and made one new humanity (Ephesians 2:14-16). This unity in diversity is itself an educational witness to the power of the gospel.

Finally, the church today has the responsibility to resist fragmentation and individualism. Many believers are tempted to treat faith as a private matter, consuming religious content online or engaging sporadically in corporate life. Yet Hebrews 10:25 warns against forsaking the assembly. Education in the church depends on a gathered community, where believers worship together, encourage one another, and share life. The church must call its members back to embodied fellowship, reminding them that discipleship is communal, not solitary.

In sum, the church's role in Christian education today is indispensable. It must preach truth, equip saints, unite generations, embrace diversity, and resist isolation. Families cannot fulfill this role alone, nor can schools. Only the church, as the body of Christ, can gather God's people to be taught, shaped, and sent into the world. When the church embraces this calling, it becomes not only a place of worship but also a living classroom of discipleship, preparing believers to glorify God in every area of life.

Transition to the School

The church, as the gathered body of Christ, remains central to Christian education. Through preaching, worship, discipleship, and fellowship, believers are formed in faith and equipped for service. Yet God's design for education is not confined to the home and church alone. Throughout history, schools have also played a vital role in shaping minds and nurturing hearts. While the home plants the seed and the church waters it, schools provide further cultivation through structured instruction, discipline, and the integration of knowledge with faith.

From the earliest catechetical schools of the early church to the universities of the medieval period and the Christian academies of the Reformation, schools have been established to ensure that education is rooted in the fear of the Lord. In modern times, Christian schools continue this mission, seeking to teach not only academic subjects but also biblical truth that frames all knowledge.

Having considered the home as the foundation and the church as the fellowship of discipleship, we now turn to the school as the third context of Christian education. Here we will examine how Christian schooling has been understood, practiced, and challenged, and how it continues to shape the next generation for faithful service to Christ.

Christian Education in the School

Schools have long been recognized as one of the most influential contexts of education. They shape not only the intellect but also the values, character, and worldview of learners. For this reason, Christians throughout history have established schools to ensure that instruction in knowledge is rooted in the fear of the Lord. While the home is the first classroom and the church is the gathered fellowship of discipleship, the school provides structured opportunities for learning across a broad range of subjects, integrated with biblical truth.

The Bible itself affirms the importance of knowledge and disciplined study. Solomon writes, *"The heart of the prudent getteth knowledge; and the ear of the wise seeketh knowledge"* (Proverbs 18:15). Education is not a human invention but part of God's design for growth in wisdom. Yet Scripture also makes clear that knowledge divorced from the fear of the Lord is empty: *"The fear of the Lord is the beginning of wisdom: and the knowledge of the holy is understanding"* (Proverbs 9:10). A truly Christian school must therefore unite intellectual formation with spiritual formation, teaching truth in light of God's Word.

From the earliest centuries, Christians recognized the value of schools. The catechetical school in Alexandria, founded in the second century, combined biblical study with philosophy and other disciplines, training leaders for the church. Augustine, Jerome, and other church fathers were shaped by both secular and sacred studies, but they insisted that all learning must ultimately serve Christ. In the medieval period, cathedral schools and universities were established by the church, making education accessible to clergy and eventually to laypeople. These institutions integrated theology with the liberal arts, reflecting the conviction that all truth is God's truth.

The Reformers carried this vision forward. Martin Luther called for schools in every town so that children might be trained not only in reading and writing but also in Scripture and the catechism. John Calvin established the Geneva Academy to prepare ministers and lay leaders alike. For them, Christian schooling was essential to passing on the faith and strengthening the church. In later centuries, Puritans in New England founded schools and colleges, such as Harvard, with the explicit purpose of training leaders in both learning and piety.

In the modern era, Christian schools have taken diverse forms, parish schools, academies, homeschooling, and universities, but their mission remains the same: to provide education that integrates faith with knowledge. Christian schools are not simply alternatives to secular education; they are communities where Christ is acknowledged as Lord over every subject. Mathematics, science, literature, and history are taught not as neutral disciplines but as areas of study that reveal God's order, creativity, and providence.

The challenges today are great. Secular schooling often promotes worldviews that deny or marginalize God, shaping students in ways contrary to Scripture. Many parents turn to Christian schools seeking a context where biblical values are upheld, where learning is framed by truth, and where children are prepared not only for careers but for godly living. The task is demanding, for Christian schools must pursue academic excellence while remaining faithful to Scripture. Yet the opportunity is also great, for schools that are Christ-centered can shape generations who will serve God with both mind and heart.

Christian education in the school, then, is not a luxury but a calling. It stands alongside the home and the church as part of God's design for forming disciples. When schools embrace this mission, they become not merely places of information but communities of transformation, preparing young men and women to glorify God in every sphere of life.

Biblical Foundations for Schooling

Though the Bible does not describe schools in the formal, modern sense, it provides strong foundations for the idea of structured, disciplined instruction. The people of God have always been called to pursue knowledge, train the mind, and shape character in ways that honor Him. Education is not a human invention but part of God's design for nurturing wisdom and godliness in His covenant people.

From the beginning, Scripture affirms that learning is central to covenant life. Adam was instructed by God in the garden (Genesis 2:16–17), and this pattern of divine teaching continues throughout the Old Testament. Parents were commanded not only to teach their children but also to establish rhythms of instruction. Deuteronomy 6 calls for daily rehearsing of God's commands, while Psalm 78 urges one generation to declare God's works to the next. These passages show that education is not accidental but structured and woven intentionally into family and community life.

The Old Testament also gives glimpses of organized instruction beyond the family. The Levites were charged with teaching Israel God's law (Leviticus 10:11; Deuteronomy 33:10). Prophets like Samuel and Elisha gathered groups of learners, often referred to as "schools of the prophets" (1 Samuel 10:5; 2 Kings 6:1). While not schools in the modern academic sense, these communities of instruction reflect the principle that God calls for intentional spaces where His Word is studied and taught systematically.

Wisdom literature further underscores the value of disciplined study. Proverbs repeatedly calls learners to seek wisdom and instruction: *"Wise men lay up knowledge"* (Proverbs 10:14); *"The heart of the prudent getteth knowledge; and the ear of the wise seeketh knowledge"* (Proverbs 18:15). Education in this sense involves more than information; it is the shaping of character through disciplined learning under the fear of the Lord. Structured teaching is necessary so that wisdom is not left to chance but cultivated with diligence.

The New Testament builds on these foundations, highlighting the importance of both teachers and learners in the community of faith. Jesus Himself was called "Rabbi," or teacher, and He gathered disciples to be instructed systematically in the truths of the kingdom. His method included lectures (the Sermon on the Mount), parables, and private discussions, all forms of organized instruction. After His ascension, the apostles continued this pattern. Acts 19:9 records Paul reasoning daily in the school of Tyrannus, where he taught disciples systematically over two years. Here we see a clear example of a school-like context used for Christian education.

Paul's letters also emphasize the need for structured learning. He commands Timothy to entrust the truth to "faithful men, who shall be able to teach others also" (2 Timothy 2:2). He warns Titus to ensure that elders are able to "give instruction in sound doctrine" (Titus 1:9). These instructions highlight not only the importance of teaching but also the need for systematic training of future teachers and leaders, the very essence of schooling.

The biblical vision of education, then, includes several key principles:

> **It is God-centered**- The fear of the Lord is the beginning of wisdom (Proverbs 9:10).
>
> **It is generational** -Each generation must intentionally teach the next (Psalm 78:4).
>
> **It is structured.** Learning is organized and repeated, not left to chance (Deuteronomy 6:7).
>
> **It involves teachers and communities.** Prophets, Levites, apostles, and pastors were called to lead learners systematically (Acts 19:9).

When applied to schooling today, these principles mean that education must be intentional, ordered, and grounded in God's Word. Schools are not merely places to accumulate facts but communities where wisdom, discipline, and godliness are cultivated. Far from being foreign to Scripture, the concept of structured schooling flows naturally from the biblical vision of learning as discipleship.

Historical Development of Christian Schools

The history of Christian schools reflects the church's conviction that education must be rooted in the fear of the Lord and integrated with faith. From the earliest centuries to the present day, believers have established schools not only to train clergy but also to nurture children, equip laypeople, and shape entire societies with the truth of God's Word.

In the early church, catechetical schools became centers of instruction for converts and future leaders. The catechetical school of Alexandria, founded in the second century, is the most famous example. Under leaders such as Clement and Origen, this school combined biblical study with philosophy, preparing students to defend the faith in a pagan culture. These schools emphasized memorization of Scripture, moral formation, and systematic teaching, laying a foundation for later Christian education.

During the Patristic and early medieval period, cathedral and monastic schools rose to prominence. Monasteries preserved Scripture and classical learning, copying manuscripts and training novices in the disciplines of prayer, work, and study. Cathedral schools, attached to local churches, provided broader education to clergy and, eventually, to lay students. These institutions taught the trivium (grammar, logic, rhetoric) and quadrivium (arithmetic, geometry, music, astronomy), integrating them with theology. Education in this era was not fragmented but holistic, preparing students to see all truth as belonging to God.

The university movement of the 12th and 13th centuries marked another milestone. Universities such as Paris, Oxford, and Bologna were founded under church sponsorship, with theology regarded as the "queen of the sciences." Here, Christian schools reached a new level of organization and influence, training scholars and clergy who would shape European society. The integration of faith and reason, Scripture and philosophy, reflected the conviction that intellectual inquiry was part of serving God.

The Reformation brought renewed attention to Christian schools for all people, not just clergy. Martin Luther called for schools in every town, insisting that children must be taught both reading and the catechism. He declared that education was essential to faith and society alike. John Calvin established the Geneva Academy (1559), which combined classical studies with rigorous biblical instruction, preparing ministers and lay leaders. For the Reformers, Christian schools were essential to sustaining the gospel and shaping a faithful church.

In the Puritan era, Christian schooling flourished in New England. The Massachusetts Bay Colony passed laws requiring schools so that children could learn to read the Bible. Harvard College was founded in 1636 to train ministers who would uphold both learning and piety. Puritans believed that ignorance of Scripture was a danger to both church and state, and they made education a priority for all.

The modern era saw the rise of parish schools, Christian academies, and mission schools across the globe. In the 18th and 19th centuries, the Sunday school movement brought basic education to children of the poor, teaching literacy through the Bible. Missionaries established schools in Africa, Asia, and the Americas, often combining evangelism with education. In the 20th century, Christian schools and colleges multiplied, seeking to provide an alternative to secular education that denied biblical truth. Homeschooling movements also arose, with parents reclaiming the responsibility to integrate faith and learning in their homes.

Through every era, Christian schools have adapted to their cultural context while remaining committed to the integration of faith and knowledge. Whether in the catechetical schools of Alexandria, the monasteries of medieval Europe, the academies of the Reformation, or the Christian schools of today, the aim has remained constant: to provide education that is Christ-centered, holistic, and transformative.

The history of Christian schools demonstrates that education is not merely preparation for careers but formation for godly living. By preserving Scripture, shaping minds, and cultivating virtue, Christian schools have sustained the church and influenced society for centuries. Their legacy reminds us that schooling, when rooted in Christ, is a vital expression of the church's mission.

The Role of Christian Schools Today

In the modern world, Christian schools play a vital role in shaping the minds and hearts of young people for the glory of God. While families and churches remain central, schools provide a structured environment where education can be integrated across all subjects, forming not only intellect but also character. In a society where secular education often separates knowledge from faith, Christian schools serve as a countercultural witness: that all truth is God's truth, and Christ is Lord over every area of life.

One of the central roles of Christian schools today is to integrate faith and learning. In many secular systems, subjects are presented as neutral or even hostile to Christianity. Science is often taught without reference to the Creator, history without providence, literature without moral order, and ethics without God's law. Christian schools reject this fragmentation. They teach science as the study of God's creation, history as the unfolding of His providence, literature as a reflection of human longing and morality, and ethics as grounded in God's holiness. In this way, they provide a unified worldview where knowledge and faith are not separated but harmonized.

Christian schools also have the role of discipling students in character and virtue. Proverbs 22:6 instructs parents and educators to "train up a child in the way he should go: and when he is old, he will not depart from it." This training is more than academic;

it includes the formation of habits, attitudes, and values. Christian schools are called to cultivate honesty, humility, diligence, and love for neighbor. Teachers are not merely instructors of facts but models of godliness, shaping students by both word and example.

Another vital role is to equip students for service in the world. Education is not an end in itself but preparation for vocation. Christian schools should help students see their studies as preparation to glorify God in every sphere, whether in business, science, the arts, or ministry. This vocational perspective distinguishes Christian education from secular approaches that focus only on personal success. A Christian school aims not merely to produce successful individuals but faithful servants who will influence the world for Christ.

Christian schools also serve as a support and extension of the home and church. They cannot replace the responsibility of parents or the fellowship of the church, but they can reinforce both. When parents teach the faith at home and churches preach the Word in worship, schools add daily reinforcement through integrated instruction. This partnership strengthens the impact of Christian education across all contexts of a child's life.

At the same time, Christian schools face serious challenges today. Rising secularism pressures schools to conform to worldly standards. Financial struggles make it difficult for some families to access Christian education. Cultural hostility often labels Christian schools as intolerant or outdated. Yet these challenges highlight the importance of their mission. In a world where truth is often denied, Christian schools stand as witnesses that truth exists, is revealed in Christ, and shapes every aspect of life.

The opportunity is profound. When Christian schools remain faithful, they produce graduates who are both academically prepared and spiritually grounded. These men and women can enter the world not as cultural imitators but as cultural transformers, bringing the light of Christ into every vocation. The role of Christian schools today is not simply to teach subjects but to form disciples who know Christ, think biblically, and live faithfully.

In sum, Christian schools serve as vital partners in the work of Christian education. They integrate knowledge with faith, shape character and virtue, equip students for vocation, and support the work of home and church. In doing so, they carry forward the biblical and historical vision of education as discipleship. Their mission remains as urgent as ever: to raise up generations who will love God with all their heart, soul, mind, and strength, and who will glorify Him in every arena of life.

Transition to Society

The school, alongside the home and the church, provides a structured and intentional context for Christian education. Within its classrooms, faith is integrated with learning, knowledge is illuminated by truth, and students are equipped to serve God in every vocation. Yet Christian education does not end within the walls of family, church, or school. Believers live and bear witness in the broader world, where faith intersects with culture, work, and civic life.

Society itself becomes a classroom, sometimes supportive, but often challenging, where Christians must live out what they have been taught. From government and economics to media, the arts, and daily work, believers are called to engage the world as salt and light (Matthew 5:13-16). Here, Christian education moves from instruction to public witness, from the shaping of individuals to the shaping of culture.

Having explored the home, the church, and the school, we now turn to society as the fourth context of Christian education. In this part, we will consider how Christian faith engages public life, how believers are educated by and within culture, and how the church can equip disciples to live faithfully in the world for the glory of God.

Christian Education in Society

Christian education does not take place only in the home, the church, or the school. While these are the primary contexts where truth is taught, reinforced, and integrated, every believer must also live out their faith in the wider society. Workplaces, neighborhoods, media, governments, and cultural institutions all shape how people think, act, and value life. Society itself becomes a classroom, one that constantly instructs, often in ways that run counter to the truth of God. For this reason, Christian education must prepare believers not only for private devotion and church fellowship but also for faithful witness in the public square.

Scripture makes clear that God's people are called to engage the world, not retreat from it. Jesus declared to His disciples, *"Ye are the salt of the earth... ye are the light of the world"* (Matthew 5:13-14). Salt preserves and flavors; light exposes and guides. Both images point to active participation in society. Believers are not to hide their faith but to display it, influencing culture for good and pointing others to Christ. Christian education, therefore, must equip disciples to live wisely in the world, discerning truth from error and bearing witness to the gospel in every sphere of life.

The Old Testament provides examples of God's people living faithfully in society. Joseph served in Pharaoh's court, using his wisdom to save nations from famine (Genesis 41). Daniel held high office in Babylon, remaining faithful to God's law while advising pagan kings (Daniel 6). Esther influenced the Persian court, risking her life to save her people (Esther 4). These figures show that education for God's people has always included preparation to live faithfully within broader cultural systems, even hostile ones.

The New Testament likewise calls believers to be witnesses in society. Paul urged Christians in Rome to "be not conformed to this world: but be ye transformed by the renewing of your mind" (Romans 12:2). Transformation through education in God's Word enables believers to resist worldly patterns and live according to God's will. Paul also instructed the Colossians, *"And whatsoever ye do, do it heartily, as to the Lord, and not unto men"* (Colossians 3:23). Whether in family, work, or public life, discipleship is lived out in society, and education must prepare believers for that reality.

Throughout history, Christians have influenced society through education, service, and cultural engagement. The early church cared for the poor, rescued abandoned infants, and modeled communities of compassion, gaining the respect of outsiders. During the Reformation, Protestant emphasis on literacy and schools reshaped entire nations. Missionaries established hospitals, universities, and printing presses, transforming societies with both the gospel and learning. These examples show that Christian education has always had a societal impact, training believers not only for personal faith but for public witness.

Today, society presents both greater opportunities and greater challenges. On one hand, Christians live in a world of unprecedented communication and cultural influence. Media, technology, and global interconnectedness provide platforms for sharing truth. On the other hand, secularism, relativism, and hostility to biblical values threaten to marginalize faith. In this context, Christian education must prepare believers to think critically, live faithfully, and engage society with courage and wisdom.

The task of Christian education in society is therefore twofold: to protect believers from being shaped by worldly lies and to equip them to shape the world with gospel truth. This means forming disciples who can discern cultural messages, resist temptation, and stand firm in their convictions, while also training them to contribute positively to art, science, politics, business, and daily life as ambassadors of Christ.

Christian education in society is not optional but essential. Believers cannot escape the world, but they can live faithfully within it. Education that remains confined to home, church, and school risks producing disciples unprepared for the pressures and opportunities of public life. When Christian education equips believers for society, the result is salt and light, men and women who glorify God by living out their faith in every sphere of culture.

Christian Education and Cultural Engagement

Christian education must prepare believers not only to know the truth but also to live it faithfully within culture. Every society communicates its own lessons through art, media, politics, and institutions. Some of these align with biblical values; many do not. For this reason, cultural engagement is both an opportunity and a challenge. Without proper formation, Christians may be swept along by cultural currents. With faithful education, however, they can become salt and light, influencing culture for Christ while remaining unshaken by its pressures.

Scripture calls believers to discernment in cultural engagement. Paul warns in Colossians 2:8: *"Beware lest any man spoil you through philosophy and vain deceit, after the tradition of men, after the rudiments of the world, and not after Christ."* At the same time, he affirms the need to live wisely toward outsiders, "redeeming the time" (Colossians 4:5). Christian education must therefore cultivate both vigilance and engagement, guarding against falsehood while encouraging meaningful participation in society.

The early church modeled this balance. Believers rejected idolatry, immorality, and unjust practices of Roman society, yet they also contributed positively by caring for the poor, rescuing abandoned children, and showing hospitality to strangers. Their countercultural love attracted attention and transformed communities. They neither withdrew completely nor conformed blindly but engaged culture with wisdom and grace.

In later history, Christian education equipped believers to influence culture through learning, art, and institutions. The Reformation emphasized literacy so that every believer could read Scripture, but this emphasis also advanced education in society as a whole. Missionaries established schools, hospitals, and printing presses that reshaped cultures with both biblical truth and practical service. In the arts, Christian influence produced music, literature, and architecture that continue to inspire. These examples show that when Christian education equips disciples for cultural engagement, the result is not retreat but transformation.

Today, cultural engagement requires even greater intentionality. Media and technology shape minds daily, often more powerfully than sermons or classroom lessons. Entertainment, advertising, and digital platforms communicate values about identity, success, sexuality, and power, many of which conflict with biblical truth. Without discernment, believers can unconsciously absorb these messages. Christian education must therefore train disciples to evaluate culture critically, asking: Does this align with God's Word? Does it glorify Christ? Does it promote love of God and neighbor?

Yet cultural engagement also offers remarkable opportunities. Believers can use media, business, education, and the arts to reflect God's truth and beauty. A Christian educator may influence a generation of students with biblical wisdom. A Christian artist can create works that point to the Creator. A Christian business leader can model integrity and generosity in an age of corruption and greed. When Christians are equipped through education to engage culture, they can be agents of renewal in every sphere.

Engaging culture does not mean surrendering to it. It means entering it as witnesses, confident in God's truth and guided by His Spirit. Christian education must emphasize that believers are in the world but not of it (John 17:14-16). They are called to resist conformity while seeking the welfare of the city where God has placed them (Jeremiah 29:7). This requires both courage and compassion, courage to stand for truth, and compassion to serve those in need.

Ultimately, cultural engagement is part of the Great Commission. To teach all nations (Matthew 28:19-20) is not only to instruct in doctrine but also to shape societies with gospel truth. Christian education equips believers to take their place in this mission, engaging culture with discernment, creativity, and faithfulness. When believers are well-educated in Christ, they can resist being shaped by the world and instead help shape the world for His glory.

Christian Education and Citizenship

Christian education must also prepare believers for faithful citizenship. Every disciple of Christ lives not only as a member of God's kingdom but also as a participant in earthly communities. Whether through voting, work, civic involvement, or service, Christians engage in the life of their nations and cities. Citizenship is therefore not merely political but spiritual, for it reflects how believers live out their faith in public.

Scripture makes this dual citizenship clear. Paul reminds the Philippians, *"For our conversation (citizenship) is in heaven; from whence also we look for the Savior"* (Philippians 3:20). Believers belong first and foremost to God's kingdom. Yet Paul also appealed to his Roman citizenship (Acts 22:25-29) and urged Christians to pray for kings and all in authority (1 Timothy 2:1-2). Jesus Himself declared, *"Render therefore unto Caesar the things which are Caesar's; and unto God the things that are God's"* (Matthew 22:21).

Christian citizenship, therefore, involves honoring earthly responsibilities while keeping ultimate loyalty to Christ.

Throughout history, Christian education has emphasized this balance. The early church taught believers to respect governing authorities while refusing to bow to idols or compromise their faith. Martyrs like Polycarp and Perpetua embodied faithful citizenship, obedient in matters of law, yet resolute when commanded to deny Christ. Augustine, in *The City of God*, distinguished between the earthly city and the heavenly city, reminding believers that they serve their nations best when they live as faithful citizens of God's kingdom.

In later centuries, Christian education shaped civic life in profound ways. The Reformers stressed literacy not only for Bible reading but also for responsible citizenship, believing that educated Christians would strengthen both church and society. In colonial America, Puritan schools were founded to ensure that children could read Scripture and fulfill their civic duties. Missionaries often combined evangelism with teaching practical skills, preparing converts to serve their communities as honest and capable citizens.

Today, the need for Christian education in citizenship is urgent. Modern societies often separate faith from public life, pressuring believers to treat religion as private. Yet Christian education insists that faith shapes every area, including civic responsibility. Believers are called to vote with biblical conviction, serve with integrity, and work for justice and mercy. Micah 6:8 provides a clear guide: *"He hath shewed thee, O man, what is good; and what doth the Lord require of thee, but to do justly, and to love mercy, and to walk humbly with thy God?"*

This means that Christian schools, churches, and homes must teach not only Bible knowledge but also public ethics: honesty in work, respect for law, care for the poor, and responsibility in community life. Christians must be prepared to participate in civic debates with wisdom and grace, to resist corruption, and to advocate for righteousness. Faithful citizenship does not mean withdrawing from public life but engaging it in ways that reflect Christ's kingdom.

Ultimately, Christian citizenship is about bearing witness to Christ in the public square. Believers live as pilgrims, seeking a better country (Hebrews 11:16), yet they also serve faithfully in the nations where God has placed them. By teaching disciples to live as both heavenly and earthly citizens, Christian education equips them to be lights in society, pointing to the true King who reigns overall.

Christian Education and Work/Vocation

Christian education must also prepare believers to see work and vocation as part of their discipleship. Too often, education is treated as preparation merely for careers, while faith is confined to private devotion. Yet Scripture teaches that all of life, including labor, belongs to God. Work is not separate from worship but an expression of it. Christian education equips believers to understand their vocations as callings from God, shaping how they labor, lead, and serve in society.

The biblical foundation for vocation begins in creation. Before sin entered the world, God placed Adam in the garden "to dress it and to keep it" (Genesis 2:15). Work was part of humanity's original purpose, not a punishment. After the fall, labor became difficult (Genesis 3:17-19), but it did not cease to be meaningful. Scripture consistently affirms that diligence, honesty, and skill in work glorify God. Proverbs 22:29 declares, *"Seest thou a man diligent in his business? he shall stand before kings."* Work well done honors both God and neighbor.

The New Testament deepens this vision. Paul exhorts believers: *"And whatsoever ye do, do it heartily, as to the Lord, and not unto men"* (Colossians 3:23). Work is done ultimately for Christ, whether in farming, teaching, governing, or serving. Paul also warns against idleness, commanding the Thessalonians that "if any would not work, neither should he eat" (2 Thessalonians 3:10). Christian vocation is not limited to ministry roles; every honest calling is service to God when done in faith.

Church history confirms this truth. The Reformers recovered the biblical idea of vocation, rejecting the notion that only clergy lived "holy" lives. Martin Luther taught that God calls people to serve Him in every station, farmer, craftsman, mother, magistrate, each one a priestly vocation. John Calvin emphasized that vocation is the arena where believers glorify God through diligence and stewardship. The Puritans carried this further, insisting that all work was sacred when done for God's glory. For them, the workplace was a field of discipleship, where labor was both duty and devotion.

Christian education today must reclaim this vision. In many modern systems, education is viewed as a pathway to wealth, status, or personal fulfillment. Yet Christian education teaches that knowledge is service to God and to others. A doctor serves by healing, a teacher by instructing, a businessperson by providing goods and employment, and an artist by reflecting God's beauty. All work, when submitted to Christ, becomes part of His kingdom mission.

This requires schools, churches, and homes to teach students not only how to succeed professionally but also how to work Christianly. Christian education must instill virtues such as honesty, humility, diligence, and stewardship. It must also prepare believers to resist temptations of greed, exploitation, and idolatry in the workplace. Integrity in business, fairness in leadership, and compassion in service are marks of a disciple shaped by Christian education.

At the same time, vocation is not only about career but about calling in every area of life. Parenting, serving in church, volunteering in the community, and caring for neighbors are all forms of vocation. Christian education must broaden the vision of vocation beyond paycheck and position, teaching that every task, from changing diapers to managing companies, can glorify God when done with faith and love.

Ultimately, Christian education in relation to work and vocation reminds believers that they are co-laborers with Christ (1 Corinthians 3:9). Their daily labor is part of God's redemptive plan, bringing order, provision, and beauty into the world. When disciples see their work as worship, they transform workplaces into mission fields and careers into callings. Christian education equips them for this integration, enabling them to live as faithful servants of Christ in every vocation.

Christian Education and Public Witness

Christian education must also prepare believers for faithful public witness. While cultural engagement, citizenship, and vocation shape how Christians live in society, public witness concerns how they testify to Christ before the watching world. Education that does not equip disciples for bold, gracious, and truthful witness in public risks producing believers who hide their faith rather than proclaim it. The goal is not only private devotion but public declaration that Jesus Christ is Lord.

Scripture places great emphasis on witnesses. Jesus told His disciples: *"Ye shall be witnesses unto me both in Jerusalem, and in all Judaea, and in Samaria, and unto the uttermost part of the earth"* (Acts 1:8). Witness is not optional; it is part of the church's identity. Peter exhorts believers to be ready always to give an answer for the hope that is in them, with meekness and fear (1 Peter 3:15). Paul declares that Christians are "ambassadors for Christ" (2 Corinthians 5:20), representing Him in the world. Public witness is, therefore, both responsibility and privilege, and Christian education must train believers for it.

The early church demonstrated the power of public witness. In the face of persecution, believers refused to deny Christ, testifying through both words and deeds. Their courage, charity, and moral integrity astonished a pagan world. Tertullian records that outsiders marveled, saying, "See how they love one another!" Their witness was not confined to sermons but embodied in daily life, attracting many to the faith.

History is filled with examples of Christian education producing courageous witnesses. The Reformers risked their lives to proclaim biblical truth against corruption. Missionaries like William Carey and Hudson Taylor brought the gospel to nations far from their own, combining education with evangelism. In more recent history, leaders such as Martin Luther King Jr. drew on biblical convictions to speak prophetically to issues of justice, showing that Christian witness shapes not only individuals but societies. Each example illustrates how education in God's Word equips believers to speak and live truth publicly.

Today, the need for public witness is urgent. Secular culture often pressures Christians to privatize their faith, to remain silent about biblical convictions on morality, truth, and salvation. Yet Jesus warns that no one should hide a lamp under a bushel but set it on a stand to give light to all (Matthew 5:15-16). Christian education must prepare believers to speak truth with both boldness and compassion. This includes teaching them how to articulate the gospel clearly, how to defend their faith against objections, and how to live consistently so that their lives match their words.

Public witness also includes deeds of love and service. James insists that faith without works is dead (James 2:17). Feeding the hungry, caring for the poor, seeking justice, and showing mercy are themselves testimonies to the reality of Christ. Christian education must therefore form disciples who not only speak truth but embody it through visible acts of compassion. Words and deeds together give credibility to a witness.

The challenge today is that public witness often comes at a cost. Believers may face ridicule, opposition, or even persecution. Yet Christian education must remind them that suffering for Christ is an honor (1 Peter 4:14-16) and that the Spirit empowers them to endure. Witness is not sustained by human strength but by divine grace.

Ultimately, Christian education and public witness converge in the mission of God: to make Christ known to the nations. When believers are trained in Scripture, grounded in truth, and equipped for courage, they shine as lights in a dark world. Their testimony, in word and deed, points others to the hope of salvation. In this way, Christian education fulfills its calling, not only forming disciples for private faithfulness but preparing witnesses for public faithfulness to Christ.

Transition to the Goal of Christian Education

Christian education in society equips believers to live faithfully in the world, to engage culture with discernment, to practice responsible citizenship, to serve God through vocation, and to bear public witness to Christ. Yet all of these responsibilities point to something deeper: the ultimate goal of Christian education itself.

The home, the church, the school, and society are contexts; teaching, worship, fellowship, and witness are practices, but what is all of this for? What is the end toward which Christian education moves? Scripture makes clear that the goal is not merely knowledge, social influence, or moral improvement. The true aim of Christian education is the transformation of believers into the likeness of Christ, so that God is glorified in every sphere of life.

Having explored the foundations, the practices, and the contexts of Christian education, we now turn to its goal. In the next chapter, we will consider what Christian education seeks to produce: men and women formed in faith, mind, character, and mission.

Conclusion: The Contexts of Christian Education

Christian education does not take place in a vacuum. It unfolds within God-ordained contexts that shape how truth is taught, received, and lived. The home, the church, the school, and society each provide unique environments where discipleship is nurtured. Together, they form a tapestry through which God weaves His purposes in the lives of His people.

The home is the foundation, where parents are called to diligently teach their children the ways of the Lord. Here, faith is modeled daily in love, discipline, and devotion. The church is the gathered household of God, where preaching, worship, discipleship, and fellowship strengthen and expand what is begun in the home. Schools provide structured opportunities for learning across disciplines, integrating knowledge with faith and preparing believers for vocations of service. Society is the broader classroom, testing and proving the faith of believers as they engage in culture, practice citizenship, pursue vocation, and bear public witness.

None of these contexts stands alone. The home without the church risks isolation. The church without schools may lack depth of training. Schools without the home and church risk becoming detached from discipleship. And believers who are not prepared for society will find their faith challenged and undermined. Christian education is strongest when all four contexts work in harmony, reinforcing one another, complementing one another, and pointing toward the same goal: the formation of Christlike disciples.

At the same time, each context presents challenges. Homes may neglect spiritual instruction. Churches may prioritize programs over discipleship. Schools may compromise academic integrity or biblical fidelity. Society may oppose the very truths believers are called to uphold. These realities remind us that Christian education is not automatic; it requires vigilance, intentionality, and faithfulness. Yet God is faithful, and He equips His people with His Word and Spirit to fulfill this calling.

The contexts of Christian education together reveal its comprehensive scope. Education is not confined to classrooms or Sunday sermons; it permeates every part of life. Every meal around the family table, every sermon preached, every lesson taught, every act of service in the world is part of God's design for forming disciples. Christian education, therefore, is not only about transferring knowledge but about shaping whole lives for God's glory.

As we look to the goal of Christian education, we see how these contexts serve a higher purpose. They are not ends in themselves but means to an end: the transformation of believers into the likeness of Christ. The home nurtures faith, the church strengthens it, the school cultivates it, and society tests and displays it. Together they prepare disciples who love God with all their heart, soul, mind, and strength, and who live as His witnesses in the world.

CHAPTER 4: THE GOAL OF CHRISTIAN EDUCATION

Introduction

Every endeavor has an aim. Medicine seeks healing, law pursues justice, and agriculture strives for a fruitful harvest. In the same way, Christian education has a goal, not simply to fill minds with knowledge or to preserve tradition, but to form disciples who glorify God with their whole lives. Without clarity on this goal, Christian education risks becoming reduced to academics, culture, or moralism. The true aim, however, is far greater: the transformation of believers into the likeness of Christ.

Scripture makes this purpose explicit. Paul declares that God predestined His people "to be conformed to the image of his Son" (Romans 8:29). He writes again that "we all… beholding the glory of the Lord, are changed into the same image from glory to glory" (2 Corinthians 3:18). The ultimate measure of Christian education is not testing scores, degrees, or professional success, but Christlikeness, a life shaped by faith, holiness, wisdom, and love.

The Great Commission also defines the goal. Jesus commanded His disciples to "teach all nations… teaching them to observe all things whatsoever I have commanded you" (Matthew 28:19-20). The aim is not information but obedience, not mere knowledge but discipleship. Christian education must therefore move beyond intellectual formation to holistic transformation, teaching believers to live under Christ's lordship in every aspect of life.

Church history supports this vision. Early catechesis not only transmits doctrine but trains converts in Christian living. The Reformers emphasized that education should produce not only scholars, but godly men and women equipped for service. The Puritans wrote catechisms and manuals that combined theology with practical guidance for family and community life. In every age, faithful educators have insisted that the goal of Christian education is the shaping of whole persons for God's glory.

This goal can be understood through four interconnected dimensions:

> **Spiritual formation** - nurturing faith and devotion so that believers grow in love for God and conformity to Christ.
>
> **Intellectual formation** - renewing the mind through truth so that believers think biblically and discern wisely.
>
> **Moral formation** - shaping character and virtue so that believers live in holiness, integrity, and love.
>
> **Missional formation** - equipping believers to serve others and bear witness to Christ in the world.

These four dimensions together express the full aim of Christian education. To neglect any one of them is to risk imbalance: knowledge without devotion, morality without truth, mission without holiness. But when held together, they produce mature disciples who glorify God in every sphere of life.

Today, this vision is urgently needed. In a world that prizes achievement, wealth, and self-fulfillment, Christian education must resist the temptation to adopt secular goals. Its standard of success is not measured by worldly recognition but by faithfulness to Christ. A Christian school may boast of its academic excellence, a church of its numbers, or a family of its heritage, but if these do not lead to Christlike disciples, they miss the mark. The goal remains unchanged: to know Christ, to be transformed by Him, and to make Him known.

Christian education, then, is a lifelong journey toward Christlikeness. It begins in the home, is nurtured in the church, structured in the school, and tested in society. But in all these contexts, the end is the same: that believers may be formed into faithful disciples who glorify God with heart, soul, mind, and strength. As we now explore the goal of Christian education, we will consider each of its dimensions more closely: spiritual, intellectual, moral, and missional formation, and how together they shape the whole person for God's kingdom.

Spiritual Formation (Christlikeness)

At the heart of Christian education lies the call to spiritual formation, the process of being shaped into the likeness of Christ. This is not an optional add-on to education, but its very essence. Knowledge, skills, and even morality are empty unless they flow from a transformed heart that loves God and delights to obey Him. Christian education seeks to nurture such transformation, forming disciples who are rooted in Christ and who live for His glory.

Biblical Foundations for Spiritual Formation

Scripture repeatedly emphasizes that God's purpose for His people is Christlikeness. Paul declares in Romans 8:29 that God predestined believers "to be conformed to the image of his Son." In 2 Corinthians 3:18, he describes believers as being transformed into Christ's image "from glory to glory" by the Spirit. Jesus Himself set the standard: *"The disciple is not above his master: but every one that is perfect shall be as his master"* (Luke 6:40). Education, in its deepest sense, is about learning Christ, being taught by Him, shaped by His Word, and empowered by His Spirit.

This goal is central to the Great Commission. Jesus commanded His disciples not only to make converts but to "teach them to observe all things whatsoever I have commanded you" (Matthew 28:20). Obedience, transformation, and Christlike living are the desired outcomes. Similarly, Paul's vision for the church is that leaders equip the saints "till we all come in the unity of the faith... unto a perfect man, unto the measure of the stature of the fulness of Christ" (Ephesians 4:13). Christian education, then, is ultimately about discipleship: shaping believers so that they reflect Christ in faith, holiness, and love.

Historical Perspectives on Spiritual Formation

The history of the church reflects this biblical priority. In the early church, catechesis was designed not only to teach doctrine but to train converts in prayer, worship, and holy living. Instruction was always joined with spiritual practices that formed the heart. The desert fathers and mothers, though sometimes extreme, emphasized the importance of inner transformation through prayer, fasting, and meditation on Scripture.

During the medieval period, monastic communities carried forward this emphasis on spiritual formation. The daily rhythms of prayer, work, and study were designed to shape character and devotion. While not all believers were monks, the monastic ideal of disciplined spiritual practice influenced broader Christian life, reminding the church that education was about holiness, not just knowledge.

The Reformers, while rejecting certain abuses, also emphasized spiritual formation. Martin Luther stressed that faith must produce fruit in daily life, and he composed catechisms to guide families in prayer and obedience. John Calvin emphasized the role of the Spirit in sanctification, teaching that true knowledge of God must lead to reverence and godliness. The Puritans carried this further, integrating theology with daily practice in manuals of devotion and family worship.

In every age, faithful educators have insisted that Christian education must shape not only the mind but the heart.

Practices of Spiritual Formation

Spiritual formation takes place through specific practices that shape believers over time. Among the most central are:

> **Prayer** - Prayer is both a means of communion with God and a formative practice that shapes dependence, humility, and love. Christian education teaches believers how to pray, not as a ritual only, but as a relationship. The Lord's Prayer (Matthew 6:9-13) provides the pattern, forming believers in reverence, submission, dependence, and forgiveness.
>
> **Scripture** - The Word of God is the primary instrument of transformation. Paul told Timothy that Scripture is "profitable for doctrine, for reproof, for correction, for instruction in righteousness" so that the man of God may be "thoroughly furnished unto all good works" (2 Timothy 3:16-17). Christian education centers on Scripture, not merely as a text to be studied but as God's living Word that forms hearts and lives.
>
> **Worship** - Worship shapes love. As believers gather to praise God, confess sin, and receive grace, their affections are reoriented toward Him. Songs, prayers, sacraments, and sermons all form the soul, teaching not only the mind but also

training desire. James K. A. Smith calls worship "the pedagogy of desire," a formative force in spiritual education.

Community - Spiritual formation is not solitary but communal. Believers are shaped through fellowship, accountability, and encouragement. The "one another" commands of Scripture (love one another, forgive one another, exhort one another) are lived out in community, making the church itself a context of spiritual education.

Service - True formation expresses itself in love for others. Jesus taught that greatness is found in serving (Mark 10:43-45). Christian education, therefore, includes opportunities for practical service, training disciples to embody Christ's humility and compassion.

Contemporary Challenges and Opportunities

In today's world, spiritual formation faces both obstacles and opportunities. Being busy, distractions, and secular pressures often make prayer and worship seem optional. Technology bombards believers with messages that shape desire away from God. Many Christians are tempted to separate faith from daily life, treating spirituality as a private matter rather than a whole-life calling.

Yet these challenges also provide opportunities for Christian education. Families, churches, and schools that prioritize spiritual formation offer a powerful countercultural witness. Teaching believers to practice daily prayer, to meditate on Scripture, to gather faithfully in worship, and to serve with joy equips them to resist cultural pressures. In a fragmented world, spiritual formation anchors believers in the love of God and the likeness of Christ.

The Goal: Christlikeness

Ultimately, the aim of spiritual formation is not simply piety or discipline but Christlikeness. Paul writes, *"For me to live is Christ, and to die is gain"* (Philippians 1:21). Christian education succeeds when believers can echo these words when their identity, desires, and actions are shaped by Christ Himself. Spiritual formation is lifelong, continuing until believers are fully conformed to His image in glory. But even now, Christian education seeks to form disciples who reflect Christ in every sphere of life, glorifying God through faith, holiness, and love.

Intellectual Formation (Mind Renewed by Truth)

Christian education does not stop at shaping the heart; it must also renew the mind. Spiritual formation and intellectual formation are inseparable, for a disciple of Christ must both love the Lord with all his heart and with all his mind (Matthew 22:37). Intellectual formation equips believers to think biblically, discern truth from error, and bring every thought captive to the obedience of Christ (2 Corinthians 10:5). Without this, faith may become shallow, easily swayed by false teaching or cultural pressure. With it, believers are prepared to live wisely, defend the faith, and glorify God through disciplined thought.

Biblical Foundations for Intellectual Formation

Scripture presents the mind as central to discipleship. Paul commands believers, *"Be not conformed to this world: but be ye transformed by the renewing of your mind"* (Romans 12:2). Transformation begins inwardly, shaping thought patterns according to God's truth. Likewise, Proverbs emphasizes wisdom and understanding: *"Wisdom is the principal thing; therefore, get wisdom: and with all thy getting get understanding"* (Proverbs 4:7). Intellectual formation is therefore not optional but integral to godliness.

Jesus modeled this integration of mind and heart. As a child, He "grew in wisdom" (Luke 2:52), engaging teachers in the temple with questions and answers. His teaching consistently appealed to both heart and reason, using parables, logic, and Scripture to correct falsehood and reveal truth. Paul followed this example, reasoning in synagogues and marketplaces (Acts 17:17), persuading hearers through careful argument grounded in Scripture. Intellectual engagement was not divorced from faith but an expression of it.

The Bible also calls for defending the truth intellectually. Peter exhorts believers: *"Be ready always to give an answer to every man that asketh you a reason of the hope that is in you"* (1 Peter 3:15). Apologetics, giving a reasoned defense of the faith, is part of Christian education. Intellectual formation ensures that believers can answer objections, resist false doctrine, and stand firm in truth.

Historical Perspectives on Intellectual Formation

The church has always valued the life of the mind. The early apologists, such as Justin Martyr and Irenaeus, engaged Greek philosophy with reasoned arguments for the faith. Origen and Augustine insisted that intellectual pursuits, when submitted to Christ, could serve the gospel. Augustine's *Confessions* reveal how the mind, enlightened by grace, finds rest in God alone.

During the medieval period, Christian intellectual life flourished in universities. Thinkers like Thomas Aquinas integrated theology and philosophy, affirming that reason and revelation, though distinct, ultimately harmonize under God. Their work reflects the conviction that truth is unified because its source is God Himself.

The Reformers emphasized that Scripture must shape

the mind of every believer, not just clergy. Martin Luther translated the Bible into the vernacular so that common people could read and understand God's Word. John Calvin insisted on rigorous study of Scripture, equipping pastors and laypeople to resist false teaching. For them, intellectual formation was not elitist but necessary for all Christians.

In the modern era, Christian intellectuals such as C. S. Lewis, Francis Schaeffer, and others have defended the faith in the face of secularism, showing that Christianity offers coherent answers to life's deepest questions. Their work underscores that intellectual formation remains vital for engaging culture and equipping the church.

Practices of Intellectual Formation

Intellectual formation occurs through deliberate practices that cultivate disciplined thinking in submission to Christ.

> **Study of Scripture** - The Bible is the foundation for intellectual formation. Systematic study, memorization, and meditation equip believers to think with a biblical worldview. Psalm 119:11 declares, *"Thy word have I hid in mine heart, that I might not sin against thee."*
>
> **Theological Reflection** - Beyond reading Scripture, believers are called to reflect deeply on its truths. Doctrine provides coherence and clarity, guarding against error. Catechisms, creeds, and confessions serve as tools for forming the mind in truth.

Engagement with Learning - All truth is God's truth. Mathematics, science, history, and literature, when studied through a biblical lens, reveal aspects of God's order and creativity. Christian education encourages disciplined study of all fields as acts of worship.

Critical Thinking and Discernment - Intellectual formation trains believers to test every idea by Scripture (1 John 4:1). It equips them to recognize cultural lies, philosophical errors, and false gospels, and to respond with wisdom.

Apologetics and Dialogue - Believers must be trained to articulate and defend their faith. This includes studying worldviews, engaging respectfully with those who disagree, and giving reasoned answers grounded in Scripture.

Contemporary Challenges and Opportunities

Modern society presents unique challenges to intellectual formation. Relativism denies absolute truth, materialism reduces reality to the physical, and secularism sidelines God. Media and technology often reward speed and distraction rather than deep thought. Many Christians are tempted to settle for shallow faith, driven by emotion rather than truth.

Yet these challenges also create opportunities. In an age of confusion, believers who think clearly and biblically stand out as lights. Christian schools, universities, and churches that prioritize intellectual formation can equip disciples to resist cultural lies and offer coherent hope. Resources around today's digital libraries, global networks, and apologetics movements that can strengthen intellectual discipleship.

The Goal: Minds Renewed in Christ

The ultimate aim of intellectual formation is not academic pride, but renewed minds submitted to Christ. Knowledge without humility leads to arrogance, but knowledge shaped by love leads to wisdom. Paul reminds us, *"Knowledge puffeth up, but charity edifieth"* (1 Corinthians 8:1). True intellectual formation produces believers who think clearly, discern wisely, and love deeply.

When Christian education succeeds in this dimension, believers are equipped to glorify God with their minds. They resist falsehood, embrace truth, and integrate faith with learning. They see the world through biblical lenses, understanding history, culture, and science as part of God's creation. Their minds, renewed by truth, become instruments for serving Christ in every sphere.

Moral Formation (Character and Virtue)

Christian education is not complete until it shapes character and cultivates virtue. Spiritual formation addresses the heart, intellectual formation renews the mind, but moral formation brings faith and truth into daily conduct. It answers the question: How shall we live? The goal is not merely to produce people who know the truth, but people who embody it, men and women of holiness, integrity, and love.

Biblical Foundations for Moral Formation

From the beginning, Scripture emphasizes that obedience is central to life with God. In Deuteronomy 10:12–13, Moses asks, *"And now, Israel, what doth the Lord thy God require of thee, but to fear the Lord thy God, to walk in all his ways, and to love him, and to serve the Lord thy God with all thy heart and with all thy soul, to keep the commandments of the Lord… which I command thee this day for thy good?"* Here, moral formation is not an option but a requirement of covenant life.

The wisdom literature reinforces this. Proverbs teaches that character matters more than wealth or success: *"A good name is rather to be chosen than great riches"* (Proverbs 22:1). The Psalms celebrate the blessedness of the righteous who delight in God's law (Psalm 1). The prophets continually rebuked Israel for hypocrisy, outward worship without justice, mercy, and righteousness (Micah 6:8). God's concern has always been not only what His people believe but how they live. The New Testament makes this even clearer. Jesus insists that true disciples bear fruit in their lives: *"By their fruits ye shall know them"* (Matthew 7:20). The Sermon on the Mount (Matthew 5-7) sets forth a moral vision that goes beyond external behavior to the transformation of the heart. Paul likewise emphasizes that faith must produce works: *"For the grace of God that bringeth salvation hath appeared to all men, teaching us that, denying ungodliness and worldly lusts, we should live soberly, righteously, and godly, in this present world"* (Titus 2:11-12).

In short, the Bible presents moral formation as inseparable from discipleship. Christian education must therefore train believers not only to know the truth but to live it in daily holiness, justice, and love.

Historical Perspectives on Moral Formation

The church has long recognized the importance of character formation in education. Early catechisms included moral instruction alongside doctrinal teaching, ensuring that converts understood how to live as Christians. Augustine's writings emphasized the reordering of loves, that virtue comes when the soul's desires are rightly directed toward God.

In the medieval period, monastic communities provided models of disciplined moral life. Their rules emphasized humility, obedience, honesty, and service. While not all were called to monastic life, the emphasis on virtue influenced broader Christian practice.

The Reformers continued this emphasis but placed it firmly within the context of grace. Luther and Calvin insisted that good works cannot save, but they are the necessary fruit of true faith. Calvin's Geneva Academy trained not only pastors but also citizens, integrating moral instruction with theological study. The Puritans likewise stressed that education must cultivate godly character. Their writings are full of exhortations to holiness, integrity in work, and purity in family life.

In later centuries, Christian schools and Sunday/Sabbath schools emphasized both literacy and morality, teaching children honesty, respect, diligence, and charity alongside Scripture. Missionaries often combined evangelism with moral instruction, helping new believers build communities of integrity and service. Throughout history, Christian education has always aimed at shaping lives, not just minds.

Practices of Moral Formation

Moral formation takes place through intentional practices that align belief with conduct:

> **Instruction in God's Law and Commands** - Teaching the Ten Commandments, the Sermon on the Mount, and other moral teachings of Scripture provides a foundation for Christian living. These are not burdens but guides to holy life.

Habituation and Discipline - Virtue is not formed overnight but through repeated practice. Just as athletes train their bodies, Christians train their souls through daily choices, habits of prayer, honesty in speech, and diligence in work. Education provides opportunities to practice virtue consistently until it becomes character.

Role Models and Mentors - Example is powerful. Teachers, parents, pastors, and historical figures serve as models of virtue. Paul himself said, *"Be ye followers of me, even as I also am of Christ"* (1 Corinthians 11:1). Moral formation requires visible examples of integrity and holiness.

Community Accountability - The church provides encouragement and correction, ensuring that believers grow in holiness together. Confession, discipline, and encouragement are all part of forming moral character in a community.

Service and Justice - Engaging in works of mercy and justice reinforces moral teaching. Feeding the hungry, visiting the sick, and advocating for the oppressed teach virtues of compassion, humility, and courage.

Contemporary Challenges and Opportunities

Today, moral formation faces severe challenges. Relativism denies objective morality, insisting that right and wrong are subjective. Secular education often focuses on skills and achievement while neglecting virtue. The media frequently glamorizes selfishness, greed, or immorality. Many Christians, influenced by culture, separate belief from behavior, leading to hypocrisy.

Yet the need for moral formation has never been greater. In a world longing for integrity and justice, Christians shaped by virtue provide a powerful testimony. Employers seek workers of honesty and diligence; communities need citizens of compassion and justice; families need parents of faithfulness and love. Christian education that prioritizes moral formation equips believers to meet these needs and to glorify God in society.

The Goal: Holiness and Integrity

The aim of moral formation is holiness, not outward legalism but inward integrity that reflects Christ. Peter exhorts, *"Be ye holy; for I am holy"* (1 Peter 1:16). Jesus calls His disciples to be the salt of the earth and the light of the world, shining through good works so that others may glorify the Father (Matthew 5:13-16). Moral formation enables believers to embody this calling.

When Christian education succeeds in this dimension, believers are not only hearers of the Word but doers. They display honesty in business, purity in relationships, compassion in service, and courage in witness. Their character reflects Christ, and their lives become living testimonies of the gospel. Moral formation, therefore, is not peripheral but central to the goal of Christian education.

Missional Formation (Service and Witness in the World)

The final dimension of the goal of Christian education is missional formation. If spiritual formation directs the heart toward God, intellectual formation renews the mind with truth, and moral formation shapes character in holiness, then missional formation sends believers outward in service and witness. The gospel does not end with personal transformation; it compels disciples to love their neighbors, serve their communities, and bear witness to Christ among the nations. Christian education must therefore equip believers not only to know and live the faith but also to share it.

Biblical Foundations for Missional Formation

Mission lies at the center of Scripture. From the call of Abraham to be a blessing to all nations (Genesis 12:3) to the Great Commission (Matthew 28:19-20), God's people have always been called to live outwardly for the sake of others. Jesus summarized the law with two commands: love God and love neighbor (Matthew 22:37-39). Both are inseparable; true devotion to God flows into selfless service.

Jesus modeled this in His ministry. He proclaimed the kingdom of God in word and deed, teaching truth, healing the sick, feeding the hungry, and showing compassion to the marginalized. At the end of His earthly ministry, He commanded His disciples, *"Go ye into all the world, and preach the gospel to every creature"* (Mark 16:15). The book of Acts records the church carrying out this mission, preaching Christ, serving the poor, and spreading the gospel across cultures and nations.

Paul also emphasizes the missional dimension of discipleship. He describes believers as "ambassadors for Christ" (2 Corinthians 5:20), entrusted with the ministry of reconciliation. He reminds the Ephesians that they are created in Christ "unto good works" (Ephesians 2:10). Christian education must form believers with this same outward orientation, preparing them to serve others and proclaim Christ wherever God places them.

Historical Perspectives on Missional Formation

Throughout church history, education has always been linked to mission. The early catechumenate prepared converts not only for baptism but for public witness in a hostile world. Martyrs like Polycarp and Perpetua were educated in the faith so that they could confess Christ boldly, even unto death.

Monastic movements, while emphasizing prayer and holiness, also engaged in service and mission. Monks preserved learning, cared for the sick, and evangelized pagan tribes. The medieval church established hospitals, schools, and charities as part of its mission to serve society.

The Reformation renewed focus on the priesthood of all believers, emphasizing that every Christian was called to serve God in daily life. Education was central to this vision, equipping ordinary believers to read Scripture, teach their children, and witness in their communities.

The Puritans carried this further, stressing that families and churches must raise children for godliness and service.

In the modern era, missionary movements expanded the reach of Christian education globally. Figures such as William Carey, Adoniram Judson, and Hudson Taylor combined evangelism with education, establishing schools, printing presses, and medical missions. For them, education was a means of forming disciples who would in turn serve and witness in their own cultures. This legacy continues today in Christian schools, seminaries, and mission organizations around the world.

Practices of Missional Formation

Missional formation is not abstract; it is cultivated through concrete practices that train believers to live outwardly for others:

> **Service Projects and Acts of Mercy** - Opportunities to care for the poor, visit the sick, and serve the community, teach compassion and humility. These practices embody the love of Christ in tangible ways.
>
> **Evangelism Training** - Believers must be equipped to share the gospel clearly and confidently. This includes learning how to articulate the core message of Christ, answer objections, and invite others to faith.
>
> **Cross-Cultural Engagement** - Exposure to different cultures, whether through missions, service trips, or diverse communities, broadens

perspective and equips disciples to witness globally.

Integration of Faith and Vocation - Missional living includes viewing one's career as a mission field. Teachers, doctors, businesspeople, and artists all serve as witnesses when they integrate faith with daily work.

Prayer for Mission - Prayer is central to mission. Interceding for the lost, for missionaries, and for global needs trains believers to align their hearts with God's purposes in the world.

Contemporary Challenges and Opportunities

Today, missional formation faces unique challenges. Secularism often labels public witness as intolerance, while consumerism tempts believers to focus inwardly on personal success. Many Christians feel unprepared to share their faith in a skeptical culture. At the same time, globalization, technology, and migration have brought the nations to our doorstep, creating unprecedented opportunities for mission.

Christian education must therefore form believers who are both courageous and compassionate. Courage is needed to proclaim Christ faithfully in a world that may mock or oppose the gospel. Compassion is needed to serve neighbors with humility and love, demonstrating the reality of Christ through actions as well as words. Together, courage and compassion produce credible witnesses who embody the gospel.

The Goal: Disciples on Mission

The ultimate aim of missional formation is to produce disciples who live as witnesses in the world. Jesus told His followers, *"As my Father hath sent me, even so send I you"* (John 20:21). Christian education succeeds in this dimension when believers embrace their calling as sent ones, whether across the street or across the world.

Missional formation ensures that Christian education does not become self-centered. It reminds us that discipleship is for the sake of the world. Believers who are spiritually rooted, intellectually renewed, and morally shaped must also be missionally oriented, ready to serve, witness, and glorify God in every place. This outward direction completes the goal of Christian education, forming disciples who are not only transformed themselves but who also become instruments of transformation in the world.

The Hope of Eternity

While Christian education forms disciples in the present, its ultimate orientation is toward the future. Spiritual formation, intellectual renewal, moral shaping, and missional service are all vital, but they find their fullest meaning in the hope of eternity. Christian education is not simply about preparing believers for fruitful living in this world; it is about preparing them for everlasting life in the presence of God. This eternal hope gives direction, endurance, and joy to every aspect of Christian education.

Biblical Foundations for Eternal Hope

Scripture consistently sets the believer's eyes on eternity. Paul reminds the Corinthians, *"For our light affliction, which is but for a moment, worketh for us a far more exceeding and eternal weight of glory"* (2 Corinthians 4:17). Education that prepares disciples only for temporal success misses this greater purpose. The true goal is to prepare believers for glory, to prepare them as citizens of heaven (Philippians 3:20) who eagerly await the day when Christ will return and make all things new.

Jesus Himself framed discipleship in light of eternity. He urged His followers, *"Lay up for yourselves treasures in heaven, where neither moth nor rust doth corrupt, and where thieves do not break through nor steal"* (Matthew 6:20). Eternal hope reorients priorities, teaching believers to live not for fleeting gain but for everlasting reward. Christian education must therefore constantly lift the eyes of learners beyond the present world to the eternal kingdom.

The climax of Scripture is not merely moral improvement or social reform but eternal communion with God. John's vision in Revelation shows a redeemed people dwelling with God in a new heaven and new earth: *"And they shall see his face; and his name shall be in their foreheads... and they shall reign for ever and ever"* (Revelation 22:4-5). Christian education, rightly understood, prepares believers for this destiny to see God face to face and to reign with Christ eternally.

Historical Perspectives on Eternal Hope

The hope of eternity has always shaped Christian teaching. Early catechisms instructed converts not only in doctrine and conduct but also in the hope of resurrection and eternal life. The Apostles' Creed ends with the confession: "I believe... in the resurrection of the body, and the life everlasting." Instruction in eternal hope gave believers courage to endure persecution and joy in the face of suffering.

The church fathers often emphasized that this world is a preparation for the world to come. Augustine, in *The City of God*, distinguished between the earthly city, marked by pride and self-love, and the heavenly city, where love of God reigns. For Augustine, education must form citizens of the heavenly city, teaching them to live now in light of eternity.

The Reformers and Puritans likewise stressed eternal hope. Luther often reminded believers that this life is a "school for eternity," shaping us for everlasting fellowship with God. Puritan writings are filled with exhortations to live in readiness for heaven. Richard Baxter's *The Saints' Everlasting Rest* encouraged readers to fix their hearts on the eternal inheritance, reminding them that present laborers are only preparation for eternal joy.

Practical Dimensions of Teaching Eternal Hope

Christian education must intentionally cultivate hope in eternity through several practices:

> **Teaching on Heaven and Resurrection** - Believers must be taught that death is not the end but the doorway to eternal life. Instruction on resurrection, judgment, and new creation gives disciples a solid anchor for hope.
>
> **Encouraging Perseverance in Suffering** - Education that emphasizes eternal hope equips believers to endure hardship with joy, knowing that suffering produces glory (Romans 8:18).
>
> **Cultivating Eternal Perspective in Daily Choices** - Eternal hope shapes how believers use time, resources, and opportunities. Christian education must train disciples to invest in what lasts forever: faith, love, and service, rather than in fleeting pleasures.
>
> **Forming Worshipful Anticipation** - Worship that anticipates the eternal kingdom (through hymns, liturgy, and preaching) trains believers to long for

Christ's coming and to live in hope.

Integrating Mission with Eternal Vision - The hope of eternity fuels evangelism and service. Believers labor to share the gospel because they long for others to share in eternal life. Christian education must instill this missional urgency.

Contemporary Challenges and Opportunities

In our present age, hope in eternity is often neglected. Secular culture dismisses eternal realities, focusing only on the here and now. Even within the church, there is a temptation to emphasize earthly success, prosperity, influence, and achievement while neglecting eternal destiny. Without a vision of eternity, education risks producing disciples who are well-prepared for careers but unprepared for glory.

Yet this context also provides opportunity. In a world marked by uncertainty, suffering, and despair, the hope of eternity shines brightly. Christians who live with an eternal perspective offer an alternative to fear and hopelessness. Christian education that emphasizes eternity provides disciples with courage to face trials, motivation to serve faithfully, and joy that cannot be shaken.

The Goal: Living in Light of Eternity

Ultimately, the hope of eternity completes the goal of Christian education. Spiritual, intellectual, moral, and missional formation are all directed toward preparing believers for eternal life with God. As Paul writes, *"Christ in you, the hope of glory"* (Colossians 1:27). The goal is not simply better people but redeemed people who are destined for eternal communion with Christ.

Christian education, then, is a foretaste of eternity. Every prayer, every lesson, every act of service is training for the day when believers will see Christ face to face. The hope of eternity gives meaning to the struggles of discipleship and assures that the labor of Christian education is never in vain (1 Corinthians 15:58).

When this hope is central, Christian education not only equips believers for faithful living now but prepares them for everlasting joy. It forms disciples who live with eyes fixed on Christ, hearts set on heaven, and lives poured out in service until the day they enter into the fullness of His glory.

Conclusion: The Goal of Christian Education

The goal of Christian education is comprehensive, reaching from the present life into eternity. It is not satisfied with shallow knowledge, outward conformity, or temporary success. Its aim is the full transformation of believers so that they glorify God in every sphere of life and are prepared for eternal communion with Him.

We have seen that this goal unfolds in five interwoven dimensions. Spiritual formation turns the heart toward God, nurturing love, worship, and Christlikeness. Intellectual formation renews the mind, enabling believers to think biblically, discern truth, and resist falsehood. Moral formation shapes character and virtue, producing holiness, integrity, and justice in daily life. Missional formation sends disciples outward into the world, equipping them to serve others and bear faithful witness to Christ. Finally, the hope of eternity lifts the eyes of believers beyond this present age, anchoring them in the promise of everlasting life and shaping their present conduct with eternal perspective.

Each of these dimensions is essential, but no one can stand alone. To emphasize devotion without truth risks sentimentality. To value intellect without holiness risks pride. To stress morality without mission risks self-righteousness. To focus on mission without eternity risks burnout and despair. Yet when all five are held together, Christian education fulfills its purpose: forming mature disciples of Jesus Christ who love God fully, serve others faithfully, and live in hope unshakable.

Throughout history, the church has embraced this holistic vision. From the catechumens of the early church to the Reformers, Puritans, and modern missionaries, faithful educators have labored not merely to pass on information but to shape whole lives for God's glory. Their example challenges us to pursue the same aim in our homes, churches, schools, and societies today.

In our own age, this vision remains as urgent as ever. Surrounded by secularism, relativism, and distraction, the church must resist the temptation to adopt worldly definitions of success. Christian education must not be reduced to career training, moralism, or social influence. Its measure of success is far greater: disciples who are spiritually rooted, intellectually renewed, morally upright, missionally engaged, and eternally hopeful.

Ultimately, the goal of Christian education is Christ

Himself. As Paul declared, *"My little children, of whom I travail in birth again until Christ be formed in you"* (Galatians 4:19). The aim is that believers may grow "unto a perfect man, unto the measure of the stature of the fulness of Christ" (Ephesians 4:13), and that they may live with eyes fixed on "the hope of glory" (Colossians 1:27). Christian education is a lifelong journey toward this end, culminating in the day when we see Him face to face and are made like Him (1 John 3:2).

Until that day, every lesson taught, every sermon preached, every prayer prayed, and every act of service contributed to this goal. Christian education is not in vain, for it prepares disciples not only for faithful living now but for eternal joy with Christ. Its final purpose is that God be glorified through a people fully formed in His image, in heart, mind, character, mission, and hope, both now and forever.

CHAPTER 5: FROM COVENANT TO KINGDOM

Biblical Stories with Lasting Lessons

Every great truth of Scripture is best understood not only through principles but through stories. The Bible is full of men and women whose lives, struggles, failures, and victories illustrate God's purposes in ways that mere definitions cannot. Where previous chapters examined the foundation, purpose, and practice of Christian education, this chapter turns our attention to the narrative side of learning because sometimes, the best lessons are told through lives.

Stories speak to the heart. When we read about Abraham leaving everything to follow God, or Lot hesitating on the edge of destruction, we don't just see doctrine; we see faith tested in the fires of real life. When we watch Hosea love an unfaithful wife, we glimpse God's covenant love. When we meet the woman at the well, we discover the radical grace of Christ that reaches into shame and restores dignity. These stories remind us that Christian education is not just information; it is transformation.

In these pages, we will revisit familiar biblical narratives with fresh eyes. We will explore them not only as historical accounts, but as living lessons.

Insights from Scripture, research, and reflection will be woven together so that each story becomes both a window into God's truth and a mirror for our own lives.

As you walk through the stories in this chapter, ask yourself: *What is God teaching me through their journey? What warnings do I need to heed? What hope do I need to embrace?* From covenant beginnings with Abraham to the promise of Christ's kingdom, these stories guide us in faith, leadership, discipleship, and endurance, reminding us that God is still writing His story through us today.

Story 1: Abraham

Covenant, Family, and Faith

1. What does it mean to trust God when you don't know what lies ahead?
2. How does Abraham's family journey reveal both faith and human weakness?
3. What can we learn from the promises God made to Abraham?
4. Why does God sometimes test us, and how should we respond?
5. How does Abraham's story connect to the bigger story of Christ?

Let's look at the story of Abraham, often called the father of faith. His story isn't just ancient history; it's a mirror for our own struggles with trust, obedience, and waiting on God.

Imagine being asked to leave your home, your family, and everything familiar. God told Abraham, "Go from your country, your people, and your father's household to the land I will show you" (Genesis 12:1). No map. No details. Just a promise. Would you go?

Abraham went. That first step was faith in action. He didn't have a full plan; he had God's word. Faith, in its purest form, is trusting the One who knows the way, even when we don't.

God promised Abraham three things: land, descendants, and blessing. For a man with a barren wife, those words seemed impossible. Yet Scripture tells us, "Abram believed the Lord, and he credited it to him as righteousness" (Genesis 15:6).

But Abraham's faith was not flawless. In Egypt, fearing for his life, he lied about Sarah being his sister. Later, he and Sarah tried to "help" God's plan by having a child through Hagar. These missteps remind us that faith does not mean perfection.

Ishmael's birth brought conflict and pain, yet God still cared for him and promised to make him into a nation. This shows us that while our choices carry consequences, God's mercy still reaches into our mistakes.

Years passed, and Abraham and Sarah still had no child together. Then God repeated His promise: Sarah would bear a son. She laughed at the thought; it seemed absurd. But God's question echoed: "Is anything too hard for the Lord?" (Genesis 18:14).

Against all odds, Isaac was born. His very name means "laughter." The child of promise turned Sarah's doubt into joy, reminding us that God's timing may not match ours, but His word never fails.

Just when Abraham thought the hardest part was over, God tested him again. "Take your son, your only son Isaac, whom you love, and sacrifice him" (Genesis 22:2). This was unthinkable. Isaac was the miracle child, the fulfillment of God's promise.

Abraham obeyed. Step by agonizing step, he walked to the mountain, trusting that God would somehow provide. His words to Isaac are haunting yet hopeful: "God himself will provide the lamb" (Genesis 22:8).

At the altar, Abraham raised the knife, but God stopped him. A ram was caught in the thicket, a substitute for Isaac. This moment foreshadowed the greatest sacrifice: Christ, the Lamb of God, offered in our place.

Abraham's willingness to give up what he loved most teaches us that true faith holds nothing back. God never desired Isaac's death. He desired Abraham's heart.

Beyond personal tests, Abraham was also a man of intercession. When God revealed His plan to destroy Sodom, Abraham pleaded: "Will you sweep away the righteous with the wicked?" (Genesis 18:23). His bold prayers show us what it means to stand in the gap.

Through intercession, Abraham revealed God's mercy. He was willing to spare the whole city for the sake of just ten righteous people. Though Sodom was destroyed, Abraham's prayer teaches us to never stop praying for mercy on behalf of others.

Everywhere Abraham traveled, he built altars. These altars were reminders that worship belongs in every part of life. What "altars" do we leave behind, signs of faith that others can see?

Abraham's story reminds us that God doesn't choose perfect people; He chooses willing people. His flaws did not disqualify him because his trust in God remained.

The New Testament calls Abraham the model of faith: "He did not waver through unbelief regarding the promise of God... being fully persuaded that God had power to do what he had promised" (Romans 4:20-21).

Abraham's covenant was bigger than himself. Through him came Israel, and ultimately through his lineage came Jesus Christ. His story stretches from covenant to kingdom.

Abraham shows us that faith is a journey. There are detours, doubts, and delays. But God's faithfulness is greater than our weakness. When we trust Him, He leads us not just to blessings for ourselves, but to blessings for generations.

His story closes with this truth: faith may stumble, but God's covenant never fails. Abraham believed, obeyed, and interceded, and through him, the story of redemption moved forward to Christ.

Reflection Questions

1. How does Abraham's obedience challenge your own trust in God's direction?
2. What lessons can we learn from Abraham's mistakes in Egypt and with Hagar?
3. How does Isaac's birth remind us about God's timing versus ours?
4. What does Abraham's test with Isaac teach us about surrender?
5. How does the ram caught in the thicket point us to Christ?
6. Why is intercession (like Abraham's prayer for Sodom) important for us today?
7. What kind of "altars" (spiritual markers) are you leaving behind in your life?
8. How does Abraham's covenant connect to

Jesus and the kingdom of God?

9. In what ways is faith a journey rather than a one-time decision?

10. What part of Abraham's story speaks most directly to your life right now?

Story 2: Lot and Sodom

Judgment, Mercy, and Compromise

1. Why did Lot choose to live in Sodom, even though it was known for wickedness?
2. What does his story reveal about the dangers of compromise?
3. How does Abraham's prayer for Sodom show us the power of intercession?
4. What lessons can we learn from the destruction of Sodom and the fate of Lot's wife?
5. How do we see God's mercy in Lot's deliverance?

Let's look at the story of Lot, Abraham's nephew. Lot's journey is one of choices, choices that seemed wise in the moment but carried painful consequences. His life is a sobering reminder that where we choose to live and how we choose to live do matter deeply.

The story begins when Abraham and Lot grew too wealthy in flocks and herds to remain together. Abraham gave Lot the first choice of land. Lot looked toward the lush Jordan Valley, described as "like the garden of the Lord" (Genesis 13:10). On appearance alone, it seemed like the perfect choice.

But appearances deceive. Scripture adds, "The people of Sodom were wicked and were sinning greatly against the Lord" (Genesis 13:13). Lot chose with his eyes, not with discernment.

How often do we make decisions this way, guided by what looks profitable, comfortable, or convenient, while ignoring the spiritual dangers? Lot's choice teaches us that compromise often begins with attraction to what looks good.

Soon, Lot wasn't just near Sodom; he was living in it. The pull of the city's prosperity outweighed the warnings of its corruption. Archaeologists note that ancient cities like Sodom were centers of wealth, but also of injustice, idolatry, and exploitation.

Meanwhile, Abraham remained in Canaan, walking with God. And when God revealed His plan to destroy Sodom, Abraham's heart was moved. He boldly interceded: "Will you sweep away the righteous with the wicked?" (Genesis 18:23).

Abraham bargained down from fifty righteous to ten. His prayer revealed God's mercy: even a handful of righteous people could have spared the city. But not even ten were found.

Two angels came to Sodom at night, and Lot urged them into his house. But the men of the city surrounded it, demanding to abuse the visitors. This horrifying moment revealed just how far Sodom had sunk into depravity.

Lot tried to protect his guests, even offering his daughters in desperation, a shocking glimpse into how much Sodom's values had influenced him. Living too close to sin had clouded his judgment.

The angels struck the mob with blindness and urged

Lot to gather his family. But his sons-in-law laughed, thinking he was joking. Sin had so dulled their hearts that even the warning of destruction sounded unbelievable.

Morning came, and the angels pressed Lot: "Hurry! Take your wife and your two daughters who are here, or you will be swept away" (Genesis 19:15). Yet Lot hesitated. Even after all the warnings, he lingered.

Out of mercy, the angels took hold of Lot, his wife, and his daughters by the hand and led them out of the city (Genesis 19:16). What a picture of grace, God pulling us out when we cannot move ourselves.

The command was clear: "Don't look back, and don't stop anywhere in the plain!" (Genesis 19:17). But Lot's wife looked back. Her heart still longed for Sodom, and in that moment, she turned into a pillar of salt.

Her fate reminds us that partial obedience is not obedience at all. When God delivers us, He calls us to leave sin behind completely, not to look back with longing.

Lot and his daughters escaped to the mountains, but even there, the story ends in tragedy. Fear drove his daughters to desperate actions, resulting in descendants who would later oppose Israel.

What began with a choice for fertile land ended in heartbreak, compromise, and loss. Lot lost his wife, his home, his possessions, and his influence all because he pitched his tent too close to sin.

Yet even here, mercy is evident. Scripture says, "God remembered Abraham, and he brought Lot out of the catastrophe" (Genesis 19:29). Lot's deliverance came not from his own faithfulness, but from God's faithfulness in response to Abraham's prayers.

Lot's hesitation shows us how easy it is to cling to what God is trying to free us from. Deliverance requires urgency. We cannot serve God while holding on to the world.

The destruction of Sodom is a sobering reminder of God's justice. Sin, unchecked and unrepentant, leads to ruin. But Lot's rescue reminds us that God delights to save, even pulling us by the hand if necessary.

In the end, Lot's life is both a warning and a testimony: don't compromise with sin, don't hesitate when God calls, and don't look back once He delivers you. Instead, run forward into the freedom He provides.

Reflection Questions
1. What does Lot's choice of Sodom reveal about decision-making based only on appearances?
2. How did living in Sodom influence Lot's thinking and behavior?
3. What can we learn from Abraham's intercession for Sodom?
4. Why do you think Lot's sons-in-law dismissed the warning of destruction?
5. What does Lot's wife teach us about divided hearts and looking back?
6. How is God's mercy shown in the angels taking Lot and his family by the hand?
7. In what ways do people today "hesitate" like Lot when God calls them to change?

8. What dangers of compromise does Lot's story highlight for believers?
9. How do you see the balance of God's justice and mercy in this story?
10. What practical steps can you take to avoid "pitching your tent" near spiritual danger?

Story 3: Hosea and Gomer.

The Prophet Commanded to Marry a Prostitute.

1. Why would God ask a prophet to marry an unfaithful woman?
2. What does Hosea and Gomer's marriage symbolize about God's relationship with His people?
3. How does this story reveal both judgment and mercy?
4. What lessons about love and forgiveness can we learn from Hosea's obedience?
5. How does Hosea's story foreshadow Christ's redeeming love for the church?

Let's look at one of the most unusual and heart-wrenching stories in Scripture, the story of Hosea, a prophet commanded by God to marry a woman who would be unfaithful to him. At first glance, this seems shocking, even unfair. But behind it lies a powerful message of God's love and Israel's unfaithfulness.

God told Hosea, "Go, take to yourself an adulterous wife and children of unfaithfulness, because the land is guilty of the vilest adultery in departing from the Lord" (Hosea 1:2). Hosea's marriage was not just personal; it was prophetic.

Gomer, Hosea's wife, symbolized Israel. Just as she would break Hosea's heart with her unfaithfulness,

Israel had broken God's heart by chasing after idols. The prophet's home became a living illustration of divine truth.

In ancient Israel, marriage was sacred, the foundation of covenant life. To marry someone known for unfaithfulness would have been humiliating. Hosea bore the shame of his marriage to show Israel what their sin looked like to God.

Together, Hosea and Gomer had children whose names carried messages of judgment. Their first son was named Jezreel, meaning "God will scatter." This pointed to Israel's coming defeat and exile.

Their daughter was named Lo-Ruhamah, meaning "Not loved." God was declaring that He would withdraw His compassion from the rebellious nation.

Their second son was named Lo-Ammi, meaning "Not my people." It was a heartbreaking declaration: Israel had rejected God so deeply that they no longer lived as His covenant people.

Yet, woven into this judgment was hope. God promised, "In the place where it was said to them, 'You are not my people,' they will be called 'children of the living God'" (Hosea 1:10). Even in the darkest pronouncements, His mercy shone through.

Gomer, true to her nature, left Hosea and fell back into unfaithfulness. Some scholars suggest she may have been enslaved or trapped in prostitution again. To the world, she was worthless. But God told Hosea to go and bring her back.

Hosea obeyed. He bought Gomer back for fifteen shekels of silver and some barley (Hosea 3:2). Imagine the scene: a prophet of God paying for his own wife, standing in the marketplace, reclaiming the one who betrayed him.

This act symbolized redemption. Just as Hosea paid a price to restore his unfaithful wife, God would pay the ultimate price to redeem His unfaithful people.

Hosea told Gomer she must live with him in faithfulness, but his love for her was unconditional. This pointed to God's love, a love that disciplines but also restores.

What does this teach us? That God's love is not based on our worthiness. He loves us even when we are unfaithful, and He calls us back when we stray.

The story also shows us the pain of sin. Hosea felt the agony of betrayal, just as God feels when His people turn away. Sin is not just breaking a rule; it's breaking God's heart.

Scholars note that Baal worship in Israel involved rituals of sexual immorality. By chasing after idols, the people weren't just breaking commandments; they were acting like Gomer, abandoning covenant love.

Hosea's marriage became a living sermon: Israel, you are Gomer. God is Hosea. And even though you are unfaithful, He is willing to buy you back.

This story foreshadows Christ, who would redeem His bride, the church. But instead of silver or barley, He would pay with His blood on the cross.

Hosea's obedience also challenges us personally. Could we love someone who has wounded us so deeply? Could we forgive in such a costly way?

The answer is found not in human strength but in God's. Only His love can empower such radical grace. Hosea's story invites us to see how much we've been forgiven, and in turn, extend mercy to others.

In the end, Hosea and Gomer's story is not just about heartbreak; it's about hope. It reminds us that God's covenant love is stronger than our sin, and His redemption reaches even the most broken places.

Reflection Questions

1. Why do you think God chose Hosea's marriage as a way to illustrate His message?
2. What do the names of Hosea's children reveal about Israel's condition?
3. How does Hosea's act of buying back Gomer point us to redemption in Christ?
4. In what ways does sin resemble unfaithfulness in a relationship?
5. How does this story change the way you see God's love for His people?
6. Why is it significant that God's message included both judgment and hope?
7. How do you see yourself in Gomer's unfaithfulness and in God's mercy?
8. What can we learn from Hosea's willingness to forgive and restore?
9. How does Hosea's story challenge you to extend grace to others?

10. What hope does this story give you about God's patience with your own struggles?

Story 4: The Shunammite Woman - Hospitality, Faith, and God's Reward

1. Have you ever given generously without expecting anything in return?
2. What does the story of the Shunammite woman reveal about faith in times of both blessing and heartbreak?
3. How does God honor simple acts of kindness?
4. What lessons can we learn about perseverance when life suddenly takes an unexpected turn?
5. How does this story connect to God's power to restore what seems lost?

Imagine opening your home to a stranger, simply because you sense God's presence in them. That's exactly what the Shunammite woman did when she noticed Elisha, the prophet, regularly passing through her town.

She wasn't wealthy in ways that made her proud; she was generous in ways that revealed her heart. She urged Elisha to stay for meals whenever he passed by. Over time, hospitality became her ministry.

But she didn't stop at meals. She told her husband, "Let's build a small room on the roof and put in it a bed, a table, a chair, and a lamp for him" (2 Kings 4:10). Her kindness gave God's servant a place of rest.

Think about how her gift was simple but practical. A

bed to rest. A lamp for light. A chair to sit. Sometimes faith is not about spectacular acts, but about meeting everyday needs with love.

Elisha was moved by her generosity and asked his servant Gehazi what could be done for her. But she had not asked for anything. She was content. That's when Gehazi revealed, "She has no son, and her husband is old" (2 Kings 4:14).

For any woman in her culture, this was a deep wound. Children were seen as a legacy and security. Yet she had never voiced her pain. Have you ever carried a silent longing that others don't know?

Elisha spoke God's promise: "About this time next year, you will hold a son in your arms" (2 Kings 4:16). Her response was honest: "No, my lord… don't mislead your servant!" She wanted to believe, but the wound of disappointment made hope hard.

And yet, God kept His word. She gave birth to a son, the very child she had stopped daring to dream of. Sometimes God surprises us with blessings we thought were no longer possible.

Years passed, and the boy grew. One day, while in the field with his father, he cried, "My head! My head!" By noon, he was dead in his mother's arms.

Can you imagine the devastation? The gift she hadn't even asked for, the miracle child she thought she had lost forever; now gone. Her joy turned to heartbreak.

But notice her response. She didn't plan a funeral. She carried her son to Elisha's room, laid him on the prophet's bed, shut the door, and went out. She wasn't in denial; she was in faith.

She told her husband she was going to see Elisha. When asked why, she said only, "It is well." Her words didn't match her grief; they matched her trust.

Along the road, Gehazi came to meet her, but she would not stop for him. She went straight to the prophet, grabbed his feet, and poured out her pain. This is what faith looks like: bringing your deepest sorrow straight to God.

Elisha went to her house. He prayed, stretched himself over the child, and pleaded with God. Life slowly returned. The boy sneezed seven times and opened his eyes.

The Shunammite fell at Elisha's feet, overwhelmed with gratitude. Her son, once dead, was alive again. Her faith had been tested by loss but rewarded by restoration.

This story teaches us that God honors both hospitality and perseverance. She gave without asking for anything, and God gave her more than she dreamed. She trusted when hope seemed gone, and God returned life to what she thought was lost.

Many of us can relate to her journey. We've had silent prayers, longings buried deep, blessings given, only to feel them slip away. Her story reminds us: don't stop at despair, run to God.

Her words, "It is well," echo through generations. They aren't a denial of pain, but a declaration of faith. Even in heartbreak, she believed God could still act.

The Shunammite woman teaches us that faith is not only about receiving blessings but also about trusting God in loss. Her story is both painful and hopeful, real and miraculous.

In her, we see a picture of endurance, generosity, and faith that clings to God until He moves. And through her, we are reminded that the God who gives life can restore it, even when we think all is lost.

Reflection Questions

1. What does the Shunammite woman's hospitality teach us about everyday faith?
2. Why do you think she never asked Elisha for anything, despite her silent longing?
3. How do her doubts when Elisha promised a child reflect our own struggles with hope?
4. What does her response to her son's death show us about faith in crisis?
5. How can the phrase "It is well" be both honest and faith-filled?
6. What does her persistence in going straight to Elisha teach us about bringing pain to God?
7. How does God's restoration in this story foreshadow His power to bring life out of death?
8. What personal longing or loss in your life do you see reflected in her story?
9. How can her faith journey encourage you to trust God even when hope feels gone?
10. In what ways can you practice generosity like hers in your own daily life?

Story 5: Habakkuk - Wrestling with Justice, Waiting in Faith

1. Why did Habakkuk question God so boldly about injustice?
2. How does this book help us process suffering and unanswered prayers?
3. What can we learn from God's response about His sovereignty over history?
4. Why is faith so central in Habakkuk's message?
5. How can Habakkuk's final prayer shape the way we trust God in hard times?

Have you ever looked at the world and asked, "God, why are You letting this happen?" That's exactly how Habakkuk begins his short but powerful book. He is the prophet who dared to wrestle with God's justice.

His opening words are raw: "How long, Lord, must I call for help, but you do not listen? Or cry out to you, 'Violence!' but you do not save?" (Habakkuk 1:2). It's the cry of someone who feels unheard in the face of chaos.

In Habakkuk's time, Judah was crumbling under corruption. Leaders were unjust, the poor were oppressed, and violence filled the land. From a human perspective, it seemed as though God was silent.

God's answer shocked Habakkuk. Instead of promising immediate relief, He said He was raising the Babylonians, a ruthless empire, to bring judgment on

Judah. To Habakkuk, this seemed even more unfair. How could God use a nation more wicked than Judah to punish His people?

This tension forms the heart of the book: why does God allow evil, and how can He remain just while working through flawed human instruments?

Scholars note that Habakkuk was unique among prophets. Instead of speaking God's words to the people, he spoke the people's questions back to God. His book reads like a dialogue, a conversation full of honesty and wrestling.

Habakkuk didn't hide his confusion. He poured out his doubts. And in doing so, he teaches us that faith isn't pretending to have all the answers, it's bringing our hardest questions to God.

God responded again, this time with a vision: "The righteous will live by faith" (Habakkuk 2:4). This verse becomes a cornerstone of Christian theology, later echoed by Paul in Romans, Galatians, and Hebrews.

God told Habakkuk to write the vision clearly so it could be passed on: His justice may seem delayed, but it is certain. "Though it linger, wait for it; it will certainly come and will not delay" (Habakkuk 2:3).

Here is a lesson in patience. God's timing is not our timing. While we see chaos, He is weaving a bigger story. His plans may seem slow, but they are never late.

God also pronounced woes against the oppressors: greed, exploitation, violence, and idolatry would all be judged. No empire, no matter how strong, escapes His justice.

Habakkuk's perspective began to shift. Though he still didn't fully understand, he realized that God's sovereignty stretched far beyond his immediate circumstances.

In chapter 3, Habakkuk responded not with more complaints but with a prayer of worship. He recalled God's mighty acts in history, how He parted the seas, shook the nations, and delivered His people.

Sometimes, when the present feels unbearable, the best thing we can do is look back at what God has already done. Remembering His faithfulness anchors us in hope.

Habakkuk's final words are some of the most powerful in Scripture: "Though the fig tree does not bud and there are no grapes on the vines... yet I will rejoice in the Lord, I will be joyful in God my Savior" (Habakkuk 3:17-18).

This is faith at its core: rejoicing in God not because circumstances are good, but because God Himself is good.

Habakkuk didn't get every answer he wanted, but he got something better: an unshakable trust in God's character.

His journey moves from complaint to confidence, from questioning to worship. That is the transformation faith brings when we wrestle honestly with God.

For us today, Habakkuk's story speaks into times of injustice, suffering, and delay. It permits us to ask hard questions, but also calls us to anchor ourselves in faith when answers don't come quickly.

Habakkuk shows us that faith doesn't erase questions; it sustains us while we wait for God's greater plan to unfold.

Reflection Questions

1. Why do you think God allowed Habakkuk to voice such raw complaints in Scripture?
2. How does Habakkuk's honesty encourage you in your own prayer life?
3. What does "the righteous will live by faith" mean in your daily walk with God?
4. How do you balance bringing hard questions to God with trusting His plan?
5. What can we learn from God's timing when He said, "Though it linger, wait for it"?
6. How does remembering God's past faithfulness help in present struggles?
7. Why do you think Habakkuk ends his book with worship instead of more questions?
8. How does Habakkuk's journey mirror your own struggles with faith and doubt?
9. What does this story teach us about God's justice over nations and empires today?
10. How can Habakkuk's declaration, "Yet I will rejoice in the Lord," shape your response to trials?

A Personal Message to the Reader

Dear Reader,

By now, you have journeyed with me from the foundations of Christian education to the living stories that shape our understanding of God's ways. You have explored what it means to build faith on covenant truth, to wrestle with questions of justice, and to see how the lives of ordinary men and women became extraordinary testimonies of God's mercy and power.

From Chapter 1, we saw how Christian education is not simply about facts, but about transformation, a lifelong shaping of the mind and spirit toward Christ. In Chapters 2 and 3, we wrestled with the purpose, the methods, and the call to teach faithfully. By Chapter 4, the focus turned more directly to practice and responsibility, reminding us that discipleship is not passive but active.

And now in Chapter 5, we've begun walking through the biblical stories themselves. You have seen Abraham's faith, not perfect but persistent. You have stood with Lot at the gates of Sodom and witnessed both the danger of compromise and the power of intercession. You have watched Hosea love an unfaithful wife as a living picture of God's redeeming love. You have welcomed the Shunammite woman's hospitality and felt her heartbreak turn to joy. And through Habakkuk, you have learned that faith means waiting on God even when answers are slow in coming.

These are not just stories to be studied; they are mirrors held up to our own lives. Abraham's doubts remind us of our own impatience. Lot's choices warn us about how easy it is to drift into compromise. Hosea's obedience challenges us to love with radical grace. The Shunammite woman's faith stirs us to trust God even when life seems unfair. And Habakkuk's bold prayer invites us to bring our questions honestly before God while still declaring, "Yet I will rejoice in the Lord."

I want to pause here and ask you: *What has spoken most to your heart so far? Which story reflects your current season? Where do you see yourself in Abraham's waiting, Lot's hesitation, Hosea's heartbreak, the Shunammite's persistence, or Habakkuk's questions?*

Remember, the goal of these pages is not only to inform your mind but to transform your walk. Education in Christ is not just about knowing, it is about living. My prayer is that what you've read so far has already begun to shape how you see God, how you approach your faith, and how you live out His calling in your daily life.

As we continue forward into the next stories, I encourage you to hold onto the lessons that have resonated with you. Write them down. Pray over them. Share them with someone else. Let these stories not remain on the page but take root in your journey.

God is still writing His story in your life. And just as Abraham, Lot, Hosea, the Shunammite woman, and Habakkuk discovered, His faithfulness is always greater than our weakness.

With gratitude for walking this far with me,
Dr. Rushayne Stewart

Story 6: The Woman at the Well - Living Water and True Worship

1. What cultural barriers made Jesus' conversation with the Samaritan woman so surprising?
2. Why was the woman at the well searching for fulfillment in relationships?
3. What does "living water" mean, and why did Jesus offer it to her?
4. How does this story reveal the heart of true worship?
5. In what ways does the woman's transformation challenge us in our own witness?

Picture the scene: it's noon, the hottest part of the day. A woman approaches Jacob's well in Samaria, carrying her jar. She comes alone, avoiding the stares and whispers of others. She is used to being judged.

She expects silence. Instead, she hears a voice: "Will you give me a drink?" It's Jesus. A Jewish man. A rabbi. To her surprise, He speaks directly to her.

This was shocking. Jews and Samaritans despised one another, and men didn't usually engage women in public. By asking for water, Jesus crossed cultural, gender, and religious barriers in one sentence.

The woman is stunned. "You are a Jew, and I am

a Samaritan woman. How can you ask me for a drink?" (John 4:9). Her tone carries both suspicion and pain; she's not used to kindness.

Jesus replies with an offer beyond her imagination: "If you knew the gift of God and who it is that asks you for a drink, you would have asked him, and he would have given you living water" (John 4:10).

Living water. She doesn't understand yet, but Jesus is pointing to something far deeper than the well. He's talking about eternal satisfaction, the Spirit who quenches the thirst of the soul.

The woman laughs off the idea at first. "Sir, you have nothing to draw with, and the well is deep." Her practical eyes see only the physical water.

Isn't that how we often think? We focus on what's tangible: jobs, money, relationships, forgetting the deeper thirst within us that only God can fill.

Jesus presses further: "Everyone who drinks this water will be thirsty again, but whoever drinks the water I give them will never thirst" (John 4:13-14). He is offering her life itself, grace that satisfies the soul forever.

She responds with eagerness, still half-confused: "Sir, give me this water so that I won't get thirsty and have to keep coming here to draw water."

Then Jesus shifts the conversation: "Go, call your husband and come back." He touches the sore spot of her life, the reason she comes to the well at noon, avoiding others.

"I have no husband," she says quietly. Jesus reveals the

truth: she has had five husbands, and the man she now lives with is not her husband. Her thirst has been for love, but every well she has drawn from has left her empty.

Notice what Jesus does. He exposes her sin without condemning her. He speaks truth, but in a way that invites healing rather than shame.

The woman tries to change the subject, asking about worship: "Our ancestors worshiped on this mountain, but you Jews claim the place we must worship is in Jerusalem."

Jesus answers with one of the deepest truths in Scripture: "A time is coming when true worshipers will worship the Father in the Spirit and in truth" (John 4:23). Worship is not about location, but about relationship.

The woman then says, "I know that Messiah is coming." And Jesus reveals His identity: "I, the one speaking to you, I am he" (John 4:26).

Imagine her heart in that moment. The Messiah she had heard about since childhood was standing before her, speaking directly into her broken life.

She drops her jar, the very reason she came to the well, and runs back to town, telling everyone, "Come, see a man who told me everything I ever did. Could this be the Messiah?" (John 4:29).

The outcast becomes an evangelist. The woman who avoided people now runs toward them with hope. Many in her town believe because of her testimony.

Her story reminds us that Jesus meets us at our wells, at

the places of our shame, loneliness, and need. He offers living water that no relationship, success, or earthly thing can provide. And once we taste it, we cannot help but share it.

Reflection Questions

1. Why was Jesus' request for water so surprising in that culture?
2. What does the woman's life reveal about the ways people search for fulfillment?
3. How does Jesus' offer of "living water" speak to your own needs?
4. Why is it significant that Jesus revealed His identity as Messiah to her first?
5. What does this story teach us about how to share truth without condemnation?
6. How does the woman's transformation challenge you in your own witness?
7. What does "worship in spirit and in truth" mean for your relationship with God?
8. What "jars" (burdens, pursuits, distractions) might you need to leave behind to follow Christ?
9. How can you identify with the woman's experience of being seen and known by Jesus?
10. How does this story encourage you to see others beyond their past and offer them grace?

Story 7: The Disciples of Jesus - Call, Struggle, and Transformation

1. What does it mean to be a disciple of Jesus?
2. How did the first disciples respond to His call?
3. What struggles did they face as they followed Him?
4. How did Jesus transform them from ordinary men into leaders of the church?
5. What lessons about discipleship apply to our lives today?

Discipleship is one of the central themes of the New Testament. To be a disciple is more than being a student; it means being a follower, an apprentice, someone who shapes their entire life around their teacher. For Christians, discipleship means learning from Jesus, living like Jesus, and leading others to Him.

Jesus' call to the first disciples was simple but life-changing: "Come, follow me, and I will make you fishers of men" (Matthew 4:19). With those words, He invited fishermen on the shores of Galilee to leave their nets and join Him in a mission that would change the world.

Think about Peter, Andrew, James, and John. They were ordinary workers, not scholars or leaders. Yet when Jesus called, "At once they left their nets and followed him" (Matthew 4:20). Discipleship always begins with a step of obedience.

Levi (Matthew), the tax collector, was sitting at his booth when Jesus called him. He left everything: his wealth, his position, his comfort, to follow Christ. This reminds us that discipleship may cost us the life we know, but it leads us to the life God intends.

To follow Jesus wasn't glamorous. The disciples walked dusty roads, faced opposition, and often misunderstood His teachings. They argued about who was the greatest. They doubted when storms rose. Peter denied Him. Thomas questioned Him.

Yet discipleship is not about perfection. It's about persistence. Even when they failed, the disciples kept following. Jesus' patience with them shows us that discipleship is a journey of growth, not instant arrival.

Jesus taught them with words and with His life. They watched Him heal the sick, welcome outcasts, and pray to His Father. He didn't just lecture them; He modeled the kingdom of God before their eyes.

At times, His lessons were hard. He said, "Whoever wants to be my disciple must deny themselves and take up their cross daily and follow me" (Luke 9:23). True discipleship means surrender, laying down our will for His.

The disciples also learned that discipleship means mission. Jesus sent them out two by two, giving them authority to heal and proclaim the kingdom. Following Christ wasn't passive; it was active, requiring them to serve.

They struggled to understand His mission. Many expected Him to overthrow Rome and establish political power. But He showed them a different kingdom, a kingdom of humility, sacrifice, and eternal life.

When Jesus was arrested, the disciples scattered. Peter denied Him three times. In those dark hours, it seemed like all was lost. Yet even this failure became part of their discipleship journey, showing them their weakness and their need for grace.

After the resurrection, everything changed. The risen Jesus restored Peter, strengthened Thomas's faith, and gave them the Great Commission: "Go and make disciples of all nations" (Matthew 28:19).

From fearful followers, they became bold witnesses. Empowered by the Holy Spirit at Pentecost, they preached the gospel, healed the sick, and planted the early church. Their transformation proves that discipleship leads to multiplication.

What began with a few fishermen and a tax collector became a global movement. The disciples didn't just learn from Jesus; they carried His mission forward into the world.

So, what is discipleship for us today? It is still the same: answering the call, learning from Jesus, following Him daily, and making more disciples.

Discipleship is not an optional part of Christianity; it is the very heart of it. To believe in Jesus is to follow Him. To follow Him is to be changed by Him. And to be changed by Him is to lead others to Him.

In practical terms, discipleship means spending time with Jesus in prayer and Scripture, living out His teachings in daily life, and walking in community with other believers.

It also means embracing the cost. Following Jesus may mean letting go of comfort, reputation, or control. But as the disciples discovered, the reward is greater than anything left behind.

Just as Jesus was patient with His disciples, He is patient with us. He doesn't expect instant perfection. He calls us to keep walking, keep learning, keep trusting.

The story of the disciples reminds us that God calls ordinary people, transforms them by His Spirit, and uses them to change the world. The same call is extended to us: "Follow me."

Reflection Questions

1. What does the word "disciple" mean, and how does it differ from just being a student?
2. Why do you think the first disciples followed Jesus so quickly?
3. What can we learn from the disciples' failures and struggles?
4. How does Luke 9:23 challenge our understanding of what it means to follow Jesus?
5. What role did mission play in the disciples' growth?
6. How did the resurrection transform their understanding of discipleship?
7. What does the Great Commission mean for us as modern disciples?
8. What daily practices help you grow as a disciple of Jesus?

9. What "nets" or comforts might Jesus be calling you to leave behind?

10. How does this story inspire you to disciple others in your own circle?

Story 8: Biblical Leadership - Servanthood from Moses to Paul

1. What makes leadership "biblical" rather than worldly?
2. How did leaders like Moses, David, and Paul model servant leadership?
3. Why does Scripture emphasize humility and service in leadership?
4. What are the dangers of leadership without accountability to God?
5. How can biblical leadership principles be applied in our churches, workplaces, and families today?

Leadership is often associated with power, authority, and influence. But in Scripture, leadership is defined very differently. Biblical leadership begins with servanthood, rooted in obedience to God and love for others.

Moses is one of the clearest examples. He didn't see himself as a natural leader. When God called him at the burning bush, Moses protested: "Who am I that I should go to Pharaoh?" (Exodus 3:11). Yet God reminded him that leadership is not about self-confidence, but God-confidence.

Moses led Israel not by his own strength but by relying on God. He interceded for the people, pleaded for mercy when they sinned, and carried the burden of their complaints. His story teaches us that leaders are shepherds, not dictators.

But Moses also struggled. His anger at Meribah caused him to strike the rock instead of speaking to it, and as a result, he could not enter the Promised Land. Leaders are held to high accountability because their actions ripple across entire communities.

David's leadership was marked by both triumph and failure. As king, he united Israel, expanded its borders, and established Jerusalem as its center. Yet his sin with Bathsheba and the fallout that followed revealed how personal failures can damage public leadership.

From David, we learn that leaders must not only be courageous but also repentant. Psalm 51 is a testimony that even in failure, true leaders turn back to God in humility.

Moving to the New Testament, Jesus redefined leadership completely. When His disciples argued about greatness, He told them, "The greatest among you will be your servant" (Matthew 23:11). He washed their feet to model what servant leadership looks like.

This is radically different from worldly models. In the world, leaders demand honor; in the kingdom, leaders bow low to lift others.

The apostle Paul carried this principle forward in his ministry. He called himself a "servant of Christ" and described leadership as stewardship, not ownership. He poured himself out like a drink offering for the sake of the gospel.

Paul's letters also show us that leadership is about equipping others. He trained Timothy, Titus, and countless others to carry on the mission. Biblical leadership multiplies; it doesn't hoard authority.

Another theme we see in Scripture is that leaders must lead with vision rooted in God's Word. Proverbs 29:18 says, "Where there is no vision, the people perish." Leadership without direction leaves people wandering.

But true vision is not self-made ambition; it is revelation from God. Moses had a vision of a promised land. Nehemiah had a vision of rebuilding Jerusalem's walls. Paul had a vision of reaching the Gentiles with the gospel.

Biblical leadership also requires courage. Joshua was told repeatedly, "Be strong and courageous" (Joshua 1:6). Leading God's people is not easy; it demands faith to stand firm when others are afraid.

At the same time, leadership is relational. Leaders walk with their people, listen to them, and share in their burdens. Paul described his leadership as being "like a nursing mother" and "like a father" to the Thessalonians (1 Thessalonians 2:7-11).

One of the dangers of leadership is pride. King Saul lost his throne because he feared people more than God and disobeyed His commands. Leaders who put ego above obedience risk losing everything.

This is why Scripture repeatedly calls leaders to humility. James writes, "God opposes the proud but shows favor to the humble" (James 4:6). Humility is not weakness; it is strength under God's control.

Leadership also requires perseverance. Paul endured shipwrecks, beatings, and imprisonment, yet he finished his race faithfully. Leaders must expect trials and keep their eyes on the mission God has given them.

The ultimate model of biblical leadership is Jesus Himself. He led by serving, ruled by sacrificing, and conquered by laying down His life. His cross is the ultimate picture of leadership through love.

Today, whether in the church, workplace, or family, leadership that reflects Christ is desperately needed. We need leaders who will serve, not exploit; who will guide, not manipulate; who will point others to God, not themselves.

Biblical leadership calls each of us, whether we lead many or few, to follow Christ's example. To lead like Jesus is to serve with humility, walk in integrity, and keep God's mission above all else.

Reflection Questions

1. How does Moses' story show that leadership depends more on God's strength than our own?
2. What can we learn from David's failures about accountability in leadership?
3. How did Jesus redefine leadership for His disciples?
4. In what ways did Paul model servant leadership?
5. Why is vision important in leadership, and how can we ensure it comes from God?
6. What dangers of pride in leadership do we see in Saul's story?
7. How do humility and service create stronger leaders?

8. How can perseverance strengthen leaders when they face trials?
9. What lessons from biblical leaders can be applied to your role in church, work, or family?
10. How does Jesus' example of leadership challenge your own approach to influence and service?

Story 9: The Second Coming of Christ - Hope and Urgency

1. What does the Bible teach us about the return of Christ?
2. Why is the Second Coming a source of both hope and urgency for believers?
3. How do Jesus' parables prepare us to live in readiness?
4. What comfort can this promise give us in a world filled with uncertainty?
5. How should the Second Coming shape the way we live today?

Have you ever waited for someone you love to come home? The clock seems slower, your heart beats faster, and you keep checking the door. That sense of anticipation gives us a glimpse of what the Second Coming of Christ means for believers.

The Bible is filled with promises of His return. Jesus said plainly, "And if I go and prepare a place for you, I will come back and take you to be with me" (John 14:3). For Christians, this is not a vague hope; it's a guaranteed reality.

Yet the Second Coming is also a mystery. Jesus Himself said, "But about that day or hour no one knows... only the Father" (Matthew 24:36). We cannot circle a date on the calendar, but we are called to live as though it could be today.

The early church lived with this urgency. They greeted one another with the word "Maranatha" "Come, Lord!" They saw His return not as something far away, but as the heartbeat of their hope.

For us, life can dull that urgency. Bills, routines, and struggles can make eternity feel distant. But every headline of war, injustice, or disaster reminds us that this world is not our final home.

Jesus taught His disciples parables about readiness. In the parable of the ten virgins (Matthew 25), some had oil for their lamps, and some did not. The lesson is clear: we must live prepared, not scrambling at the last minute.

The parable of the talents also reminds us that readiness is not passive. While waiting, we are called to serve faithfully, to use what God has given us for His kingdom.

The Second Coming brings hope for those who suffer. Paul wrote, "We eagerly await a Savior... who, by the power that enables him... will transform our lowly bodies so that they will be like his glorious body" (Philippians 3:20-21).

For the grieving, it means reunion. For the oppressed, it means justice. For the weary, it means rest. Christ's return answers every ache of the human heart.

But it also brings accountability. Jesus said He will return like a thief in the night (1 Thessalonians 5:2). We cannot predict it, but we must be ready, living in holiness, not half-hearted compromise.

Sometimes people fear the Second Coming. But for believers, it is not meant to produce fear; it is meant to bring hope. It's the promise of homecoming.

That said, it is a warning to those who reject Christ. Revelation describes His coming as both salvation and judgment. To follow Christ is to be ready with joy. To reject Him is to face His return unprepared.

Personally, I find this truth both comforting and challenging. Comforting because no matter what chaos swirls in the world, I know Christ is coming to set things right. Challenging because it calls me to examine my own walk daily.

It makes me ask: am I living with lamps full of oil, or am I distracted by temporary things? Am I investing my life in God's kingdom, or wasting it on what will not last?

The Second Coming is not just about the end of time; it's about how we live in the meantime. Every act of kindness, every prayer whispered, every seed of the gospel planted carries eternal weight.

Peter wrote, "Since everything will be destroyed in this way, what kind of people ought you to be? You ought to live holy and godly lives" (2 Peter 3:11). Our readiness is reflected in our daily choices.

Waiting for Christ doesn't mean sitting idle; it means working, loving, serving, and shining as lights in a dark world.

Like a bride waiting for her groom, the church is called to live with anticipation. Hope should color how we see everything: our trials, our victories, and even our ordinary days.

The cry of the early church is still ours: "Amen. Come, Lord Jesus" (Revelation 22:20). Until that day, we live by faith, holding fast to His promise.

The Second Coming reminds us of this truth: history is not random, our struggles are not wasted, and our future is secure. Christ is coming again. That is our hope, and that is our call to live ready.

Reflection Questions

1. What does Jesus' promise in John 14:3 mean to you personally?
2. Why is it important that no one knows the exact day or hour of His return?
3. How do Jesus' parables about readiness challenge your daily life?
4. What aspects of Christ's return bring you the most comfort?
5. What aspects stir you to urgency or self-examination?
6. How do you balance living in the present while preparing for eternity?
7. What does 2 Peter 3:11 teach us about holy living in light of the Second Coming?
8. How can you encourage others with the hope of Christ's return?
9. In what ways does the promise of His return help you endure trials today?
10. If Christ returned today, what would you want Him to find you doing?

A Personal Message to the Reader

Dear Reader,

By now, you've traveled through a wide landscape of Scripture. You've seen covenant promises, warnings against compromise, portraits of mercy, and glimpses of hope that reach all the way to Christ's return. These stories are not random; they are stepping stones, guiding us from God's covenant with Abraham to the fulfillment of His kingdom through Jesus Christ.

What strikes me most as I reflect on these journeys is how patient God is with His people. He doesn't abandon Abraham when he falters, or the disciples when they stumble, or even His people when they cry out like Habakkuk. Instead, He draws near, teaches, restores, and leads them forward. That same patience is extended to you and me.

The Second Coming reminds us that history itself is moving toward God's great conclusion. Yet between the covenant made long ago and the kingdom still to come, there is our present moment, the space where we choose how to live, who to follow, and what legacy to leave.

So I ask you, as a fellow traveler on this road: *How are these stories shaping the way you walk with God right now?* Are they challenging you to trust Him more deeply, to obey Him more fully, or to share His love more boldly?

We are not simply students of these stories; we are participants in the same story God is still writing. Let what you've read so far inspire you to live with greater courage, deeper humility, and stronger faith. And as we turn to the next accounts, Joseph, Ruth, David, Jonah, Esther, and the Prodigal Son, be ready to see yourself once again in their struggles and victories, and to hear God's voice speaking through them to you.

With hope for the journey ahead,
Apostle Dr. Rushayne Stewart

Story 10: Joseph - From Pit to Palace

1. How can God use painful experiences to shape our destiny?
2. What does Joseph's story teach us about betrayal and forgiveness?
3. How did Joseph remain faithful in temptation and adversity?
4. What role does God's providence play when life seems unfair?
5. How does Joseph's rise from pit to palace encourage us in our own struggles?

Joseph's life begins with dreams. At just seventeen, he dreamed of greatness, sheaves bowing down to his sheaf, stars bowing down to his star. His dreams weren't just youthful fantasies; they were glimpses of God's plan. However, dreams often stir jealousy. Joseph's brothers hated him because he was their father's favorite, and his coat of many colors only fueled their envy.

One day, when Joseph came to check on them in the fields, their jealousy boiled over. They stripped him of his coat, threw him into a pit, and debated his fate. Betrayal doesn't always come from strangers; sometimes it comes from those closest to us.

Instead of killing him, they sold him to Midianite traders for twenty pieces of silver. Imagine Joseph's fear as he was carried away, his cries echoing while his brothers turned their backs.

Betrayal turned into slavery. Joseph was sold in Egypt to Potiphar, an officer of Pharaoh. Yet even in captivity, "the Lord was with Joseph" (Genesis 39:2). This truth is a thread through his entire story: God's presence is greater than our circumstances.

Joseph served faithfully in Potiphar's house. His integrity and diligence earned trust, and he was put in charge of everything. But faithfulness doesn't exempt us from trials.

Potiphar's wife desired him and tried to seduce him. Joseph refused, saying, "How then could I do such a wicked thing and sin against God?" (Genesis 39:9). His faith was stronger than his desire.

Angered by rejection, she falsely accused him of assault. Potiphar believed her, and Joseph was thrown into prison. From favored son to slave, from trusted servant to prisoner, it must have felt like his life was unraveling.

Yet again, "the Lord was with Joseph" (Genesis 39:21). Even in prison, Joseph's faithfulness shone. He interpreted the dreams of Pharaoh's cupbearer and baker, correctly predicting their fates.

Still, the cupbearer forgot him for two years. Imagine the loneliness of waiting, knowing your gift, yet feeling forgotten. Have you ever been overlooked despite doing right? Joseph knew that pain.

Then came the turning point. Pharaoh himself had troubling dreams; seven fat cows devoured by seven thin ones, seven full heads of grain swallowed by seven thin ones. No one could interpret them.

Suddenly, the cupbearer remembered Joseph. Brought before Pharaoh, Joseph declared, "I cannot do it... but God will give Pharaoh the answer he desires" (Genesis 41:16). His humility pointed to God, not himself.

Joseph interpreted the dreams: seven years of plenty would be followed by seven years of famine. He advised Pharaoh to store grain during the years of abundance.

Impressed, Pharaoh made Joseph second in command over Egypt. The prisoner became a prince in one day. This is God's providence. He can turn pits into palaces.

During the famine, Joseph's brothers came to Egypt seeking food. They bowed before him, fulfilling his childhood dreams. But instead of revenge, Joseph tested their hearts and eventually revealed himself with tears.

"I am your brother Joseph, the one you sold into Egypt! And now, do not be distressed... because it was to save lives that God sent me ahead of you" (Genesis 45:4–5). Forgiveness triumphed over bitterness.

Joseph's perspective is one of the greatest lessons in Scripture: "You meant evil against me, but God meant it for good" (Genesis 50:20). His pain was real, but God's purpose was greater.

Think about that for your own life. What pits have you been thrown into? What betrayals have left scars? Joseph's story tells us that God can weave even the darkest threads into His greater plan.

Joseph saved not only Egypt but also his family, preserving the line that would lead to Christ. His personal trials became part of God's global redemption story.

From pit to palace, Joseph teaches us to trust God's providence, to remain faithful in temptation, and to forgive those who wrong us. His life is proof that nothing, not betrayal, not suffering, not waiting, can stop God's plan.

Reflection Questions

1. What do Joseph's dreams reveal about God's ability to guide our future?
2. How does Joseph's betrayal by his brothers speak to the pain of family conflict?
3. Why is Joseph's refusal of Potiphar's wife such an important moment of integrity?
4. How did Joseph remain faithful even when falsely accused and imprisoned?
5. What does Joseph's waiting in prison teach us about patience and God's timing?
6. How did Joseph's humility before Pharaoh show true leadership?
7. Why was forgiveness such a key part of Joseph's story?
8. What does Genesis 50:20 teach us about God's providence in our own lives?
9. How can Joseph's story encourage you when you feel overlooked or betrayed?
10. In what ways does Joseph's journey point forward to Jesus, who also suffered to bring salvation?

Story 12: David and Bathsheba - Sin, Repentance, and God's Mercy

1. What led King David, a man after God's heart, to fall into serious sin?
2. How does this story reveal the danger of temptation and compromise?
3. What role did the prophet Nathan play in confronting David?
4. How does David's repentance model true confession before God?
5. What does this story teach us about God's mercy and the consequences of sin?

King David's story is filled with victories, courage, and deep faith. He was the shepherd boy who faced Goliath, the psalmist who poured out his heart to God, the leader who united Israel. Yet even the strongest of believers can fall.

One spring, when kings went off to war, David stayed behind in Jerusalem. That decision to step away from his duty set the stage for disaster. From the rooftop of his palace, he saw her: a beautiful woman bathing. Her name was Bathsheba, the wife of Uriah, one of David's own soldiers.

Desire clouded judgment. Instead of turning away, David sent for her. Their meeting led to adultery. What began with a lingering look became a life-altering sin.

Soon Bathsheba sent word: she was pregnant. Panic set

in. David tried to cover it up by bringing Uriah home, hoping he would spend time with his wife. But Uriah, loyal to his fellow soldiers, refused.

Desperation grew into darker sin. David arranged for Uriah to be placed at the front lines of battle, where he was killed. Adultery led to deception, and deception led to murder.

What David tried to hide, God saw clearly. Scripture says, "But the thing David had done displeased the Lord" (2 Samuel 11:27). Sin may be hidden from people, but never from God.

God sent the prophet Nathan to confront David. Nathan told a parable about a rich man who stole a poor man's only lamb. David was furious at the injustice until Nathan declared, "You are the man!"

In that moment, David's heart was pierced. He realized the depth of his sin. Unlike Saul, who excused his failures, David confessed: "I have sinned against the Lord" (2 Samuel 12:13).

His confession is captured in Psalm 51, a raw and powerful prayer: "Have mercy on me, O God... blot out my transgressions... Create in me a pure heart, O God" (Psalm 51:1,10).

True repentance isn't just admitting to wrong; it's turning back to God with humility and a broken heart. David's prayer shows us that God values honesty over excuses.

Nathan assured David that God had forgiven him, but forgiveness did not erase consequences. The child born to Bathsheba died, and David's household would face ongoing turmoil. Sin has ripple effects.

Yet even in judgment, mercy was present. Later, Bathsheba bore another son, named Solomon, who would become Israel's wisest king and continue the royal line that led to Jesus. **Out of brokenness, God still brought redemption.**

David's story reminds us that even people of great faith can fall if they let their guard down. Temptation often comes when we are idle, unaccountable, or careless.

It also reminds us that God's grace is greater than our worst failures. David was restored, not because he deserved it, but because he humbled himself before God.

Psalm 32, another song of David, reflects his joy after forgiveness: "Blessed is the one whose transgressions are forgiven, whose sins are covered" (Psalm 32:1). Forgiveness lifted the weight of guilt from his soul.

For us, the story warns of the seriousness of sin, but it also offers hope. No sin is too great for God's mercy when we come in true repentance.

It teaches us that sin carries consequences, but grace offers restoration. God does not abandon His children when they fall; He lifts them when they confess.

David's life after this failure was not free of struggle, but he continued to walk with God. His legacy was not erased; he is still remembered as "a man after God's own heart" (Acts 13:22).

The story of David and Bathsheba is both sobering and encouraging: sobering because of how easily sin can entangle, encouraging because of how deep God's mercy reaches.

Reflection Questions
1. Why was David's decision to stay behind in Jerusalem so significant?
2. How does this story illustrate the danger of letting temptation grow unchecked?
3. What does David's attempt to cover up his sin reveal about human nature?
4. How did Nathan's parable effectively confront David?
5. What makes David's repentance in Psalm 51 a model for us today?
6. Why did forgiveness not remove the consequences of David's sin?
7. How does the birth of Solomon show God's ability to bring redemption out of brokenness?
8. What warnings from David's failure can help us guard against temptation?
9. How do David's psalms of repentance encourage you in times of failure?
10. What does this story teach us about God's balance of justice and mercy?

Story 13: Jonah - Running from God and the Call to Obedience

1. Why did Jonah run from God's call to preach in Nineveh?
2. What does Jonah's story teach us about obedience and surrender?
3. How does God use storms and trials to bring us back to Him?
4. What do we learn about God's compassion through His dealings with Nineveh?
5. In what ways do we sometimes resemble Jonah in our own lives?

Jonah's story begins with a clear command: "Go to the great city of Nineveh and preach against it, because its wickedness has come up before me" (Jonah 1:2). God gave Jonah a mission, but Jonah didn't want it.

Nineveh was the capital of Assyria, Israel's enemy. Known for cruelty and violence, the Assyrians were feared and despised. Jonah didn't want them saved; instead, he wanted them judged.

Instead of going to Nineveh, Jonah went the opposite direction. He boarded a ship headed for Tarshish, as far from God's command as possible. Have you ever run the other way when God called you to something hard?

But God pursued him. A great storm arose, and the sailors panicked. They cried out to their gods, but nothing helped. Meanwhile, Jonah was asleep below deck, trying to escape not only his mission but also his conscience.

The sailors cast lots, and the lot fell on Jonah. He admitted, "I know that it is my fault that this great storm has come upon you" (Jonah 1:12). **Disobedience doesn't just affect us; it affects those around us.**

Reluctantly, the sailors threw Jonah into the sea, and immediately the storm calmed. The sailors, struck with awe, offered sacrifices to the Lord. Even in Jonah's rebellion, God's glory was revealed.

But Jonah wasn't finished. God provided a great fish to swallow him, and Jonah spent three days and nights inside its belly. Alone in darkness, he prayed.

His prayer in Jonah 2 is filled with desperation and hope: "From the depths of the grave I called for help, and you listened to my cry" (Jonah 2:2). Even when we run, God hears us when we cry out.

The fish spat Jonah out onto dry land, and God gave him a second chance: "Go to the great city of Nineveh and proclaim to it the message I give you" (Jonah 3:2). God doesn't give up on His purposes, nor does he give up on us.

This time, Jonah obeyed. He entered Nineveh and preached a simple but urgent message: "Forty more days and Nineveh will be overturned" (Jonah 3:4).

To his shock, the people listened. From the king to the poorest, they fasted, repented, and cried out to God for mercy. The king declared, "Let everyone call urgently on God. Let them give up their evil ways" (Jonah 3:8).

God saw their repentance and relented. He spared the

city. This should have been a victory, but Jonah was furious. He didn't want mercy for Nineveh; he wanted wrath.

Jonah sat outside the city, sulking. He prayed, "Isn't this what I said, Lord, when I was still at home? That is why I tried to forestall by fleeing to Tarshish. I knew that you are a gracious and compassionate God" (Jonah 4:2).

Think about that, Jonah was angry at God's mercy. His heart was harder than the Ninevites'. Sometimes we resist grace because it offends our sense of justice.

God patiently taught Jonah through a plant that grew to shade him, then withered. Jonah cared more for the plant than for the thousands of people in Nineveh.

God's closing words pierce the heart: "Should I not have concern for the great city of Nineveh, in which there are more than a hundred and twenty thousand people…?" (Jonah 4:11).

The story ends abruptly, with Jonah still wrestling. The Bible doesn't tell us his final response, leaving the question hanging for us: Will we align our hearts with God's compassion, or will we cling to our grudges?

Jonah's story is more than a tale of a runaway prophet and a big fish. It's about God's relentless mercy for nations, for cities, for individuals, even for stubborn prophets.

It shows us that God doesn't just call us to obedience for His sake; He calls us for the sake of others. Someone's salvation may depend on our willingness to obey.

Ultimately, Jonah points us to Christ, who also spent three days in the depths, but unlike Jonah, Jesus obeyed perfectly, giving His life so that mercy could reach us all.

Reflection Questions

1. Why did Jonah resist God's call to preach in Nineveh?
2. What does Jonah's flight to Tarshish reveal about human reluctance to obey God?
3. How does the storm at sea show the consequences of disobedience?
4. What do Jonah's prayers in the fish's belly teach us about repentance?
5. Why do you think Nineveh responded so quickly to Jonah's message?
6. Why was Jonah angry at God's compassion for Nineveh?
7. How does the plant in Jonah 4 illustrate God's lesson to Jonah?
8. What does Jonah's unfinished ending invite us to consider about our own hearts?
9. How do you see God's mercy in your own life when you've resisted Him?
10. What steps of obedience might God be calling you to take today?

Story 14: The Prodigal Son - Grace, Forgiveness, and the Father's Love

1. Why is the parable of the prodigal son one of Jesus' most powerful teachings?
2. How does the younger son's journey reflect our own struggles with sin and pride?
3. What does the father's response teach us about God's heart toward repentant sinners?
4. Why is the older brother's reaction important to the story?
5. How does this parable speak to forgiveness, restoration, and grace in our own lives?

Jesus told the story of a man with two sons to illustrate the heart of God. It is not just the tale of one family; it is a mirror for every family, every sinner, and every heart longing for home.

The younger son shocked his father with a bold request: "Father, give me my share of the estate" (Luke 15:12). In that culture, this was like wishing his father dead. He wanted an inheritance without a relationship. Just like many of us who want to inherit heaven and glory without having a relationship with God.

The father divided the property, and the younger son left for a distant country. With pockets full and pride high, he chased pleasure, wasting everything on wild living.

When the money ran out, so did his friends. A famine struck, and the once-proud son found himself feeding pigs, an unthinkable job for a Jew. Hunger gnawed at his stomach, and shame gnawed at his heart.

He longed to eat the pigs' food. That's when reality hit: even his father's servants lived better than this.

"I will set out and go back to my father," he resolved. He rehearsed a speech: "Father, I have sinned against heaven and against you. I am no longer worthy to be called your son; make me like one of your hired servants" (Luke 15:18-19).

With weary steps, he began the long walk home, each step weighed with guilt and fear. Would his father reject him? Would the door be slammed in his face?

But while he was still a long way off, his father saw him. The father had been watching, waiting. Compassion flooded his heart, and he ran to his son, embracing him before the boy could finish his speech.

The son tried to confess, but the father interrupted with joy: "Quick! Bring the best robe, put a ring on his finger and sandals on his feet. Bring the fattened calf and kill it. Let's feast and celebrate" (Luke 15:22-23).

The robe, ring, and sandals weren't just gifts; they were symbols of restored sonship. The father didn't treat him as a servant but welcomed him back as a beloved son.

The celebration began, but not everyone was happy. The older brother, hearing music and dancing, grew angry. He had been faithful, obedient, and hardworking, yet he felt overlooked.

"All these years I've been slaving for you and never

disobeyed your orders. Yet you never gave me even a young goat so I could celebrate with my friends" (Luke 15:29). His words revealed resentment, a heart that served but didn't rest in love.

The father gently replied, "My son, you are always with me, and everything I have is yours" (Luke 15:31). But he reminded him why they celebrated: "This brother of yours was dead and is alive again; he was lost and is found" (Luke 15:32).

The parable ends without telling us if the older brother joined the feast. The story leaves us with a question: Will we share in God's joy when the lost are found, or will we withhold grace?

This story is not only about a wayward son, it's about all of us. At some point, we've all wandered, squandered, or harbored resentment.

The father represents God, whose love waits, watches, and runs toward us when we turn back to Him. His grace interrupts our guilt with restoration.

The younger son represents those who run far from God, chasing fulfillment in the world but finding emptiness instead.

The older son represents those who stay outwardly faithful but inwardly bitter, forgetting that relationship with the Father is the greatest gift of all.

The story shows us that grace is undeserved, forgiveness is complete, and God's love is extravagant. He doesn't just tolerate repentant sinners; He celebrates their return.

The parable of the prodigal son is an invitation to every

reader: whether you're far away or close but resentful, the Father's arms are open. The feast is waiting. Will you come in?

Reflection Questions (After Reading)
1. What does the younger son's request for inheritance reveal about his heart?
2. How does his journey to the pigsty illustrate the emptiness of life without God?
3. What do the father's actions teach us about God's love and forgiveness?
4. Why do the robe, ring, and sandals matter in restoring the Son?
5. How does the older brother's resentment mirror struggles in our own hearts?
6. What does the father's response to the older brother teach us about grace?
7. How does this parable challenge both "wanderers" and "workers"?
8. Which character, father, younger son, or older brother, do you most relate to right now?
9. How does this story deepen your understanding of God's grace in Christ?
10. What step can you take today to embrace the Father's love more fully?

Grace and Mercy - God's Twins of Love

Grace and mercy are often spoken of together in Scripture, and for good reason: they are like twins, inseparable and complete only when held side by side. Grace is God giving us what we do not deserve. Mercy is God withholding what we do deserve. Together, they reveal the fullness of His love.

The apostle Paul reminds us, "For it is by grace you have been saved, through faith, and this is not from yourselves, it is the gift of God" (Ephesians 2:8). Grace is God's unearned favor, lavished upon us in Christ. We could never work for it, never buy it, never repay it. It is a gift freely given.

At the same time, Scripture tells us, "The Lord is compassionate and gracious, slow to anger, abounding in love. He will not always accuse, nor will He harbor His anger forever; He does not treat us as our sins deserve or repay us according to our iniquities" (Psalm 103:8-10). This is mercy. God does not give us the judgment we rightfully deserve.

Grace gives us salvation. Mercy spares us from condemnation. Grace takes us to places we could never reach. Mercy pulls us back from the punishment we had earned. One without the other would be incomplete, but together, they display God's heart.

The cross of Jesus Christ is the ultimate picture of both grace and mercy. At the cross, mercy triumphed over judgment: our sins were placed upon Christ, so we would not bear them. At the same time, grace was poured out: we received adoption, forgiveness, and eternal life through Him.

Titus 3:5-7 says it clearly: "He saved us, not because

of righteous things we had done, but because of His mercy. He saved us through the washing of rebirth and renewal by the Holy Spirit, whom He poured out on us generously through Jesus Christ our Savior, so that, having been justified by His grace, we might become heirs having the hope of eternal life."

What God shows us, He also calls us to show others. Jesus taught, "Be merciful, just as your Father is merciful" (Luke 6:36). And Paul exhorts us to live in grace: "Let your conversation be always full of grace, seasoned with salt, so that you may know how to answer everyone" (Colossians 4:6).

We cannot claim to have received God's grace and mercy and refuse to extend them to others. Forgiven people forgive. Loved people love. Those who have been shown patience must show patience. To live in grace and mercy is to reflect the very nature of God.

Grace and mercy go hand in hand because they are both rooted in God's character. Exodus 34:6 describes Him as "The Lord, the Lord, the compassionate and gracious God, slow to anger, abounding in love and faithfulness." Compassion, mercy, and grace are not what He occasionally does; they are who He is.

So let us live as people of grace and mercy. Let us forgive when wronged, show kindness when hurt, and offer compassion when others fall short. The same God who meets us daily with mercy (Lamentations 3:22–23) and grace (Hebrews 4:16) calls us to extend His love to the world.

When we practice grace and mercy, we mirror the heart of Christ. And in doing so, we become living testimonies of His gospel, the good news that though we were undeserving, God loved us, spared us, and lifted us by His grace and mercy, forever twin gifts of His love.

CHAPTER 6: DOCTRINE

The Meaning of Doctrine

The word *doctrine* simply means "teaching." In Scripture, doctrine refers to the truths God has revealed and the church is called to preserve, teach, and live by. Paul told Timothy, "Watch your life and doctrine closely. Persevere in them, because if you do, you will save both yourself and your hearers" (1 Timothy 4:16). Doctrine is not human opinion; it is the faithful handing down of God's truth from one generation to the next.

Doctrine matters because what we believe shapes how we live. Right doctrine leads to right living, while false teaching leads people astray. That's why the apostles were devoted to "the apostles' doctrine and fellowship, in the breaking of bread and in prayers" (Acts 2:42). Doctrine is not just a set of dry statements; it is the foundation of discipleship and Christian growth.

Historically, the church has had to wrestle with questions of doctrine whenever confusion or false teaching arose. The early believers asked: Who is Jesus? What does it mean that He is the Son of God? How is the Holy Spirit related to the Father and the Son? Each generation sought to faithfully explain what Scripture already taught. Doctrine, then, is the church's effort to articulate clearly what God has made known in His Word.

Doctrine also unites believers across cultures and time. When Christians confess the same truths, the lordship of Jesus, the authority of Scripture, and the saving power of the cross, we are bound together as one body. Doctrinal statements like the creeds of the early church or the confessions of later generations were written not to divide, but to preserve unity in truth.

Finally, doctrine is practical. It teaches us who God is, who we are, and how we are to live in the world. It protects us from error, strengthens us in trials, and gives us hope for the future. Sound doctrine is like an anchor; it keeps the church steady in the midst of cultural storms and personal struggles. Without doctrine, faith becomes vague and unstable; with doctrine, it becomes rooted and fruitful.

The Godhead in Scripture (Matthew 28:19)

When Christians speak of the Godhead, they are referring to the fullness of God's nature, who He is as revealed in Scripture. The apostle Paul uses this term in Acts 17:29 (KJV), declaring that the Godhead is not like gold or silver shaped by human design. Instead, the Godhead is the eternal, living God, revealed through His Word and His works.

One of the clearest expressions of the Godhead appears in Jesus' Great Commission: "Go therefore and make disciples of all nations, baptizing them **in the name** of the Father and of the Son and of the Holy Spirit" (Matthew 28:19). This verse ties together discipleship, mission, and identity with the very being of God.

Notice the language: Jesus commands baptism "in the

name" (singular), not "names" (plural). Yet three are listed: Father, Son, and Holy Spirit. This grammatical detail shows unity (one God) and diversity (three persons). The oneness of God is never compromised, yet His threefold self-revelation is made explicit.

For early Christians, Matthew 28:19 wasn't just a formula; it was a declaration of the God they worshiped and followed. To be baptized into the name of the Father, Son, and Holy Spirit was to enter into the very life of God Himself.

Historical evidence supports that this triadic baptismal formula was used very early. The *Didache* (a first–second century church manual) instructs: "Baptize in the name of the Father, and of the Son, and of the Holy Spirit" (Didache 7:1). This mirrors Matthew's Gospel, showing that the early church took these words literally.

Some modern critics have suggested Matthew 28:19 may have been expanded later. However, leading textual scholars point out that there are no manuscript variants omitting the triadic phrase. Every known Greek copy of Matthew includes it. In addition, early sources like the Didache and the writings of church fathers confirm its use.

This consistency across texts and traditions makes a strong case for authenticity. The triadic formula was not invented centuries later; it was present in the very earliest practices of the church.

Across the New Testament, the Father, Son, and Spirit consistently work together. The Father sends the Son into the world out of love (John 3:16). The Son promises to send the Spirit as Comforter and Teacher (John 14:26; 15:26). And Paul blesses believers with "the grace of the Lord Jesus Christ, the love of God, and the fellowship of the Holy Spirit" (2 Corinthians 13:14).

These patterns show that Christian faith from the beginning was relational and triadic. Believers experienced God not in isolated parts but in the unity of Father, Son, and Spirit.

Importantly, this confession did not deny the Jewish conviction of one God (Deuteronomy 6:4, the Shema). Early Christians did not abandon monotheism; rather, they came to understand that the one God had revealed Himself fully through Jesus and by the Spirit.

Matthew 28:19 thus reveals both continuity and newness. Continuity, because God is still one; newness, because His inner life is disclosed through the Father's mission, the Son's sacrifice, and the Spirit's presence.

The Godhead can also be seen at work in Jesus' baptism (Matthew 3:16-17). There, the Son is baptized, the Spirit descends like a dove, and the Father's voice declares, "This is my beloved Son." The scene is profoundly triadic, showing unity in diversity.

In the Gospel of John, the relationship between Father, Son, and Spirit is further explained. The Son is sent by the Father (John 5:19-23), yet is one with Him (John 10:30). The Spirit is sent by both the Father and the Son to guide believers (John 14:26; 15:26).

The book of Acts also reflects this unity. At Pentecost (Acts 2), the Father's promise (Joel 2:28), the Son's exaltation, and the Spirit's outpouring all converge. The mission of the church is born out of the Godhead's action.

Paul's letters frequently reference Father, Son, and Spirit in close association. In Ephesians 4:4-6, he writes: "There is one body and one Spirit... one Lord, one faith, one baptism; one God and Father of all." Again, unity and diversity are affirmed together.

The Godhead, then, is not a philosophical invention but a biblical reality. Theologians later coined the word Trinity to describe what was already lived and confessed by the church. The language developed, but the worship and practice were in place from the beginning.

Understanding the Godhead is not merely intellectual; it is deeply practical. To be baptized into the triune name means to live under the Father's love, the Son's grace, and the Spirit's fellowship. It means our identity as Christians is grounded in God's own life.

It also shapes prayer and worship. We pray to the Father, through the Son, in the Spirit. We worship God in His fullness, not separating His persons nor confusing them, but honoring Him as one God revealed in three.

For believers today, the Godhead is both mystery and invitation. Mystery, because we can never fully comprehend how God is one yet three. Invitation, because we are welcomed into a relationship with the living God who is love in Himself.

In the end, Matthew 28:19 anchors us in the truth that God's mission, salvation, and identity are inseparable from His triune life. The Godhead is not a doctrine to be filed away; it is the reality of the God we worship, the God who calls us, and the God who walks with us every day.

The Doctrine of the Trinity

The word *Trinity* does not appear in the Bible, yet the concept became central to Christian faith because it describes the way Scripture reveals God. The term comes from the Latin *Trinitas*, used by Tertullian in the early third century, to capture the biblical reality of one God in three persons.

The church did not invent the Trinity; it discovered it by reflecting on the biblical witness. Christians worshiped one God, yet confessed Jesus as Lord and experienced the power of the Spirit. To remain faithful to Scripture, the early church had to articulate how these realities fit together.

In the second century, theologians like Justin Martyr spoke of the Logos (the Word, Jesus Christ) as eternally with God and active in creation (John 1:1-3). This showed that Christians already believed in the divine status of Jesus long before the word "Trinity" was coined.

Tertullian of Carthage (c. 200 AD) is the first writer we know to use the word *Trinitas*. He described God as "one substance, three persons" (*una substantia, tres personae*), giving language that would shape later doctrine.

This language arose in response to errors. Some claimed Jesus was merely human and later adopted as God (adoptionism). Others, like Sabellius, argued that Father, Son, and Spirit were simply roles or modes of the one God (modalism). The church rejected both extremes, affirming that the Son and Spirit are truly distinct yet fully God.

The third century brought growing clarity, but also new controversies. Arius, a priest in Alexandria, taught that the Son was not eternal but created by the Father before the world. His slogan was: "There was a time when the Son was not."

The church responded at the Council of Nicaea in 325 AD. Over 300 bishops gathered and confessed that the Son is *homoousios* of the same substance, with the Father. This was a turning point: Jesus Christ was declared fully God, not a creature.

But debates continued. Some argued that the Spirit was lesser than the Father and Son. The church wrestled with how to speak of three without sliding into tritheism (three gods) or collapsing into one person.

The Cappadocian Fathers, Basil the Great, Gregory of Nazianzus, and Gregory of Nyssa, helped resolve this tension. They taught that God is one essence *(ousia)* in three persons *(hypostases)*. This formula became the heart of orthodox Trinitarian doctrine.

In 381 AD, the Council of Constantinople affirmed the full divinity of the Holy Spirit, completing the Nicene faith. The Spirit, like the Son, is not created but proceeds eternally from the Father (and, in Western tradition, from the Son as well).

From this point on, the doctrine of the Trinity became a standard confession of Christian faith, expressed in creeds such as the Nicene Creed, the Athanasian Creed, and later Protestant confessions.

Importantly, the Trinity was not just abstract theology; it shaped worship and prayer. Christians prayed to the Father, through the Son, in the Spirit. Baptism and blessing were administered in the triune name. Doctrine flowed from devotion.

The Trinity also reveals something profound about God's nature: that God is love (1 John 4:8). Love requires relationship, and within the Godhead, love is eternal. The Father loves the Son, the Son loves the Father, and the Spirit is the bond of that love.

This means God did not create the world because He was lonely; He already had perfect fellowship within Himself. Creation was an overflow of divine love, not a remedy for divine lack.

The Trinity also grounds salvation. The Father planned it, the Son accomplished it on the cross, and the Spirit applies it to our hearts. Each person of the Trinity is fully involved, showing that our salvation is truly God's work from start to finish.

In missions, the Trinity is the sending God. The Father sent the Son, the Son sent the Spirit, and now the Spirit sends the church. Our mission is a continuation of the triune God's mission in the world.

Throughout history, heresies often returned in new forms. Modern groups have sometimes denied the Trinity, claiming it to be unbiblical. Yet the testimony of Scripture and centuries of worship affirm its truth: the Trinity is the church's faithful interpretation of the Bible's witness.

The Trinity also has ethical implications. Just as the three persons live in unity, Christians are called to live in unity with one another. The church is meant to reflect the relational harmony of Father, Son, and Spirit.

Ultimately, the Trinity is a mystery. No analogy, whether water/ice/steam or roles like father/son/husband, can fully capture it. But mystery does not mean contradiction. It means God is greater than human categories, yet He has truly revealed Himself.

To confess the Trinity is to confess the God of Scripture: one God in three persons, eternal, loving, and saving. It is not a philosophical puzzle but the heartbeat of Christian faith. To worship the Trinity is to worship the God who is Father, Son, and Holy Spirit, forever one, forever true.

Oneness and the Apostolic/Pentecostal Doctrine (Acts 2:38)

Among modern Christian movements, the Oneness or Apostolic Pentecostal tradition stands out for its emphasis on the name of Jesus in baptism and the unity of God. Rooted in the revival fires of early 20th-century Pentecostalism, Oneness believers see themselves as returning to the simplicity and power of the New Testament church.

The foundation text is Acts 2:38. After Peter's sermon at Pentecost, the people asked what they should do. His answer was clear: "Repent, and be baptized every one of you in the name of Jesus Christ for the remission of sins, and you will receive the gift of the Holy Spirit."

For Apostolic Pentecostals, this verse contains the full gospel response: repentance, water baptism in Jesus' name, and Spirit baptism with evidence of speaking in tongues, as described in Acts 2.

They note that throughout Acts, baptism is consistently described as being performed "in the name of Jesus" (Acts 8:16; 10:48; 19:5). For them, this repetition shows the apostles obeyed Matthew 28:19 by invoking the name of Jesus, the revealed name of Father, Son, and Spirit.

Oneness theology emphasizes the absolute oneness of God. Drawing from Deuteronomy 6:4-"Hear, O Israel: The Lord our God, the Lord is one" they reject the idea of three co-equal persons in favor of one God who revealed Himself in different ways.

Jesus, according to this view, is the full manifestation of God. He is the Father in creation, the Son in redemption, and the Spirit in regeneration. These are not separate persons, but different roles or manifestations of the one true God.

This perspective is often summarized as "Jesus is the name of the Father, Son, and Spirit." Thus, when believers are baptized in Jesus' name, they are obeying Matthew 28:19, because the singular "name" is revealed as Jesus.

Oneness teachers point out that in Colossians 2:9, Paul declares, "In Christ all the fullness of the Godhead dwells bodily." For them, this verse proves that everything about God is found in Jesus.

They also emphasize Philippians 2:9-11: God gave Jesus the name above every name, and at that name every knee will bow. Salvation, they argue, must therefore be identified explicitly with the name of Jesus.

Historically, the Oneness movement gained traction after the 1913 Arroyo Seco Camp Meeting in California, when evangelist R.E. McAlister preached on Acts 2:38 and baptism in Jesus' name. From there, many Pentecostals embraced this understanding, forming what became known as the "Jesus' Name" movement.

Leaders like **Frank J. Ewart** and later **David K. Bernard** provided theological frameworks for Oneness belief, arguing that it aligns with apostolic teaching and early Christian practice.

Opponents often accused Oneness believers of denying Christ's divinity. In reality, Oneness theology strongly affirms that Jesus is fully God and fully man; what they deny is the idea of eternal distinctions within the Godhead.

Critics also argue that the triadic baptismal formula in Matthew 28:19 contradicts the Jesus-name formula. Oneness scholars respond by saying Matthew's singular "name" is fulfilled in Jesus, while Acts shows how the apostles practiced baptism in obedience to Christ.

Beyond baptismal formulas, Oneness Pentecostals stress the necessity of Spirit baptism, with tongues as the initial sign. Acts 2, Acts 10, and Acts 19 are cited as normative examples for believers today.

This emphasis creates a strong sense of continuity with the book of Acts. For Apostolics, they are not merely repeating history; they are living it. The same Spirit that fell on Pentecost still falls today, empowering believers for holy living and bold witness.

The oneness doctrine also shapes worship and prayer. Songs, prayers, and sermons are directed to Jesus as the one true God. Their services are known for passionate praise, expressive prayer, and a strong focus on the presence of God.

Ethically, this belief calls for holiness in lifestyle. Apostolics often emphasize separation from worldliness in dress, entertainment, and conduct, seeing themselves as distinct, Spirit-filled witnesses.

Theologically, Oneness Pentecostalism stands as a challenge to Trinitarian Christianity, forcing renewed reflection on the role of Jesus' name, the meaning of baptism, and the unity of God. While mainstream Christianity holds to the Trinity, Oneness insists that God's identity is best understood in Jesus alone.

Whether one agrees or not, Oneness devotion to Scripture, mission, and holiness cannot be ignored. Their rapid global growth, especially in Africa, Asia, and Latin America, shows the power of their message to resonate with believers longing for an Acts-like Christianity.

In sum, the Apostolic/Oneness doctrine is built on three pillars: God is absolutely one, Jesus is the full revelation of that one God, and salvation is experienced through repentance, baptism in Jesus' name, and the infilling of the Spirit. It is a call to return to what they see as the apostolic pattern of Acts 2:38.

Reflection Questions on Doctrine

1. What does Matthew 28:19 teach us about the unity and diversity within the Godhead?
2. How do passages like John 3:16, John 15:26,

and 2 Corinthians 13:14 illustrate the Father, Son, and Spirit working together?

3. Why did early Christians feel the need to clarify their beliefs in formal creeds, and what role did the Trinity play in that process?

4. How did the Council of Nicaea (325 AD) and the Cappadocian Fathers shape the church's understanding of the Trinity?

5. What does the Trinity reveal about God's nature as love (1 John 4:8)?

6. How does Acts 2:38 reflect the Apostolic Pentecostal emphasis on repentance, baptism, and Spirit-filled living?

7. In what ways do Oneness believers interpret baptism "in the name of Jesus" as the fulfillment of Matthew 28:19?

8. How do Trinitarian and Oneness traditions differ in their explanation of the relationship between Father, Son, and Spirit?

9. What can we learn from both Trinitarian and Oneness perspectives about devotion to Scripture, mission, and the centrality of Jesus?

10. Why is sound doctrine important for Christian unity, spiritual growth, and faithful discipleship today?

Concluding Reflection on Doctrine

Doctrine is more than abstract theology; it is the heart of Christian belief and practice. The Godhead reminds us that Scripture reveals one God who works as Father,

Son, and Spirit. The Trinity helps us confess this mystery with clarity, protecting the church from error and grounding our worship in truth. Oneness theology, with its focus on the name of Jesus and Acts 2:38, challenges us to never lose sight of the centrality of Christ in salvation and mission.

Together, these perspectives call us to approach doctrine with humility, reverence, and devotion. Doctrine anchors us in God's truth, unites us as His people, and equips us to live faithfully in the world. At its core, sound doctrine is not about winning arguments, it is about knowing God more deeply, worshiping Him more truly, and living in a way that reflects His love and holiness.

CHAPTER 7: PRAYER

Introduction to the Prayer Chapter

Prayer is the soul's meeting place with God. It is where heaven and earth touch, where the infinite bends to listen to the finite, and where the child speaks to the Father with confidence that He cares. Every great movement of God in Scripture and in history has begun with prayer, because prayer is the posture of dependence and the language of trust.

From Genesis to Revelation, God's people are described as those who call upon His name. Prayer is not just one discipline among many; it is the lifeblood of faith. To neglect prayer is to cut ourselves off from the very source of strength, guidance, and peace. To embrace prayer is to walk in step with the Spirit and to live in constant awareness of God's presence.

In this chapter, we will move beyond seeing prayer as a duty and begin to see it as a privilege. We will explore what prayer is, what it means to cultivate a prayer life, the blessings that flow from it, and the qualities of a person who lives close to God in prayer. Scripture will guide us, but so will the witness of believers throughout history who discovered that prayer could transform not only individuals but whole communities.

This chapter is not an academic lecture; it is an invitation. I hope that as you read, you will not only learn about prayer but will also be stirred to pray. May these pages inspire you to draw closer to the God who is always listening, always present, and always ready to meet you in the quiet moments of your heart.

Prayer

Prayer is one of the most fundamental expressions of the Christian life. From Genesis to Revelation, the people of God are depicted as those who call upon His name. Prayer is not an optional accessory; it is at the very heart of faith.

In the Old Testament, Abraham pleaded with God for Sodom, Moses interceded for Israel, Hannah poured out her soul in grief, and David composed psalms of lament and praise. Prayer has always been the language of the relationship between God and His people.

In the New Testament, prayer is equally central. Jesus Himself prayed often, rising early to commune with the Father (Mark 1:35), praying all night before choosing the disciples (Luke 6:12), and crying out in Gethsemane before His crucifixion (Matthew 26:39).

The early church was birthed in prayer. Acts 1 shows the disciples gathered in prayer before Pentecost, and Acts 2:42 notes they "devoted themselves to the apostles' teaching and to fellowship, to the breaking of bread and to prayer."

Prayer is not only asking but also listening. Elijah on Mount Horeb discovered that God spoke not in the wind, earthquake, or fire, but in a gentle whisper (1 Kings 19:12). True prayer is dialogue, not monologue.

The Psalms demonstrate the breadth of prayer: lament,

thanksgiving, confession, and praise. Prayer is not limited to joyful moments; it encompasses the full range of human emotion.

Jesus taught His disciples how to pray in what we now call the Lord's Prayer (Matthew 6:9-13). This model includes worship, submission, petition, confession, and intercession.

Prayer is relational before it is functional. It is not about getting things from God, but about being with God. As the Puritan Thomas Watson once wrote, "Prayer is the key of heaven, but faith turns the key."

Historically, prayer has sustained the church through persecution, famine, and revival. Augustine, Luther, Wesley, and countless others testified that the strength of their ministry was rooted in prayer.

Prayer is also spiritual warfare. Paul exhorts believers to "pray in the Spirit on all occasions with all kinds of prayers and requests" as part of the armor of God (Ephesians 6:18).

In Revelation, the prayers of the saints are pictured as incense rising before God's throne (Revelation 5:8), showing that no prayer is lost, but each is treasured by Him.

Prayer is both individual and corporate. Jesus prayed alone, but He also prayed with His disciples. The church gathers in prayer to seek God's direction and power.

Modern Christian writers, such as E.M. Bounds, emphasize that "Prayer is not learned in a classroom but in the closet." It is practiced, not merely studied. Ultimately, prayer is about drawing near to God, aligning our will with His, and experiencing His presence in daily life.

To speak of prayer is to speak of the heartbeat of Christian spirituality; it is the breath of the soul.

What is Prayer (Definition)

Prayer can be defined simply as communication with God. It is speaking, listening, and relating to the Creator who made us. More specifically, prayer is an act of worship that glorifies God and aligns the believer with His will. Jesus prayed, "Not my will, but yours be done" (Luke 22:42).

Biblically, prayer includes adoration (Psalm 103:1), confession (1 John 1:9), thanksgiving (Philippians 4:6), and supplication (Philippians 4:6).

The Hebrew word *tefillah* and the Greek word *proseuche* both carry the idea of earnest communication, whether petition, praise, or intercession.

John Calvin defined prayer as "the chief exercise of faith." In prayer, trust is expressed, and dependence on God is acknowledged. Prayer is not manipulating God but submitting to Him. It is not about changing His mind but about being changed ourselves.

Some prayers are words; others are silent groans (Romans 8:26). The Spirit helps us pray when we cannot. Jesus described prayer not as performance but as intimacy: "When you pray, go into your room, close the door and pray to your Father" (Matthew 6:6). Prayer is both spontaneous and structured. The Lord's Prayer provides a model, while the Psalms give liturgical patterns. Both are valid expressions of prayer. The Westminster Catechism defines prayer as "an offering up of our desires unto God, for things agreeable to His will, in the name of Christ, with confession of our sins, and thankful acknowledgment of His mercies."

Prayer is also covenantal. God promises to hear His people when they call (2 Chronicles 7:14). Modern theologian Karl Barth wrote: "To clasp the hands in prayer is the beginning of an uprising against the disorder of the world." Prayer, then, is active, not passive.

Prayer is both a private devotion and a public declaration. It affirms dependence on God in every context. The definition of prayer is incomplete without relationship: it is grounded in the fact that God calls Himself Father and invites us to speak as His children.

In sum, prayer is not just a religious duty; it is communion with the living God.

What it Means to Have a Prayer Life

Having a prayer life goes beyond occasional prayers; it is cultivating a lifestyle of communion with God. Paul exhorts believers to "pray without ceasing" (1 Thessalonians 5:17). This doesn't mean constant words, but constant awareness of God's presence.

A prayer life means prioritizing regular times of prayer, just as Daniel prayed three times a day (Daniel 6:10). It involves consistency. Like breathing, prayer becomes a rhythm of life, not an emergency measure in crisis only.

Jesus modeled a prayer life by withdrawing often to solitary places to pray (Luke 5:16). If the Son of God needed this, so do we. A prayer life includes both speaking and listening. God desires conversation, not just requests. Developing a prayer life requires discipline. Early mornings, set times, and intentional focus help us grow in consistency.

A prayer life is not defined by eloquence. Jesus warned against babbling. It is defined by sincerity (Matthew 6:7). Community helps sustain a prayer life. Believers encourage one another when they gather for prayer. Having a prayer life means seeing every situation as an opportunity to turn to God, whether in joy, grief, or uncertainty.

It requires humility, acknowledging that apart from Him, we can do nothing (John 15:5). A prayer life transforms daily routines into sacred moments; walking, working, or driving become occasions for prayer. Technology and busyness often distract us, but a disciplined prayer life helps us recenter on God. Saints throughout history, from monks to reformers, testify that a structured prayer life anchors the soul.

Ultimately, a prayer life means living in continual fellowship with God, aligning our hearts with His presence and power.

Benefits of Having a Prayer Life

A prayer life draws us closer to God, deepening intimacy with Him. "Draw near to God, and He will draw near to you" (James 4:8). Prayer provides peace. Paul writes, "The peace of God, which transcends all understanding, will guard your hearts and your minds in Christ

Jesus" (Philippians 4:7). Prayer gives wisdom. James 1:5 promises that if we ask God, He will give generously without finding fault.

Prayer strengthens faith. By praying and seeing God answer, believers grow in trust and reliance.

Prayer provides comfort in suffering. The Psalms show how prayer gives voice to pain and brings healing. Prayer protects from temptation. Jesus told His disciples, "Watch and pray so that you will not fall into temptation" (Matthew 26:41). Prayer brings breakthrough. Elijah prayed for rain, and it came after three years of drought (1 Kings 18:42–45).

Prayer unites believers. Corporate prayer creates fellowship and shared mission. Prayer opens doors for mission. Paul asked for prayer "that God may open a door for our message" (Colossians 4:3).

Prayer invites the power of the Holy Spirit. Pentecost came after the disciples prayed in unity.

Prayer changes circumstances, but more importantly, it changes us. Prayer brings clarity. Many testify that decisions made in prayer are marked by divine guidance.

Prayer fosters gratitude, turning our focus from problems to God's provision. Prayer brings joy. Jesus said, "Ask and you will receive, and your joy will be complete" (John 16:24).

In short, prayer enriches every dimension of life, spiritual, emotional, and relational.

A Prayerful Person

A prayerful person is one who walks with God daily. Their life reflects reliance on Him. Prayerful people are marked by humility, acknowledging their dependence on God. They are often at peace because they bring their anxieties to God instead of carrying them alone.

A prayerful person has discernment because they seek God's wisdom regularly. They are persistent, not giving up even when answers are delayed. Prayerful people often radiate compassion because prayer softens the heart. They tend to be bold in faith because prayer makes them confident in God's promises.

A prayerful person influences others, drawing people closer to God by example. They are often patient, because prayer teaches waiting. Their words are seasoned with grace, shaped by time spent with the Father. A prayerful person is sensitive to the Spirit's leading, willing to obey even in small things. They are resilient in trials because they have already learned to lean on God.

A prayerful person doesn't need recognition; their strength comes from time alone with God. History remembers prayerful people, like Daniel, who prayed despite opposition, or George Müller, whose prayers sustained orphanages by faith alone. Ultimately, a prayerful person reflects Christ Himself, who lived a life of constant communion with the Father.

Reflection Questions on Prayer

1. Why do you think prayer is called "the breath of the soul" in Christian tradition? How does this metaphor help you understand its importance?

2. In your own words, how would you define prayer after reading this chapter?

3. What does Jesus' example of prayer (Mark 1:35; Luke 6:12; Matthew 26:39) teach us about dependence on God?

4. What does it mean to "pray without ceasing" (1 Thessalonians 5:17), and how could you practice this in daily life?

5. Which of the benefits of prayer (peace, guidance, strength, unity, joy) have you experienced personally?

6. How do you balance personal/private prayer (Matthew 6:6) with corporate/community prayer (Acts 2:42)?

7. What challenges or distractions keep you from a consistent prayer life, and how can you overcome them?

8. How does prayer prepare us for spiritual warfare (Ephesians 6:18) and protect us from temptation (Matthew 26:41)?

9. Who in Scripture or Christian history do you see as a model of a prayerful person, and what can you learn from their example?

10. How would your life look different if prayer became a stronger daily priority?

A Personal Message on Prayer

Dear Reader,

As you come to the end of this chapter, I want to remind

you that prayer is not reserved for the spiritual elite or for moments of crisis; it is for you, right now, wherever you are in your journey. Prayer is the lifeline of faith, the place where burdens are lifted, guidance is given, and love is renewed.

Perhaps you feel strong in your prayer life, or perhaps you struggle with distraction, doubt, or discouragement. Take heart: God delights in even the smallest whispers of your heart. The very act of turning to Him, however imperfect, is precious in His sight.

Remember that prayer is not about eloquence; it is about honesty. It is not about ritual; it is about relationship. The God who heard Hannah's tears, Elijah's bold cries, and the thief's desperate plea on the cross is the same God who listens to you today.

My prayer for you is that this chapter has not only explained prayer but has inspired you to pray. Let it become more than a practice, let it become your way of life. May you find joy in God's presence, peace in His promises, and strength in His Spirit as you walk with Him daily.

Above all, may your prayer life draw you closer to the heart of God, until your words, your silence, and your very life become a living prayer before Him.

With encouragement and blessing,
Dr. Rushayne Stewart

CHAPTER 8: FASTING

Introduction

Fasting has been practiced by God's people throughout Scripture as a way of humbling the heart, focusing the mind, and drawing closer to the Lord. From Moses on Mount Sinai to Daniel in Babylon, from Esther in the Persian court to Jesus in the wilderness, fasting has always been a powerful act of devotion and dependence on God.

In our modern world of abundance, convenience, and constant noise, fasting may seem foreign or even unnecessary. Yet it remains a vital spiritual discipline. Fasting is not about earning God's favor or punishing ourselves; it is about creating space for God to work more deeply in our lives. When we willingly set aside food or other comforts, we declare that our true sustenance comes from God alone.

Fasting is always connected to prayer and faith. Without prayer, fasting is simply dieting. But when paired with prayer, it becomes a spiritual weapon, a way to seek God's presence, discern His will, and align our lives with His purposes.

This chapter will explore what fasting is, its biblical roots, and how it can strengthen your walk with God. Just as prayer is the breath of the soul, fasting can be seen as its sharpening discipline, quieting the flesh so the Spirit may speak more clearly.

Definition of Fasting

Fasting can be defined as the voluntary abstinence from food, drink, or certain activities for a spiritual purpose. In Scripture, fasting is always an intentional act directed toward God, not merely the denial of physical needs.

The Hebrew word for fasting, *tsom*, literally means "to cover the mouth," while the Greek word *nēsteia* means "not eating." Both point to the physical act of abstaining, but the spiritual meaning goes much deeper.

Biblical fasting is not about outward show but inward humility. Jesus warned, "When you fast, do not look somber as the hypocrites do... But when you fast, put oil on your head and wash your face, so that it will not be obvious to others... and your Father, who sees what is done in secret, will reward you" (Matthew 6:16-18).

At its core, fasting is about replacing dependence on earthly things with dependence on God. It is about focusing the heart away from distraction and toward devotion.

While fasting often involves food, it can also include abstaining from other things that occupy our desires or attention, such as entertainment, technology, or habits, so that time and energy are redirected toward God.

In short, fasting is a discipline of the body that awakens the spirit. It is an embodied prayer that says, "Lord, You are more important than my daily bread, and my soul hungers for You above all else."

Why Do We Fast?

Fasting is first and foremost an act of worship. It is choosing to set aside natural desires in order to focus fully on God. In fasting, believers declare that they value spiritual nourishment more than physical satisfaction. We fast to humble ourselves before God. Psalm 35:13 says, "I humbled my soul with fasting." It is a posture of dependence, recognizing our weakness and need for Him.

Fasting sharpens our spiritual focus. By denying the flesh, we silence distractions and allow the Spirit to bring clarity. We fast to seek God's guidance in critical moments. Acts 13:2-3 records that the early church fasted before sending out Paul and Barnabas.

Fasting is also a way of repentance. In Jonah 3, the people of Nineveh fasted and turned from their wicked ways, and God had mercy on them. We fast in times of crisis. Esther called for a three-day fast before she approached the king to save her people (Esther 4:16).

Fasting expresses hunger for God's presence. Jesus said, "Blessed are those who hunger and thirst for righteousness, for they will be filled" (Matthew 5:6). We fast to prepare for ministry. Jesus fasted 40 days before beginning His public mission (Matthew 4:1-2).

Fasting can be a way to strengthen intercession. Daniel fasted while praying for Israel's restoration (Daniel 9:3). We fast because Scripture assumes believers will. Jesus said, "When you fast" (Matthew 6:16), not "if you fast." Fasting is a way to express seriousness before God, showing that we are not casual about our prayers.

We fast to resist temptation and subdue the flesh. Paul wrote, "I discipline my body and keep it under control" (1 Corinthians 9:27). Fasting is an act of solidarity with the suffering. Isaiah 58:6-7 links fasting with acts of justice and compassion.

We fast to stir revival. Throughout history, great awakenings often began with seasons of prayer and fasting. Ultimately, we fast because it aligns our hearts with God's will, reminding us that "man shall not live by bread alone, but by every word that proceeds out of the mouth of God" (Matthew 4:4).

What Are the Benefits of Fasting (Spiritual, Physical, Mental, and Health-wise)?

Spiritually, fasting deepens intimacy with God by removing distractions. It creates space for His voice to be heard more clearly. Fasting strengthens prayer. It does not manipulate God but sharpens our spiritual sensitivity. It increases discipline, teaching us to say no to the flesh and yes to the Spirit. Fasting reveals hidden idols, exposing what we truly depend on when food or comforts are removed.

Spiritually, fasting breaks strongholds. Jesus said some spiritual battles are won only "by prayer and fasting" (Mark 9:29). It opens the heart to humility and repentance, as seen in Nineveh (Jonah 3)

Physically, fasting gives the digestive system rest, allowing the body to reset. Studies show fasting can promote detoxification, as the body flushes out toxins. Fasting may lower inflammation, improve metabolism, and regulate blood sugar when practiced wisely.

Mental benefits include clarity and focus. Many testify to increased alertness when fasting. Fasting also develops resilience, teaching perseverance and self-control.

Emotionally, fasting helps us confront unhealthy attachments and addictions. Fasting fosters compassion. Feeling hungry reminds us of those who suffer daily.

Health-wise, fasting can promote weight management and longevity, though this is a byproduct, not the main goal. Above all, the greatest benefit is spiritual: a closer walk with God and renewed strength for the Christian journey.

What Does Scripture Teach About Fasting?

Scripture consistently presents fasting as a spiritual discipline tied to prayer and devotion.

In the Old Testament, Moses fasted 40 days when receiving the law (Exodus 34:28). David fasted in grief and repentance (Psalm 35:13). Ezra proclaimed a fast to seek protection on a journey (Ezra 8:21). Esther fasted before interceding for her people (Esther 4:16).

In the prophets, fasting was often corrected. Isaiah 58 warned against empty rituals and taught that true fasting involves justice and compassion. Daniel fasted by abstaining from delicacies while praying for Israel (Daniel 10:2–3).

In the New Testament, Jesus fasted in the wilderness before facing Satan (Matthew 4:2). Jesus also taught His disciples to fast privately and sincerely (Matthew 6:16-18). The early church fasted before making important decisions (Acts 13:2-3; 14:23). Paul described fasting as part of his ministry life (2 Corinthians 6:5). Scripture connects fasting with humility, repentance, and seeking God's favor.

It is never portrayed as earning salvation but as deepening a relationship with God. Fasting in Scripture always involves prayer; it is never mere abstinence. The consistent biblical theme: fasting is a spiritual discipline meant to align us with God's purposes.

Who Should Fast and Why?

Fasting is for all believers, not just prophets, leaders, or "spiritual elites." In Joel 2:15-16, the entire community was called to fast, men, women, children, and even newlyweds.

Jesus said, "When you fast," assuming His followers would practice it (Matthew 6:16). Leaders should fast for wisdom in guiding others (Acts 13:2-3). Families can fast together, teaching children dependence on God.

Pastors and intercessors fast to seek God's power for ministry. Individuals facing major life decisions should fast for clarity. Those battling temptation can fast as a means of strengthening the spirit. Churches fast corporately in times of revival or crisis.

Missionaries and evangelists fast to prepare spiritually for outreach. Fasting is not restricted by age but should be done wisely with health in mind. Even those who cannot fast from food can fast from other things, media, entertainment, or habits. Everyone should fast because it expresses dependence on God, not self.

We fast not to impress God or people, but to humble

ourselves. Simply put: every believer is invited to fast, because every believer needs God's presence and power.

Fasting and Prayer Go Hand in Hand

Fasting without prayer is merely dieting; prayer without fasting may lack intensity. Together, they create a powerful partnership.

In Scripture, fasting is almost always paired with prayer (Ezra 8:21; Nehemiah 1:4; Daniel 9:3). Jesus Himself fasted and prayed in the wilderness, preparing for His mission (Matthew 4:1–2).

The apostles prayed and fasted before sending missionaries (Acts 13:3). Fasting intensifies prayer, showing God our seriousness. Prayer guides fasting, keeping it focused on God rather than self.

Fasting weakens the flesh; prayer strengthens the spirit. Together, they align us with God. Daniel fasted while praying for Israel's restoration, and God sent an angel with an answer (Daniel 10).

Fasting and prayer bring breakthrough in the situation. Jesus said, "This kind can come forth by nothing, but by prayer and fasting" (Mark 9:29). Prayer covers the mind with truth, while fasting disciplines the body.

Together, they sharpen discernment, helping us hear God's voice more clearly. Prayer brings intimacy with God; fasting removes barriers to that intimacy. When joined, fasting and prayer stir revival and transformation in individuals and communities.

History testifies that great awakenings were birthed through fasting and prayer. Ultimately, fasting and prayer are inseparable because both are acts of dependence on God, one through petition, the other through discipline.

Reflection Questions on Fasting

1. In what ways does fasting humble us before God, and why is humility so central to spiritual growth (Psalm 35:13)?

2. When facing important decisions or challenges, how might fasting help you discern God's will (Acts 13:2–3)?

3. Which benefit of fasting (spiritual, physical, mental, or health-related) resonates most with you, and why?

4. How does Isaiah 58 reshape your understanding of fasting as more than just abstaining from food?

5. Reflect on Esther's fast (Esther 4:16). What does her example teach about fasting in times of crisis?

6. Who in your life could join you in fasting for a need or breakthrough, and how could this strengthen your faith community?

7. What are some practical ways you could fast from non-food distractions (media, entertainment, habits) to make more room for God?

8. How does prayer give focus and direction to fasting, and why are the two inseparable (Mark 9:29)?

9. When you think about Jesus' own fasting (Matthew 4:1-2), what lessons can you apply to your personal walk with God?

10. After reading this chapter, what first step can you take toward cultivating fasting as a regular spiritual discipline?

A Personal Message on Fasting

Dear Reader,

As you reach the end of this chapter, I want to remind you that fasting is not about earning God's approval or proving your strength. It is about opening your heart more fully to Him. In fasting, we are simply saying, "Lord, You are my greatest need. You are my bread, my water, my life."

Perhaps you have fasted before, or perhaps this discipline feels new and intimidating. Do not be discouraged. God does not measure your fast by length or difficulty; He looks at the posture of your heart. A simple meal missed with sincere prayer can be just as precious to Him as a long, extended fast.

Fasting is not meant to be a burden but a blessing. It draws you nearer to the Father, sharpens your prayers, and strengthens your spirit. As you deny yourself, you will discover that God fills the empty places with His presence.

I encourage you to take a step of faith. Begin where you are. Pair your fast with prayer, and invite God to speak into your life in new and deeper ways. Remember, you are joining a long line of saints, from Moses to Esther, from Daniel to Jesus Himself, who found strength, wisdom, and breakthrough in fasting.

May your fasting not only change your circumstances

but transform your heart. May it draw you closer to Christ, deepen your love for Him, and empower you to live with renewed faith and boldness.

With encouragement and blessing,
Dr. Rushayne Stewart

CHAPTER 9: WOMEN OF FAITH

Women of Influence

Introduction

Throughout Scripture, women play pivotal roles in God's unfolding story. From judges and queens to mothers and prophets, women demonstrated courage, wisdom, faith, and leadership that shaped nations and advanced God's kingdom. Though they often lived in societies that limited their voices, their obedience to God's call broke barriers and left legacies of faith.

Deborah judged Israel and led them to victory. Ruth, though a Moabite, became part of the lineage of Christ. Esther risked her life to save her people. Hannah's persistent prayer brought forth Samuel. Elizabeth gave birth to John the Baptist in her old age. Mary, humble and obedient, bore the Savior of the world. These stories remind us that leadership is not about position but about faith, obedience, and courage.

This chapter will highlight the lives of fifteen women of Scripture, each with a unique calling and testimony. Some led nations, others preserved families, some bore children against all odds, and still others gave prophetic witness to God's plan. From their examples, we will draw lessons for ministry, leadership, and life today.

Deborah - Judge, Prophetess,

and Leader of Israel

Deborah stands out as one of the most remarkable women in the Bible. At a time when Israel was oppressed and weak, she rose as both prophetess and judge, offering leadership to a nation that had forgotten its God.

Judges 4 introduces her as "Deborah, a prophet, the wife of Lappidoth, was leading Israel at that time." She held court under a palm tree, where the people came to her for wisdom and judgment. Her authority came not from position, but from God's calling. The people of Israel were suffering under Jabin, king of Canaan, and his commander Sisera, who had 900 iron chariots. For twenty years, the Israelites were cruelly oppressed until Deborah began to lead them.

As a prophetess, she heard God's voice and delivered His command to Barak: "Go, take with you ten thousand men... and I will give Sisera into your hands" (Judges 4:6-7). Barak hesitated. He told Deborah, "If you go with me, I will go; but if you don't go with me, I won't go" (Judges 4:8). This shows both his fear and his recognition of Deborah's authority.

Deborah agreed to go, but prophesied that the honor of victory would not go to Barak but to a woman. God would turn the tables, showing that His power works beyond human expectations. In the battle, Sisera's army was thrown into confusion, and he fled on foot. He found refuge in the tent of Jael, the wife of Heber. Yet Jael killed him with a tent peg, fulfilling Deborah's prophecy.

Deborah and Barak then sang a song of victory in

Judges 5, one of the oldest poems in the Bible. It celebrated God's deliverance and praised the courage of those who fought. It also honored Jael as "most blessed among women" (Judges 5:24). Deborah's leadership was marked by both wisdom and courage. She guided a hesitant commander, inspired a fearful people, and celebrated God's victory with prophetic song.

She was not a warrior with sword and shield but a leader with vision and faith. Her example reminds us that leadership is not about physical strength but about spiritual conviction. Deborah's story also challenges cultural assumptions. In a patriarchal society, God chose a woman to lead His people, showing that His calling is not limited by human tradition. Her role as judge and prophetess teaches us that leadership in God's kingdom is rooted in obedience, not gender, background, or status.

Deborah's courage shows the importance of standing firm when others hesitate. Barak's reluctance contrasts with Deborah's confidence in God's word. Today, Deborah's story inspires women and men alike to step boldly into the roles God calls them to. Whether in ministry, family, or community, her life shows that faith and obedience can change the course of history.

Deborah reminds us that when God's people cry out, He raises leaders who hear His voice and act in His power. She was truly a woman of faith and influence, and her legacy continues to speak across generations.

Ruth - Loyalty, Redemption, and God's Hidden Hand

1. How does Ruth's loyalty to Naomi model faithfulness in relationships?
2. What risks did Ruth take in following Naomi to Bethlehem?
3. How does the story of Ruth reveal God's providence in ordinary life?
4. What role does Boaz play in showing kindness and redemption?
5. How does Ruth's story point us toward Christ?

Ruth's story begins in a time of famine and loss. Naomi, her mother-in-law, left Bethlehem with her husband and sons to live in Moab. There, Naomi's sons married Moabite women, Orpah and Ruth.

But tragedy struck. Naomi's husband and both her sons died, leaving three widows in grief. In that culture, widowhood meant vulnerability, poverty, and uncertainty.

Naomi, hearing that the famine had lifted in Bethlehem, decided to return home. She urged Orpah and Ruth to stay in Moab, to find security with new husbands. Orpah wept and stayed, but Ruth clung to Naomi.

Ruth's words are some of the most beautiful in Scripture: "Where you go I will go, and where you stay I will stay. Your people will be my people and your God my God" (Ruth 1:16). This was more than loyalty; it was faith. Ruth chose Naomi's God as her God.

Imagine the courage it took. Ruth left her homeland, her culture, and her gods to walk with Naomi into an uncertain future. She embodied what discipleship looks like: leaving everything to follow.

When the two arrived in Bethlehem, Naomi was bitter. She said, "Don't call me Naomi. Call me Mara, because the Almighty has made my life very bitter" (Ruth 1:20). She felt empty, but she wasn't alone; Ruth was beside her.

To provide for them, Ruth went to glean leftover grain from the fields, a provision in God's law for the poor. It so happened that she worked in the field of Boaz, a wealthy and kind relative of Naomi's late husband.

Boaz noticed Ruth's hard work and asked about her. When he heard of her loyalty to Naomi, he showed kindness. He told his workers to leave extra grain for her and to protect her.

Ruth was astonished by his generosity. "Why have I found such favor in your eyes that you notice me a foreigner?" she asked (Ruth 2:10). Boaz saw not her nationality but her faithfulness.

Naomi rejoiced at God's providence. She told Ruth that Boaz was a "kinsman-redeemer," a relative who had the right to redeem their family line by marriage. Suddenly, hope stirred where bitterness once lived.

Naomi instructed Ruth to approach Boaz humbly, laying at his feet at the threshing floor to signal her desire for his covering. This act wasn't scandalous; it was cultural, a request for redemption.

Boaz responded with honor. He praised Ruth's noble character, promised to do what was right, and took steps to secure her redemption legally before the elders of the city.

Boaz married Ruth, and their union brought joy not only to Naomi but to all of Bethlehem. Naomi, once bitter, now held a grandson in her arms.

The women of the town said to Naomi, "Praise be to the Lord, who this day has not left you without a guardian-redeemer" (Ruth 4:14). God had turned emptiness into fullness.

Ruth's story reminds us that God works not only through miracles but through everyday faithfulness, through gleaning in fields, showing kindness, and keeping covenant loyalty.

Ruth, a foreigner, became part of Israel's story. More than that, she became part of the lineage of David, and ultimately of Jesus Christ. The outsider became part of God's greatest plan.

For readers today, Ruth challenges us to live with loyalty in our relationships, to serve faithfully even in obscurity, and to trust God's hidden hand at work in our ordinary days.

Her story also teaches us about redemption. Just as Boaz redeemed Ruth, Christ redeems us, not because we deserve it, but because of His love and grace.

Naomi's journey reminds us that bitterness is not the end of the story. God can take our emptiness and fill it again. He can turn mourning into joy.

Ruth shows us that no one is too far, too foreign, or too broken to be part of God's story. Her life proves that God weaves even pain and loss into His redemptive plan.

Reflection Questions

1. What does Ruth's loyalty to Naomi teach us about faithfulness in relationships?
2. How did Ruth's decision to follow Naomi reflect her faith in God?
3. What can Naomi's bitterness and later joy teach us about God's ability to restore?
4. How does Boaz's kindness reflect God's character?
5. Why is it significant that Ruth, a foreigner, became part of Jesus' lineage?
6. How does Ruth's story show us God's providence in ordinary circumstances?
7. What does the role of a "kinsman-redeemer" teach us about Christ's redemption of His people?
8. In what ways can we practice everyday faithfulness like Ruth?
9. How does Ruth's courage challenge you in your own walk of faith?
10. What part of Ruth's story encourages you most in seasons of loss or uncertainty?

Esther - Courage, Providence, and Deliverance of a people

1. How does Esther's story show God's providence even when His name isn't mentioned?
2. What risks did Esther take in approaching the king?
3. How did Mordecai's wisdom and courage influence Esther's choices?
4. What can this story teach us about standing firm when others' lives depend on it?
5. How does Esther's courage point us toward Christ's ultimate act of deliverance?

The story of Esther unfolds in Persia, long after Israel had been exiled. Many Jews lived scattered throughout foreign lands, often vulnerable to prejudice and persecution. Esther's story begins with a crown, but it quickly becomes a story of courage and deliverance.

When Queen Vashti refused King Xerxes' command to appear before him, she was removed from her position. To find a new queen, a search began across the empire. Among those chosen was a young Jewish woman named Hadassah, better known as Esther.

Esther was raised by her cousin Mordecai, who advised her not to reveal her Jewish identity. She entered the palace quietly, carrying her heritage in secret.

The king favored her above all others, and Esther was

crowned queen. Yet her new position came not as an escape from her people, but as the very means God would use to save them.

Trouble arose when Haman, a high official, was enraged that Mordecai refused to bow to him. His pride turned into hatred, not just against Mordecai but against all Jews. He plotted genocide, persuading the king to issue a decree to destroy them.

When Mordecai learned of this, he tore his clothes and mourned publicly. He sent word to Esther, urging her to go before the king and plead for her people.

Esther hesitated. "Any man or woman who approaches the king in the inner court without being summoned… will be put to death unless the king extends the gold scepter" (Esther 4:11). To approach the king uninvited was to risk her life.

Mordecai's reply is one of the most powerful statements in Scripture: "And who knows but that you have come to your royal position for such a time as this?" (Esther 4:14).

Esther resolved to act. She asked Mordecai and the Jews to fast for three days, and she and her servants would do the same. Then she said, "When this is done, I will go to the king, even though it is against the law. And if I perish, I perish" (Esther 4:16).

On the third day, Esther put on her royal robes and entered the king's court. The king extended the golden scepter, sparing her life. She had stepped into danger with courage—and God's providence met her there.

Instead of rushing her request, Esther invited the king and Haman to two banquets. With wisdom and patience, she prepared the right moment to reveal the truth.

At the second banquet, she exposed Haman's plot: "We have been sold, I and my people, to be destroyed, killed, and annihilated" (Esther 7:4). The enraged king had Haman executed on the very gallows he built for Mordecai.

But the decree against the Jews could not be revoked, so the king issued a new decree allowing them to defend themselves. When the day of destruction came, the Jews rose and prevailed against their enemies.

Mordecai was elevated to a position of honor, and the Jewish people celebrated deliverance. To this day, the festival of Purim commemorates God's salvation through Esther's bravery.

What's remarkable about Esther is that God's name is never mentioned in the book. Yet His fingerprints are everywhere, in timing, in favor, in courage, in deliverance. Sometimes God works most powerfully behind the scenes.

Esther's story teaches us that courage often requires risk. She could have stayed silent, but silence would have cost lives. True faith acts, even when fear whispers otherwise.

It also teaches us about providence, that God positions us in specific places, families, jobs, or seasons, not by accident, but for a purpose.

Mordecai's words echo across time: *"For such a time as this."* They remind us that our lives are part of God's bigger plan.

Esther points us to Jesus, who also risked everything, laying down His life not just to save His people from earthly death, but to save all humanity from eternal separation from God.

Her courage invites us to ask: What risks of faith might God be calling me to take for the sake of others? And will I trust His providence enough to step forward, even if it costs me?

Reflection Questions

1. Why was Esther's position as queen critical in God's plan for deliverance?
2. How did Mordecai's words challenge Esther to act courageously?
3. What risks did Esther take by approaching the king uninvited?
4. How does her story reveal God's providence, even when His name isn't mentioned?
5. What does the festival of Purim teach us about remembering God's deliverance?
6. How do you see parallels between Esther's bravery and Christ's sacrifice?
7. What does "for such a time as this" mean in your own life right now?
8. In what areas might you be tempted to remain silent when God is calling you to speak or act?
9. How can Esther's story encourage you to trust God's hidden hand in your circumstances?
10. What practical steps can you take to live with

greater courage and faith like Esther?

Naomi - From Bitterness to Blessing

Naomi's story is deeply human, marked by grief, bitterness, and eventual restoration. She shows us that faith is not always neat and tidy; sometimes it wrestles, laments, and waits for God to bring renewal.

Her journey begins in Bethlehem, where famine forced her husband, Elimelek, to move their family to Moab. What was meant as a temporary survival plan became a season of deep loss.

In Moab, Elimelek died, leaving Naomi a widow. Her two sons married Moabite women, Orpah and Ruth, but after ten years, both sons also died. Naomi was left without a husband or children, a devastating situation in her culture. With no means of survival in Moab, Naomi decided to return to Bethlehem. She urged her daughters-in-law to stay in Moab, remarry, and rebuild their lives. Orpah complied, but Ruth refused, clinging to her with unwavering loyalty.

Arriving in Bethlehem, Naomi was greeted by her old neighbors. They barely recognized her. She said, "Don't call me Naomi... Call me Mara, because the Almighty has made my life very bitter" (Ruth 1:20). Her name, meaning "pleasant," no longer seemed to fit her reality.

Naomi's honesty is striking. She did not hide her grief or pretend to be fine. Instead, she brought her pain directly into the community of God's people. Her story reminds us that lament is a part of faith.

Though bitter, Naomi did not turn away from God. She acknowledged His sovereignty, even when she didn't understand His actions. Her honesty with God became the soil for future hope.

Naomi's role in Ruth's life shows another side of her character: mentorship. Though grieving, she guided Ruth with wisdom, teaching her how to navigate life in Bethlehem. She recognized God's providence when Ruth gleaned in Boaz's field, calling him a potential redeemer. Even in her bitterness, Naomi's faith peeked through as she saw God's hand at work.

Her instructions to Ruth about approaching Boaz show that she was not passive. Naomi became an active participant in God's unfolding plan, guiding Ruth with discernment.

When Boaz redeemed Ruth and they married, Naomi's story turned from emptiness to fullness. The women of Bethlehem said, "Praise be to the Lord, who this day has not left you without a guardian-redeemer" (Ruth 4:14). Naomi held Ruth's son, Obed, in her arms. The woman said, "Naomi has a son!" Though not biologically hers, the child became her joy and restoration.

That grandson, Obed, became the grandfather of David, weaving Naomi's story into the Messianic line. What seemed like bitterness became part of God's redemptive plan. Naomi teaches us that leadership is not always about public roles or visible power. Sometimes it is about quietly guiding, mentoring, and influencing the next generation.

Her story reminds us that God can turn mourning into

joy and bitterness into blessing. Naomi was a woman of faith and influence, not because her life was free of pain, but because she trusted God through it.

Hannah - A Woman of Prayer and Dedication

Hannah's story is one of sorrow turned into song. She shows us that persistent prayer, even in pain, can become the foundation for God's greater work.

She was married to Elkanah, who loved her deeply, but Hannah was barren. In her culture, infertility was considered a disgrace, and she carried the weight of shame. To make matters worse, Elkanah's other wife, Peninnah, mocked Hannah because she had no children, the rivalry and taunting cut Hannah's heart deeply. Year after year, they went to Shiloh to worship the Lord. There, Hannah wept bitterly, pouring out her soul before God. Her grief was not hidden but brought honestly into His presence.

One day, she made a vow: "Lord Almighty, if you will only look on your servant's misery and remember me... then I will give him to the Lord for all the days of his life" (1 Samuel 1:11). As she prayed silently, Eli the priest saw her lips moving but heard no sound. Mistaking her anguish for drunkenness, he rebuked her. Hannah responded, "I was pouring out my soul to the Lord" (1 Samuel 1:15).

Hannah's explanation moved Eli, who blessed her with a word of assurance: "Go in peace, and may the God of Israel grant you what you have asked of him" (1 Samuel 1:17). Hannah's faith was evident even before her prayer was answered. She left the temple no longer downcast, trusting God with her burden. In time, God remembered Hannah, and she gave birth to a son,

Samuel. His name means "heard by God," a testimony to answered prayer.

True to her vow, Hannah dedicated Samuel to the Lord's service at Shiloh. Though it must have been painful to release him, her obedience showed her trust in God's larger plan. Hannah's prayer of thanksgiving in 1 Samuel 2 is one of the most beautiful hymns in Scripture. It celebrates God's power to reverse situations, the hungry are filled, the barren bear children, and the proud are humbled.

Hannah's prayer later inspired Mary's Magnificat in Luke 1, showing how her faith echoed across generations. Through Samuel, God raised a prophet who would anoint Israel's first kings and guide the nation. Hannah's faith shaped the future of Israel through her son. Hannah teaches us that prayer is not just about receiving but about surrendering. Her story is a model of intercession, faith, and obedience.

Her influence as a woman of faith and prayer continues to remind us that God hears the cries of His people and can turn grief into joy, bitterness into blessing, and prayer into legacy.

Sarah- A Promise Fulfilled in God's Time

Sarah, originally named Sarai, is one of the most significant women in Scripture. She was the wife of Abraham and the mother of Isaac, the child of promise. Her journey reveals both the struggles and triumphs of faith.

When God called Abraham to leave his homeland, Sarah went with him, stepping into uncertainty. She walked alongside her husband as he obeyed God's call, though she did not yet see the fulfillment of His promises.

God promised Abraham that he would become the father of many nations. Yet Sarah was barren, and as the years passed, the weight of unfulfilled promises grew heavier on her heart.

Her barrenness was not just personal grief; it was also a cultural burden. In her time, a woman's value was often tied to bearing children, and Sarah carried the shame of being childless.

In her impatience, Sarah tried to solve the problem herself. She gave her servant Hagar to Abraham, and Hagar bore Ishmael. But this decision brought tension and conflict into the household.

Despite Sarah's doubts, God reaffirmed His promise. He declared that Sarah herself would bear a son, even in her old age. When she overheard this promise, Sarah laughed. At nearly ninety years old, the idea of conceiving seemed impossible. Yet God asked, "Is anything too hard for the Lord?" (Genesis 18:14).

In time, God's word was fulfilled. Sarah gave birth to Isaac, whose name means "laughter." What began as doubt turned into joy, and her laughter became a testimony of God's faithfulness.

Sarah's story shows that faith is often a journey of wrestling with doubt and waiting for God's timing. She struggled, faltered, and even laughed in disbelief, but God's promise still prevailed.

Hebrews 11:11 commends her faith: "By faith even Sarah, who was past childbearing age, was enabled to bear children because she considered him faithful who had made the promise."

Sarah was not perfect, but she was chosen. Her life shows that God does not require flawless faith, only trust in His faithfulness. As the mother of Isaac, she became part of the covenant line through which God's promises would unfold, leading to the nation of Israel and ultimately to Christ.

Sarah also demonstrated loyalty. She followed Abraham through difficult journeys, including times of famine and danger. Her commitment reveals the endurance of her faith.

Though her impatience with God's promise led to mistakes, Sarah's life ultimately proves that God's plan cannot be thwarted by human doubt or failure.

Sarah's legacy reminds us that God's promises may take time, but they will surely come to pass. Her laughter of disbelief turned into laughter of joy, and her story continues to inspire those who wait on the Lord.

Rebekah - Chosen by God,

Mother of Nations

Rebekah enters the biblical story in Genesis 24, when Abraham sent his servant to find a wife for his son, Isaac. Her introduction is marked by divine providence and hospitality.

At the well, Rebekah offered water not only to Abraham's servant but also to his camels. This act of generosity fulfilled the servant's prayer for a sign, proving she was God's chosen bride for Isaac.

Her willingness to serve revealed her character. She was a woman of initiative and kindness, reflecting the values of faith and family.

When asked if she would go with the servant to marry Isaac, Rebekah agreed immediately: "I will go" (Genesis 24:58). Her courage to leave home and follow God's plan showed bold faith.

Upon meeting Isaac, she became his wife, and Scripture says he loved her, finding comfort after the death of his mother, Sarah. Rebekah's presence was a gift of healing to Isaac.

Like Sarah before her, Rebekah faced barrenness. For twenty years, she bore no children. Yet Isaac prayed, and God answered; she conceived twins, Jacob and Esau. Her pregnancy was difficult, and she sought the Lord. God revealed that "two nations are in your womb" and that the older would serve the younger (Genesis 25:23).

This prophecy framed her role as mother of nations, for her children became the ancestors of Israel (through Jacob) and Edom (through Esau). Rebekah's faith shines in her perseverance, but her story also reveals flaws.

She favored Jacob over Esau, setting in motion a sibling rivalry that shaped their lives.

When Isaac planned to bless Esau, Rebekah intervened. She helped Jacob disguise himself and receive the blessing instead, ensuring God's prophecy was fulfilled, but through deception.

Her actions reveal both determination and weakness. She trusted God's word but relied on her own methods, creating lasting family conflict. Yet even through her imperfections, God's plan prevailed. Jacob became the father of the twelve tribes of Israel, fulfilling the promise spoken to Rebekah.

Rebekah's story teaches us that God works through both strengths and shortcomings. She was chosen, blessed, and used in His plan despite her human failings. Her faith and courage at the well, her perseverance in barrenness, and her role as mother of Israel highlight her importance in God's covenant story.

Rebekah was a woman of influence; her choices shaped generations. Though her methods were imperfect, her life reminds us that God's purposes will stand, and He often works through ordinary people to accomplish extraordinary things.

Rachel -Beloved Wife, Mother of Joseph and Benjamin

Rachel's story is one of love, longing, and perseverance. She is remembered as the beloved wife of Jacob and the mother of Joseph and Benjamin, two of Israel's most significant tribes.

Jacob first met Rachel at a well, where she was tending

her father's sheep. Struck by her beauty and grace, he wept aloud and kissed her, a dramatic beginning to their love story (Genesis 29:9-11). Jacob agreed to work for seven years for Rachel's hand in marriage. The years "seemed like only a few days to him because of his love for her" (Genesis 29:20). This speaks to the deep bond they shared.

Yet their story was marked by deception. On the wedding night, Rachel's father, Laban, tricked Jacob into marrying her older sister, Leah, first. Jacob then worked another seven years to marry Rachel as well.

This rivalry between sisters created tension, as Leah bore children while Rachel remained barren. Her longing for children was intense, and she cried out to Jacob, "Give me children, or I'll die!" (Genesis 30:1).

Her desperation led her to give her maidservant Bilhah to Jacob, so that she might have children through her. This decision reflected cultural practices of the time, but also showed her struggle with waiting on God. At last, God remembered Rachel and opened her womb. She gave birth to Joseph, whose name means "May the Lord add." Her joy overflowed as she saw Joseph as the beginning of her answered prayers.

Joseph would later become one of Israel's greatest leaders, saving nations during famine and rising to power in Egypt. Rachel's long-awaited son became a vessel of God's providence. Rachel's faith was tested again as she longed for more children. Eventually, she conceived once more and bore Benjamin, Jacob's youngest son. Tragically, Rachel died during childbirth with Benjamin, and she was buried near Bethlehem. Her death was mourned deeply by Jacob, who set up a pillar over her tomb.

Rachel's life, though brief, left a lasting impact through her sons. Joseph and Benjamin became central to Israel's story; the tribes that bore their names were strong and influential.

Jeremiah later referenced Rachel as a symbol of mourning for her children (Jeremiah 31:15). This verse was echoed in Matthew 2:18 when Herod killed the infants in Bethlehem, linking Rachel's sorrow to the hope of Christ. Rachel's story teaches us about longing and waiting on God. Her barrenness tested her faith, but her perseverance reminds us that God's timing is perfect.

Though her life ended in sorrow, her legacy lives on through her children, especially Joseph, whose faith and leadership blessed nations.

Rachel was a woman of faith and influence, remembered for her love, her longing, and her place in God's covenant story. Even in grief, her life points us to the God who hears prayers and fulfills promises.

Leah - The Overlooked Mother of Nations

Leah's story is one of pain, perseverance, and unexpected honor. Though she was less loved than her sister Rachel, God used her to build the foundation of Israel's tribes.

Leah was the elder daughter of Laban. Unlike Rachel, who was described as beautiful and graceful, Leah was described as having "weak eyes" (Genesis 29:17). This contrast set the stage for her life of rejection and longing. When Jacob fell in love with Rachel, he worked seven years to marry her. But on the wedding night, Laban deceived him and gave him Leah instead. Jacob was shocked and angry, feeling betrayed.

The next morning, Jacob confronted Laban, but the marriage stood. Laban justified it by saying the younger sister could not be married before the elder. Thus, Leah became Jacob's wife by trickery, not by choice. Jacob married Rachel as well, but his heart always favored her. Leah carried the heavy burden of being unloved, living in the shadow of her sister.

Yet in her pain, God saw her. Genesis 29:31 says, "When the Lord saw that Leah was not loved, He enabled her to conceive, but Rachel remained childless." Leah bore Jacob's first son, Reuben, whose name means "the Lord has seen my misery." Each child she bore reflected her longing for Jacob's love. Her second son, Simeon, meant "one who hears," acknowledging that God had heard her cries. Her third son, Levi, meant "attached," as she hoped Jacob would now become closer to her, but it was with her fourth son, Judah, that Leah's perspective shifted. She said, "This time I will praise the Lord" (Genesis 29:35). Judah's name means "praise," and from his line would come King David and ultimately Jesus Christ.

Leah's story shows that even when human love fails, God's love remains steadfast. Though rejected by Jacob, she was chosen by God to play a central role in His redemptive plan.

Leah bore six of Jacob's twelve sons, Reuben, Simeon, Levi, Judah, Issachar, and Zebulun, as well as a daughter, Dinah. She became the mother of half of Israel's tribes.

Her sons shaped history. Levi's descendants became priests, Judah's descendants became kings, and through Judah came the Messiah. Leah's legacy far outshone her rejection. Though her life was marked by rivalry with Rachel and longing for Jacob's affection, Leah turned her eyes to God. Her journey teaches us that our worth is not determined by human approval but by God's calling.

Leah was a woman of faith and influence, reminding us that God sees the overlooked, loves the unloved, and uses the broken to bring forth His greatest blessings.

Elizabeth -Faithful in Waiting, Mother of John the Baptist

Elizabeth's story shines as a testimony of patience, faith, and answered prayer. Though she waited many years for a child, her faithfulness was rewarded when she gave birth to John the Baptist, the forerunner of Christ. Elizabeth was married to Zechariah, a priest from the line of Aaron. Together, they were described as "righteous in the sight of God, observing all the Lord's commands and decrees blamelessly" (Luke 1:6).

Despite their devotion, Elizabeth was barren. Like Sarah, Rebekah, and Rachel before her, she carried the pain of infertility in a culture where children were considered a blessing and barrenness a reproach. The years of waiting tested her faith, but she remained steadfast. Her life shows us that unanswered prayers are not forgotten prayers.

When Zechariah was serving in the temple, an angel appeared to him with astonishing news: Elizabeth would bear a son, and he would prepare the way for the Lord (Luke 1:13-17). Zechariah doubted because of their old age, and as a result, he was struck mute until the child's birth. But Elizabeth responded with faith and gratitude. When she became pregnant, she declared, "The Lord has done this for me. In these days he has shown his favor and taken away my disgrace among the people" (Luke 1:25).

Her pregnancy became a sign of God's mercy, not just for her but for all who longed for the fulfillment of His promises. Elizabeth also played a vital role in affirming Mary, the mother of Jesus. When Mary visited her, Elizabeth was filled with the Holy Spirit, and her unborn child leaped in her womb. She exclaimed, "Blessed are you among women, and blessed is the child you will bear!" (Luke 1:42). Elizabeth was the first to publicly recognize Mary's child as the Lord.

Her words brought encouragement to Mary, confirming that God's promises were being fulfilled. Their meeting became a moment of prophetic joy shared between two faithful women. When John was born, neighbors and relatives rejoiced. Against custom, Elizabeth insisted that his name be John, as the angel had commanded. Her obedience upheld God's word. With John's birth, Elizabeth's years of waiting turned into a legacy that would shape history. Her son became the voice crying in the wilderness, preparing hearts for Jesus.

Elizabeth's faith teaches us that delays are not denials. God's timing is perfect, and His promises are sure. Her story reminds us to trust Him even when hope seems long delayed.

Elizabeth was a woman of faith and influence.

Through her patience, obedience, and encouragement, she became part of God's redemptive plan, proving that those who wait on the Lord will see His goodness.

Mary -The Chosen Vessel of God

Mary's story is one of humility, faith, and surrender. She was a young woman from Nazareth, living in obscurity, yet God chose her to carry His Son into the world.

The angel Gabriel appeared to Mary with extraordinary news: "You will conceive and give birth to a son, and you are to call him Jesus" (Luke 1:31). He would be great and called the Son of the Most High. Mary was troubled at the angel's greeting, but she did not resist. Instead, she asked, "How will this be, since I am a virgin?" (Luke 1:34).

Gabriel explained that the Holy Spirit would come upon her and the power of the Most High would overshadow her. Her pregnancy would be a divine miracle, fulfilling ancient prophecy. Mary responded with one of the most beautiful declarations of faith in Scripture: "I am the Lord's servant. May your word to me be fulfilled" (Luke 1:38). Her surrender became the doorway for the incarnation.

Soon after, she visited her relative Elizabeth, who confirmed the truth of the angel's message. Elizabeth exclaimed, "Blessed is she who has believed that the Lord would fulfill His promises to her" (Luke 1:45). In response, Mary sang the Magnificat, a hymn of praise recorded in Luke 1:46-55. Her song celebrated God's mercy, justice, and faithfulness, showing her deep knowledge of Scripture.

Mary's obedience brought both blessing and hardship. She carried the stigma of a pregnancy outside of marriage, risking shame and even danger in her community. Yet she trusted God to work through the challenges. Joseph, her betrothed, was reassured by an angel to take her as his wife, showing God's protection over her calling.

In Bethlehem, Mary gave birth to Jesus in humble surroundings, laying Him in a manger. Her role in the nativity reminds us that God's greatest works often begin in the smallest, simplest places.

Mary pondered the events in her heart, treasuring the mysteries surrounding her Son. She lived with both wonder and uncertainty, raising Jesus while knowing He was no ordinary child. She was present at key moments of His life, from the wedding at Cana, where Jesus performed His first miracle, to the cross, where she watched her Son suffer and die.

In John 19:26-27, Jesus entrusted Mary to the care of the disciple John, showing His love and honoring her even in His final moments. After the resurrection, Mary remained with the disciples in prayer (Acts 1:14), showing her ongoing devotion and leadership in the early church.

Mary was a woman of faith and influence, not because she sought greatness, but because she surrendered fully to God's will. Her life teaches us that true leadership begins with obedience and that God can use anyone who says, "Yes, Lord."

Mary Magdalene - Witness of

Grace and the Resurrection

Mary Magdalene's story is one of transformation and devotion. Once afflicted, she became one of Jesus' most faithful followers and the first witness of His resurrection.

Luke 8:2 introduces her as a woman from whom Jesus cast out seven demons. This detail reminds us of her broken past and the depth of the healing she received from Christ. Set free, Mary devoted her life to following Jesus. She became one of the women who supported His ministry, providing resources and presence. Unlike many who followed from a distance, Mary remained close. Her gratitude for what Jesus had done in her life made her fearless in her devotion.

Mary Magdalene was present at the crucifixion when many disciples fled. John 19:25 lists her among the women standing near the cross, sharing in Jesus' suffering. Her presence at the darkest moment reveals her courage. She did not turn away in fear but stayed near the One who had transformed her life.

After Jesus' death, Mary went to the tomb early on the first day of the week to anoint His body (Mark 16:1). Her love compelled her to honor Him even in death. To her surprise, she found the stone rolled away. Confused and weeping, she thought His body had been stolen (John 20:13).

Then Jesus appeared to her. At first, she did not recognize Him, mistaking Him for the gardener. But when He said her name, "Mary," she immediately knew it was the Lord (John 20:16). This moment is profound. The risen Christ revealed Himself first not to Peter,

John, or any of the apostles, but to Mary Magdalene.

Jesus gave her a commission: "Go to my brothers and tell them, 'I am ascending to my Father and your Father, to my God and your God'" (John 20:17). Mary became the first messenger of the resurrection. She went and told the disciples, "I have seen the Lord!" (John 20:18).

Her role shows that God entrusts His greatest news to those who are faithful, regardless of status or gender. Mary Magdalene's story teaches us that no past is too broken for God to redeem, and no life is too small to carry His greatest message.

She was a woman of faith and influence because she bore witness to the most important event in history, the resurrection of Jesus Christ, and proclaimed it with boldness.

Priscilla - Teacher, Partner, and Mentor in the Early Church

Priscilla is one of the most influential women in the New Testament church. Alongside her husband Aquila, she is remembered as a teacher, mentor, and faithful servant of Christ.

Her story begins in Acts 18, where Paul met Priscilla and Aquila in Corinth. They were tentmakers by trade, and Paul stayed with them, working and ministering together. Priscilla is remarkable because her name often appears before her husband's in Scripture (Acts 18:18; Romans 16:3). This suggests her prominence in ministry and teaching.

She and Aquila were Jewish believers who had been

forced to leave Rome by an imperial edict. Despite displacement, they opened their home and their lives to the work of the gospel.

Paul not only worked with them but also referred to them as "my fellow workers in Christ Jesus" (Romans 16:3). Their partnership in ministry was recognized and honored by the apostle himself.

One of Priscilla's most significant contributions was her role in teaching Apollos, an eloquent and learned preacher. Though passionate, Apollos knew only the baptism of John. Priscilla and Aquila took him aside privately and "explained to him the way of God more accurately" (Acts 18:26). This act of mentoring helped shape a future leader of the early church. Priscilla's teaching role challenges assumptions about women's leadership in the early church. She did not lead alone but in partnership, showing that ministry can be collaborative and balanced.

Her influence extended beyond teaching. Priscilla and Aquila hosted churches in their home (1 Corinthians 16:19), making their household a hub of worship and discipleship.

This shows that leadership is not only about public preaching, but it is also about creating spaces where faith can grow and communities can thrive.

Priscilla's hospitality was a ministry. By opening her home, she nurtured the church and provided a safe place for believers to gather. She also demonstrated courage. Paul wrote that Priscilla and Aquila "risked their lives for me" (Romans 16:4). Their devotion was not theoretical; it was sacrificial.

Priscilla's leadership is marked by humility. She did not seek titles or positions; she simply used her gifts to build up the church and strengthen others in the faith. Her legacy reminds us that women in ministry can be powerful teachers, mentors, and leaders when they faithfully use their God-given abilities.

Priscilla was truly a woman of faith and influence, an example of how ordinary believers, working together, can have an extraordinary impact on the kingdom of God.

Miriam - Prophetess, Leader, and Witness of Deliverance

Miriam's story stretches from her childhood bravery to her prophetic leadership during Israel's exodus. As the sister of Moses and Aaron, she played a vital role in God's deliverance of His people.

She first appears in Exodus 2, when Pharaoh had ordered the death of Hebrew baby boys. Miriam, still a young girl, watched over her infant brother Moses as he floated in a basket on the Nile.

When Pharaoh's daughter discovered the baby, Miriam bravely approached and suggested a nurse for the child. Her quick thinking ensured that Moses was raised under his mother's care before entering Pharaoh's household. This early act of courage set the tone for Miriam's life. She was bold, wise, and willing to step forward in critical moments.

As an adult, Miriam became a prophetess and leader among the Israelites. After God parted the Red Sea and delivered Israel from Egypt, she led the women in worship with tambourines and dancing. Her song, recorded in Exodus 15:20-21, proclaimed: "Sing to the Lord, for he is highly exalted. Both horse and driver he has hurled into the sea." Miriam's worship became a testimony of victory.

In that moment, Miriam stood as a leader of celebration, reminding the people that their triumph belonged to God alone. Her leadership, however, was not without flaws. In Numbers 12, Miriam and Aaron spoke against Moses, questioning his authority. God defended Moses, and Miriam was struck with leprosy as a sign of His judgment.

The people interceded for her, and Moses prayed for her healing. After seven days outside the camp, Miriam was restored. This episode highlights both her influence and her accountability before God.

Miriam's discipline reminds us that leadership carries responsibility. Even prophets and leaders must remain humble and obedient to God's order. Despite this setback, Miriam remained respected. Micah 6:4 includes her alongside Moses and Aaron as one of the leaders God sent to bring Israel out of Egypt.

Miriam's story shows that women played essential roles in the spiritual and communal life of Israel, not only in support but in leadership and prophecy. Her courage as a child saved Moses' life, her song encouraged a nation, and her mistakes remind us of the need for humility in leadership.

Through Miriam, we learn that God calls women to leadership roles, equipping them with courage, wisdom, and spiritual gifts.

Miriam was truly a woman of faith and influence, a prophetess who witnessed God's power, led His people in worship, and stood as a reminder of His faithfulness.

Phoebe - Servant, Leader, and Supporter of the Gospel

Phoebe is mentioned briefly in Scripture, but her legacy is powerful. In Romans 16:1-2, Paul commends her to the believers in Rome, describing her as a deacon (*diakonos*) of the church in Cenchreae and a benefactor of many.

Though only a few verses describe her, those words reveal her importance in the early church. Phoebe was a trusted leader, recognized for her service and generosity. Paul's commendation suggests that Phoebe may have been the one entrusted to deliver his letter to the Romans, a significant responsibility that highlights her reliability and influence.

The word *diakonos* used for Phoebe is the same word Paul uses elsewhere to describe himself and other ministers. This shows that her role was not simply menial service but one of recognized spiritual leadership. She is also called a *prostatis*, meaning benefactor or patron. This indicates that she likely provided financial and practical support to the ministry, enabling the gospel to spread.

Phoebe's leadership demonstrates that women were actively involved in ministry roles in the early church, supporting both the practical and spiritual needs of the community. By commending her publicly, Paul affirmed her authority and asked the church in Rome to "receive her in the Lord in a way worthy of his people." This shows respect for her as a leader and servant of God.

Phoebe's story challenges the assumption that women in the early church only served behind the scenes. She was a visible, recognized, and commended leader. Though we do not have a long narrative about her life, the brief mention of Phoebe reveals the essential role women played in sustaining the church's mission.

Her role as benefactor also highlights the importance of stewardship. She used her resources not for personal gain but to support the spread of the gospel. Phoebe's willingness to serve shows that leadership is not about recognition but about faithfulness. Her quiet influence strengthened many, including Paul himself.

Her example is a reminder that every act of service, no matter how small or unseen, contributes to the growth of God's kingdom. Phoebe teaches us that women in leadership can be both practical and spiritual pillars of the church. Her support helped shape the future of Christianity in Rome and beyond.

Though her story is brief, her influence is timeless. Her life speaks of devotion, generosity, and servant-leadership that inspire believers today. Phoebe was truly a woman of faith and influence, a deacon, benefactor, and trusted servant of the gospel who used her gifts to advance God's kingdom.

Hagar - The God Who Sees

Hagar's story is one of hardship, survival, and divine encounter. Though often overlooked, she is remembered as the first woman in Scripture to give God a name, "El Roi," the God who sees me.

Hagar was an Egyptian servant in the household of Abraham and Sarah. When Sarah could not bear children, she gave Hagar to Abraham as a surrogate, following the customs of the time (Genesis 16:1-2). This arrangement placed Hagar in a difficult position. Though she bore Abraham's child, she remained a servant, and tension grew between her and Sarah.

When Hagar became pregnant, she looked down on Sarah, which only deepened the rivalry. Sarah mistreated her, and Hagar fled into the wilderness. Alone, pregnant, and desperate, Hagar encountered the angel of the Lord. He asked her, "Hagar, servant of Sarai, where have you come from, and where are you going?" (Genesis 16:8).

The angel told her to return and submit, but also gave her a promise: her son would be named Ishmael, meaning "God hears," because the Lord had heard her misery. In response, Hagar declared, "You are the God who sees me" (Genesis 16:13). She recognized that even in her affliction, she was not invisible to God.

Later, after Isaac was born to Sarah, tension flared again. Sarah asked Abraham to send Hagar and Ishmael away. Heartbroken, Hagar wandered in the desert with her son. When their water ran out, Hagar placed Ishmael under a bush and wept, unable to watch him die. In her despair, God again appeared. The angel of God called to her, saying, "Do not be afraid; God has heard the boy crying as he lies there" (Genesis 21:17).

God opened her eyes to see a well of water, saving their lives. Ishmael grew up to become the father of a great nation, fulfilling God's promise. Though not the child of the covenant, he was still the child of God's mercy.

Hagar's story is one of being seen and heard in affliction. Twice in the wilderness, God met her when she felt abandoned and hopeless. Her experience teaches us that God is near to the brokenhearted and attentive to the cries of the outcast.

Hagar reminds us that no one is invisible to God. Even when rejected by people, we are noticed, valued, and cared for by Him. She was a woman of faith and influence because her testimony still speaks: God sees, God hears, and God provides even in the wilderness.

Huldah - The Prophetess of Truth

Huldah is one of the lesser-known women of Scripture, but her influence was significant. She was a prophetess in Jerusalem during the reign of King Josiah and played a key role in one of Israel's greatest spiritual reforms.

Her story is found in 2 Kings 22 and 2 Chronicles 34. When the Book of the Law was rediscovered in the temple, Josiah was deeply troubled by the nation's disobedience. He sought God's direction. Instead of going directly to a priest or another prophet, Josiah's officials were sent to consult Huldah. This shows the respect she carried as a trusted voice of God.

Huldah lived in Jerusalem's Second District and was the wife of Shallum, the keeper of the wardrobe. Despite her ordinary setting, her prophetic authority was extraordinary. When the officials presented the scroll to her, Huldah confirmed that the words were true. She declared that judgment would come on Judah because they had forsaken God and turned to idols. Yet she also gave a personal word for King Josiah. Because his heart was humble and he wept before the Lord, he would not see the disaster in his lifetime. God would grant him peace.

Her message balanced truth and mercy. She did not soften God's word, yet she also affirmed His compassion for those who repent. Huldah's role is significant because she was one of the few women in Scripture consulted as a prophetess by national leaders. Her wisdom guided an entire kingdom. Josiah responded by renewing the covenant and leading the people in reform, removing idols and restoring worship. Huldah's prophecy became the spark for revival.

Her example reminds us that God raises women as well as men to proclaim His word, and that their voices are essential in times of crisis. Huldah demonstrates that prophetic ministry is not about popularity but about faithfulness to God's truth. She spoke with courage, knowing her words would shape the course of a nation. She also shows us that God often chooses unlikely places and people to reveal His word. A woman in Jerusalem's Second District became a voice for an entire kingdom.

For women in ministry today, Huldah is a model of courage, wisdom, and integrity. Her influence came not from position or power but from obedience to God. Huldah reminds us that revival begins with the word of God. When Scripture is rediscovered and applied, transformation follows.

She was a woman of faith and influence, one whose bold proclamation of truth brought clarity, conviction, and renewal to God's people.

Anna the Prophetess - Faithful Witness of the Messiah

Anna the Prophetess is one of the quiet yet powerful figures of the New Testament. Though only mentioned briefly in Luke 2:36-38, her story radiates faithfulness, perseverance, and hope fulfilled.

Anna was the daughter of Phanuel, of the tribe of Asher. She had lived many years, making her a respected elder among her people. Luke records that she was very old. She had been married for only seven years before becoming a widow and then lived the rest of her life devoted to God. Rather than remarry, Anna chose to dedicate herself fully to the Lord, spending her days and nights in the temple courts. She worshiped, fasted, and prayed continually. Her life became a testimony that devotion to God is not bound by age or circumstance.

Anna's ministry was not one of public preaching but of quiet intercession. In her prayers, she carried the longings of her people for redemption. On the day Mary and Joseph brought the infant Jesus to the temple to be presented to the Lord, Anna was there. Her decades of devotion led to this divinely appointed moment. When she saw the child, she recognized Him as the fulfillment of Israel's hope. Her spiritual eyes saw what many others missed.

Anna gave thanks to God immediately. Her heart overflowed with joy at seeing the Messiah she had long awaited. She then began to speak about the child to all who were looking for redemption in Jerusalem. Though her words are not recorded in detail, her testimony became part of the first witness to Jesus. Anna shows us that faithfulness in hidden places prepares us for moments of revelation. Her quiet life of prayer was rewarded with the vision of God's salvation. Her story demonstrates that no season of life is wasted when given to God. Even widowhood and old age became opportunities for her to serve.

Anna also models the power of intercession. While leaders and rulers came and went, her consistent prayers became part of the foundation for God's work in her generation. For modern believers, Anna is a reminder that unseen devotion is not forgotten. God honors perseverance, especially in prayer and fasting. She was a woman of faith and influence because she bore witness to Christ when He was just a child, proclaiming redemption to those who longed for hope.

Conclusion - Women of Faith, Women of Influence

The stories of Deborah, Ruth, Esther, Naomi, Hannah, Sarah, Rebekah, Rachel, Leah, Elizabeth, Mary, the mother of Jesus, Mary Magdalene, Priscilla, Miriam, Phoebe, Hagar, the Shunammite woman, and Anna remind us that women have always held a vital place in God's story.

These women were prophets, judges, queens, mothers, mentors, servants, and intercessors. Some led nations into victory; others nurtured families and guided future generations. Some were lifted by joy, while others endured rejection and grief. Yet all were remembered because of their faith, their obedience, and their influence.

Their examples shatter the notion that leadership or ministry is reserved for a select few. God used women of every background, wealthy and poor, young and old, Israelites and foreigners, to carry forward His purposes. He saw them, called them, and equipped them for tasks that shaped history.

The lessons are clear:

> **Faith is powerful.** Sarah's barrenness became laughter, and Hannah's tears became songs.
>
> **Courage is contagious.** Esther risked her life, and Deborah led a nation into battle.
>
> **Devotion is influential.** Mary surrendered to God's will, and Anna prayed faithfully for decades.
>
> **Service is leadership.** Phoebe, Priscilla, and the Shunammite woman used their resources and gifts to strengthen the people of God.

Above all, these women point us to the God who is faithful. He honors faith, redeems brokenness, hears prayers, and calls both women and men to be vessels of His kingdom.

A Personal Message to the Reader

Dear Reader,

As you reflect on these women, I invite you to see yourself in their stories. Perhaps you feel like Naomi, wrestling with bitterness; or like Hannah, praying for an answer; or like Deborah, standing at the edge of leadership, called to be courageous. Wherever you are, know this: God sees you, just as He saw Hagar in the wilderness. He calls you, just as He called Esther, "for such a time as this."

Your influence may not make headlines, but it can change lives. Your faith may seem small, but it can move mountains. The God who worked through these women is the same God who works through you.

May you carry forward their legacy of faith and influence. Lead with courage, pray with persistence, serve with humility, and live with hope. For in every season, God is still writing His story, and He invites you to be a part of it.

With encouragement and blessing,
Dr. Rushayne Stewart

Reflection Questions

1. Which woman's story (Deborah, Ruth, Esther, Naomi, etc.) speaks most to your current season of life, and why?
2. How does Deborah's courage challenge you to step into leadership or responsibility God may be calling you to?
3. What can Ruth's loyalty and humility teach

you about faithfulness in relationships and devotion to God?

4. How does Esther's willingness to risk her life for her people inspire you to act courageously "for such a time as this"?

5. Naomi struggled with bitterness before experiencing restoration. How does her story encourage you in times of loss or disappointment?

6. Hannah, Sarah, Elizabeth, and others prayed persistently for children and saw God answer. What does their perseverance in prayer teach you about waiting on God's timing?

7. What can we learn from women like Priscilla, Phoebe, and the Shunammite woman about servant-leadership and using our resources for God's kingdom?

8. How does Mary's surrender to God's will ("I am the Lord's servant") challenge you in your own walk of faith?

9. Mary Magdalene was the first to witness the resurrection. How does her devotion remind you of the importance of faithfulness, even in difficult times?

10. How can the legacy of these women, ordinary yet influential, encourage you to believe that God can use your life to make a difference?

Prayer of Blessing

Heavenly Father,

We thank You for the women of Scripture whose lives still inspire us today, Deborah, Ruth, Esther, Naomi, Hannah, Mary, and so many others who walked in faith, courage, and obedience. Their stories remind us that You call and equip women to lead, to serve, to teach, to pray, and to shape the future of Your people.

Lord, I lift up every woman reading these words. Bless her with wisdom like Deborah, loyalty like Ruth, courage like Esther, perseverance like Hannah, and devotion like Mary. May her heart be steady in prayer, her voice bold in truth, and her hands willing in service.

Strengthen women in ministry and leadership today. Open doors of opportunity, silence voices of doubt, and fill them with the confidence of Your Spirit. Let their lives reflect the light of Christ in their families, churches, workplaces, and communities.

May every woman know she is seen, valued, and empowered by You. And may her influence ripple through generations, leaving behind a legacy of faith, hope, and love.

In the name of Jesus,
Amen.

EPILOGUE

Still Standing, Still Called

A Closing Reflection

Throughout these pages, we have walked through faith, prayer, fasting, doctrine, and the lives of women who shaped history. From Abraham to Ruth, from Hannah's tears to Esther's courage, from the Godhead to the power of prayer and fasting, we have seen that God is faithful in every generation.

This book has not been just about learning *information*; it has been about experiencing transformation. Each story, each doctrine, each testimony has been written so you may know this truth: **the God of Scripture is the same God who walks with you today.**

A Call to the Reader

Dear reader, the time has come to take what you have learned and live it out. The pages are ending, but your story is not. You are now invited to become the next testimony of faith. You are called to rise with the courage of Deborah, pray with the persistence of

Hannah, serve with the devotion of Priscilla, and lead with the humility of Christ.

Don't close this book as though the journey is over. Close it knowing that the torch has been placed in your hands. The world is waiting for your obedience, your faith, your influence.

A Prophetic Charge

Like Esther, you were born *for such a time as this.* Like Ruth, your loyalty to God will bring forth generations of blessing. Like Mary Magdalene, you are called to proclaim the risen Christ with boldness. And like the early church, you are empowered by prayer and fasting to carry the gospel into the world.

Stand firm in doctrine. Stand strong in prayer. Stand faithful in fasting. Stand courageous in leadership. And above all, stand rooted in Christ.

REFERENCES

Anthony, M. J., & Benson, W. S. (2003). *Exploring the history & philosophy of Christian education: Principles for the 21st century.* Wipf & Stock.

Barclay, W. (1962). *Educational ideals in the ancient world.* Collins.

Baker, N. (2013). *Educating all God's children: What Christians can—and should—do to improve public education for low-income kids.* Brazos Press.

Christian Education Nation. (2021). *What is Christian education?* Retrieved from https://www.cen.edu.au/index.php/shortcode/what-is-christian-education

Fulgham, N. B. (2013). *Educating all God's children: What Christians can—and should—do to improve public education for low-income kids.* Brazos Press.

Gangel, K. O. (1995). *Competent to lead: The biblical qualifications of a church leader.* Moody Press.

Hendricks, H. (1987). *Teaching to change lives.* Multnomah.

Hyde, R. (2018). *The importance of a Christian education.* Liberty University Online Academy Blog. Retrieved from https://www.liberty.edu/index.cfm?id=1101871&blogpid=33000&pid=9720

Lamport, M. (1998). *The hand-me-down faith: The challenge of Christian education across generations.* Baker

Academic.

Luther, M. (1956). *Luther's works* (J. Pelikan, Ed.). Concordia Publishing House.

Miller, R. C. (1963). *The theory of Christian education practice*. Abingdon Press.

Simmons, E. S. (2015). Christian education in the urban setting: Facing realities and overcoming challenges. *Journal of Adventist Education*, 77(5), 4–9.

Spitzer, B., & Aronson, J. (2015). Minding and mending the gap: Social psychological interventions to reduce educational disparities. *British Journal of Educational Psychology*, 85(1), 1–18.

Tyndale University. (2021). *Challenges for educators in the church*. Retrieved from https://www.tyndale.ca/seminary/christian-education-formation/vision/challenges

White, E. G. (1886). *Fundamentals of Christian education*. Pacific Press.

The Holy Bible, Authorized King James Version.

FINAL BLESSING

Heavenly Father,

Thank You for the gift of learning, for the sacred call to teach, and for the grace that transforms every lesson into a moment of ministry. You are the source of all wisdom, the Author of truth, and the Great Teacher who guides us in knowledge and love.

Lord, bless every reader of this work. May the seeds of faith and formation planted through these pages take root in their hearts and flourish in their homes, classrooms, churches, and communities. May every lesson they teach be filled with compassion, every word they speak be seasoned with grace, and every act of service be marked by humility.

Strengthen their hands for the work ahead. Renew their minds daily with Your Word. Let prayer be their power, mercy their language, and Christ their example.

May they walk in the unity of the Spirit, teaching not for recognition but for transformation; not for applause but for Your glory. And when their work feels heavy, remind them that You are their rest and their reward.

Now may the grace of our Lord Jesus Christ, the love of God the Father, and the fellowship of the Holy Spirit rest upon every teacher, leader, and learner who walks in truth.

Go forth in faith. Go forth in purpose. Go forth in love. In Jesus mighty name,
Amen.

ABOUT THE AUTHOR

Dr. Rushayne Stewart

Dr. Rushayne Stewart is a devoted preacher, Christian counselor, and Pastor whose passion for development and service spans continents and cultures. Holding advanced degrees in both Christian Psychology/Counseling and Christian Education, Dr. Stewart brings a unique blend of academic excellence and heartfelt ministry to every setting, whether in the pulpit or the community.

With years of experience in ministry, social services, and leadership development, Dr. Stewart has taught, inspired, and mentored students, educators, and faith leaders worldwide. As a speaker and Christian counselor, he inspires others to pursue learning as a sacred calling, one that nurtures not only the intellect but the soul.

Rooted in Scripture and driven by compassion, Dr. Stewart believes education is more than instruction; it is transformation. Through a Christ-centered approach, he continues to empower individuals to grow in wisdom, faith, and purpose, building lives that reflect the heart and mind of Christ.

Keep in touch with Dr. Rushayne Stewart via email rushaynestewart24@icloud.com. Social Media: Facebook - Rushayne Stewart. You can follow him on Amazon.

www.ingramcontent.com/pod-product-compliance
Lightning Source LLC
LaVergne TN
LVHW051110080426
835510LV00018B/1973

GEORGE BOWLEY

© Penrose Publishing Ltd

First Published 2013 by Penrose Publishing Ltd, York House, York Road, Felixstowe IP11 7QG, www.penrose-publishing.co.uk

ISBN
Paperback 978-1-909879-29-4
Kindle 978-1-909879-30-0
Kobo 978-1-909879-31-7
PDF 978-1-909879-32-4